CULTURES OF CANNABIS CONTROL

An International Comparison of Policy Making

David Brewster

BRISTOL UNIVERSITY PRESS

First published in Great Britain in 2023 by

Bristol University Press
University of Bristol
1–9 Old Park Hill
Bristol
BS2 8BB
UK
t: +44 (0)117 374 6645
e: bup-info@bristol.ac.uk

Details of international sales and distribution partners are available at bristoluniversitypress.co.uk

British Library Cataloguing in Publication Data
A catalogue record for this book is available from the British Library

ISBN 978-1-5292-1496-3 hardcover
ISBN 978-1-5292-1497-0 ePub
ISBN 978-1-5292-1498-7 ePdf

Cover design: Nicky Borowiec
Front cover image: iStock/NickS
Bristol University Press uses environmentally responsible print partners
Printed and bound in Great Britain by CPI Group (UK) Ltd, Croydon, CR0 4YY

FSC
www.fsc.org
MIX
Paper | Supporting responsible forestry
FSC® C013604

Contents

List of Tables

About the Author

David Brewster is Lecturer at Kanazawa College of Art and Fellow at the Centre for Criminology, University of Hong Kong. His research interests are in comparative studies of drug policy and criminal justice, and he has published in *The British Journal of Criminology*, the *International Journal of Drug Policy* and the *European Journal of Criminology*, among others.

Acknowledgements

This book is the culmination of work that has taken place over a number of years, originally forming the basis of my doctoral thesis and since revisited, revised and expanded on. During the PhD programme and thereafter, I have become indebted to many individuals without whom this book would simply not have been possible. First, I would like to extend my thanks to the Economic and Social Research Council for their financial support during the PhD programme, to Lee Gregory for encouraging me to pursue publishing a monograph, and to the team from Bristol University Press for their kindness and patience in guiding me through the publishing process.

Most importantly, the empirical fieldwork that informs this book would not have been possible without all the individuals in England & Wales and the Netherlands who participated in the research. While they remain anonymous, I can only hope that I have done justice in representing their voices. My sincere thanks also go to Ronald van Steden for allowing me to stay and work at Vrije Universiteit Amsterdam during the period of empirical research in 2013, as well as to the countless others who assisted in introductions, went out of their way to help me or otherwise made doing research on cannabis policy an unforgettable experience. I would also like to thank all those who provided critically constructive feedback at various stages over the years, in particular Rob Jones.

Finally, engaging in a PhD and writing a monograph produces many sorts of stress and distress, and I am truly grateful to have family and friends who have always been there when support was needed and kept me going when times were tough. My immense gratitude also goes to my two PhD supervisors, Gordon Hughes and Trevor Jones, along with my progress reviewer, Adam Edwards. From the moment I joined Cardiff University as a fresh-faced 18-year-old undergraduate student, and continuing to this day, Gordon, Trevor and Adam have been a pillar of support, always believing in me, inspiring me and willing me on in my personal and academic development. So to all those who made this book possible, thank you.

1

Introduction

For almost a century, prohibitive regimes have been the dominant mode of cannabis control across the world. Yet despite what one might expect, it cannot be said that policy approaches have been uniform throughout this period, and certainly over the past couple of decades cannabis policy across the globe has become ever more fragmented.

The diversity that can be found is reflective of the differentiated meanings that are attached to the use of cannabis, which are constantly shifting over time and space. For some, it is the source of moral degradation which corrupts the mind and body; it is the cause of developmental, mental health and crime problems; it is the gateway to other drugs, such as cocaine, heroin and methamphetamine; and it is a key driver of organized crime activities and destabilizing conflict. Yet for others, its use is a matter of individual liberty and human rights; it is a source of creativity and means for spiritual enlightenment; it is the cure for an ever-increasing range of ailments; it is a means for economic gain; and it is a valuable resource in agriculture, textiles and manufacturing.

This raises interesting questions about why certain ideas about cannabis and their manifestation in policy have triumphed over others, and what sorts of processes and relations facilitate or hinder the ascension or repression of particular approaches. In thinking about this, it is evidently not the case that cannabis policies are necessarily constituted from logically coherent and consistent dispositional tendencies; rather, it is often the case that multiple, sometimes contradictory, meanings coexist in policy and public discourse, both within the governable space of an individual country and more broadly in the international community. In this regard, for example, it is striking that while at a federal level in the United States there continue to be aggressive criminal justice frameworks and approaches, at the time of writing, 18 states, the District of Columbia and two territories have legalized cannabis for recreational purposes; or that lawmakers in the Philippines – a country in which it is conservatively estimated that 8,663 people were killed between 2016 to 2020 for suspected drug offences – have attempted to introduce more 'progressive' legislation than countries such as the United Kingdom in respect of medical cannabis (Punay, 2020; UN High Commissioner for Human Rights, 2020).

So how can we understand the continuities and fragmentation in cannabis control that have emerged across and within different countries? This book seeks to explore and explain inter- and intra-national policy convergence and divergence in cannabis control through an examination of policy-making processes.

Comparative criminology and control culture

Through focusing on cannabis policy-making processes, this book speaks to, challenges and aims to clarify core comparative criminological questions surrounding the nature and extent of convergence and divergence in different polities' response to crime and disorder under contemporary, late modern conditions.

In the context of vast social, economic, political and technological shifts associated with globalization in the 20th and 21st centuries, conceptualizing the threads that tie together the norms, values, practices, social relations and systems apparent in responses to crime and disorder – in totality, 'control culture' – has led to a variety of competing accounts of the 'master patterns' that characterize the field (for example, Cohen, 1985; Young, 1999; Christie, 2000; Hallsworth and Lea, 2011). Among these, David Garland's (2001) *The Culture of Control* has had an authoritative appeal, and even now, beyond the 20th anniversary of its first publication, this seminal work continues to leave a strong imprint on contemporary understandings of control culture and the governance of crime.

In brief, Garland (2001) asserts that from the early 20th century until around the 1970s, responses to crime in the United Kingdom and the United States were enveloped within a system of penal-welfarism, which had at its core a 'rehabilitative ideal'. This paradigm was premised around three interlocking axioms: the understanding of crime as conceptually unproblematic and geographically and socially delimited; the basing of policy and practice on causal theories which understand crime as a symptom of deep-seated social problems; and the attachment to notions of crime control as the province of experts (Garland and Sparks, 2000; Loader, 2006; Loader and Sparks, 2007). However, owing to wide-ranging social, political and economic transformations that brought new and altered risks, threats, ways of being and ways of thinking, penal-welfarism has since been eclipsed by a set of ambivalent strategies (Garland, 2001).

On the one hand, the administrative burdens associated with the 'normality of high crime rates' have generated a need to employ 'adaptive' strategies (Garland, 1996, 2001). These include 'defining deviance down' to divert offences away from the formal criminal justice system (Garland, 2001) and a managerial shift towards counting the 'outputs' and efficiency of 'services' rather than actual 'outcomes' (Feeley and Simon, 1994). Moreover, they include the ways in which control agencies have become more professional, bureaucratized and dependent on digital technologies with an emphasis on risk management and prevention (Zedner, 2007). Finally, adaptive strategies encompass the growing diversification and responsibilization of crime control above, below, beyond and within the state (Hughes, 2007; Jones, 2012). Within governance studies, this latter aspect has featured strongly, with one prominent line of thought emphasizing the 'withering' of the nation state in governing problems of crime and security under late modern conditions. In this vein, the state is but one 'node' within a network-distributed form of governance (Burris et al, 2005).

At the same time, however, the political ramifications of appearing 'soft' or 'weak' on crime have generated pressure to reaffirm the 'myth' of state sovereignty in the provision of law and order through non-adaptive strategies of 'denial' and 'acting out' (Garland, 1996, 2001). Such strategies employ more expressive and emotive discourses in debates on crime control, with retributive philosophies of punishment and incarceration becoming embedded in policy approaches. It is in this vein that a further dominant tendency in governance studies has asserted the centrality of the nation state in crime control, with the state amassing ever greater powers with which to curtail individual liberties and exert surveillance and control over its citizens (for example, Hallsworth and Lea, 2011).

Emerging from this 'policy predicament' is a culture of control formed around three central elements. The first of these is a recoded penal-welfarism in which the penal aspect has become 'more punitive, more expressive, more security-minded', while the welfare aspect has become 'more conditional, more offence-centred, more risk conscious' (Garland, 2001: 175). The second element is a criminology of control, which has seen the rise of competing conceptualizations of criminality in reaction to the perceived failures of the rehabilitative ideal. The 'criminologies of everyday life' have become less concerned with a person's welfare and more centred on managing risk and space, while the 'criminologies of the other' assume a deeply divisive position between 'us' – hard-working, upstanding citizens – and 'them' – 'opaquely monstrous creatures beyond or beneath our knowing' (Garland, 2001: 184). Third, the culture of control is characterized by an economic style of reasoning whereby managerialist concerns of costs and efficiencies have replaced a focus on social welfare.

Garland's (2001) *The Culture of Control* became an extremely influential narrative through which to interpret the trajectory of policy responses, particularly in respect of punitive 'non-adaptive' strategies of control. While Garland's original work focused explicitly on the United Kingdom and the

United States, observable similarities in other countries subsequently led to criminologists claiming that a 'punitive turn' and culture of control had emerged elsewhere (see Estrada, 2004; Hamai and Ellis, 2006; Downes and van Swaaningen, 2007). As such, whether overtly intended or inadvertently resulting from the piecemeal efforts of the academic community, the picture to emerge was one in which the advent of globalizing late modern conditions was, irrespective of context, tied to convergence around a common (punitive) culture of crime control.

However, this in turn saw somewhat of a backlash from certain quarters, with criticisms that accounts such as *The Culture of Control* were 'grimly pessimistic' and 'determinedly dystopic' (Zedner, 2002: 342, see also O'Malley, 2000; Loader and Sparks, 2004; Huchinson, 2006). Critical commentators argued not only that in these accounts 'little room is left for the impact of contestation and resistance' (O'Malley, 2000: 162), but also that they lead to a type of thinking whereby 'processes of social control appear to have a logic of their own which leads ineluctably towards an ever more restrictive system of regulation' (Matthews, 2002: 220). In response, Garland (2004: 167–8) recognized the underemphasis on 'counter-doxic struggles' and acknowledged that the field 'is not composed of fully settled practices and firmly established policies but rather of competing actors and ongoing struggles, often with delicately balanced forces and power ratios whose equilibria are subject to change'.

However, the notion that there has been convergence in contemporary crime control culture was also critiqued on the basis of a neglect of the qualities of different contexts and how these generate exceptional and diverging tendencies, with commentators using national case studies of contexts such as the United States to highlight their particular historical and social characteristics, which appeared to clearly demarcate them from other countries (for example, Tonry, 2009).

This debate speaks to core theoretical and methodological issues that lie at the heart of comparative criminology, particularly the juxtaposition between accounts which emphasize *either* the context-independency *or* the context-dependency of social phenomena. In other words, does the conception of a *singular* culture of control adequately capture what is happening across different contexts under late modern conditions? Or is it only possible to explain phenomena of control in a given context through reference to its specific, exceptional social relations and characteristics?

Yet, as Edwards and Hughes (2005) suggest, this represents a false dilemma – one that this book seeks to further redress. While the argument of 'false universalism' may rightly raise attention to the problem of assuming neat cross-cultural convergence around a singular culture of control, the assertion of cultural exceptionalism also leaves itself open to accusations of 'false uniqueness'. The implied existence of an infinite, incomparable array of cultures of control seems equally implausible as a monolithic culture, especially given the extent of global social, economic and political dependency and connectivity (Edwards and Hughes, 2005; Edwards et al, 2013a).

Indeed, in responding to criticisms of punitive determinism, and complementary to his acknowledgement of a need to recognize and capture contestation and resistance, Garland reiterated the complex nature of the field – as a whole – under study. Thus, while critical commentators have tended to focus on the punitive turn, Garland (2004: 170) argues for a reflection 'on the non-punitive modes of managing crime that … deep transformations [in society] make possible'. In this sense, punitive 'knee-jerk' reactions by the state are but one strategy of control, coexisting with others. The implication is that while in some contexts, non-adaptive strategies may be more prominent in governing styles, in others, adaptive strategies – including those which responsibilize and empower actors below, beyond and above the nation state – may be more dominant.

In sum, the strength of Garland's thesis is in its ability to capture and explain the contradictions that exist in contemporary crime control, not least in terms of both the weakening and the strengthening of the nation state. Yet it is clear that questions remain about how we can navigate the pitfalls of false universalism and false uniqueness in accounting for the diverse manifestations of crime control in different governable spaces (Brewster, 2020). As Garland himself recognizes, there is a need to critically examine how differing geopolitical spaces have 'adapted and reacted to the new risks, insecurities, and opportunities inherent in the social organization of everyday life under late modern conditions' (2004: 179–80).

This is ever more pertinent given that some of the core premises on which *The Culture of Control* was developed have since shifted; not least in this regard are: the significant decline in official crime rates across many advanced countries; the patterns of divestment in criminal justice institutions; and the re-emergence of rehabilitation onto policy agendas (Cullen, 2013; Hough, 2013; Farrell et al, 2014; Youdell and McGimpsey, 2015). There have also been other, broader, social changes in many countries, representing both continuities and breaks with the patterns observed by Garland and others at the end of the millennium. These include: global economic instability; the rise of nationalist populism and antiglobalization movements; growing social insecurities and distrust towards political authorities; changing patterns of global geopolitical power; rapid advances in digital technologies; the growing influence and role of international corporations in democratic processes and the lives of private citizens; and, at least in respect of living memory, the unprecedented outbreak of a global health epidemic.

Despite the extent of change, the core structures which govern social life in advanced liberal democracies have not been reconstituted, and it remains the case that works such as *The Culture of Control* still provide a useful set of tools for capturing and explaining broader currents in the criminal justice sphere. Nevertheless, as Garland acknowledges, by their very nature such grand theories 'don't capture the multi-layered texture of [actors'] meanings, the complexity of historical events, the role of contingency, the operation of counter-forces, or the variations of local outcome' (Garland, 2018: 15). Thus, there is a tendency to conceal the multifaceted and variegated nature of responses across different national and local levels of decision-making (Edwards and Hughes, 2005). Given the growing appreciation of such dynamics (Garland, 2018), there is a need to empirically clarify how cultures of control unfold, which can be achieved by examining the nature and extent of convergence and divergence across and within different jurisdictions. This mirrors the call of Stenson and Edwards (2004: 219) 'for further accounts of the uneven ways in which political rationalities and government technologies are configured in different localities by competing coalitions of actors'.

Thus, in advancing the valuable contributions of *The Culture of Control*, two central propositions can be stated about control culture under late modern conditions: (1) it is both possible and expected to observe *some degree of convergence internationally*; and (2) we can simultaneously expect *some degree of divergence intra-nationally* between different spheres of governance within each jurisdiction.

In moving beyond the stalemate between accounts of control culture which champion either context-dependency or context-independency, an approach based on a critical realist philosophy of social science and focuses on the political competition to govern (Sayer, 2000; Edwards, 2016) is advocated. This entails capturing both social relations that are necessary to policy making in a liberal democracy – and ought to be found in any such context – and those relations which are contingent on a given governable space – and possess the potential for generating variation across and within national contexts. This will alert us to the capacities of policy stakeholders and communities – and the 'negotiated orders' (Edwards and Hughes, 2012) between them – in advancing as well as adapting, resisting and subverting policy within and beyond the nation state (see also Edwards and Hughes, 2005; Edwards, 2016). Through grasping the challenges and opportunities that such relations generate in policy-making processes, it becomes possible to gain a much firmer understanding of the current and future possibilities and constraints for political responses to social objects that are subject to formal control in different governable contexts.

Cannabis control culture and researching policy-making processes

The preceding discussion shows that an empirical examination of policy approaches to cannabis is an extremely interesting avenue to pursue.

Notwithstanding alternative ways in which the cannabis plant has been conceptualized and responded to over the approximate 2,500 years in which there is evidence of its use as a mind-altering substance (Ren et al, 2019), the establishment of global prohibitive frameworks throughout the 20th century powerfully marked the substance as an object of crime control and appeared to signal convergence around a culture of control. While *The Culture of Control* was criticized for its 'silence' on these issues (O'Malley, 2002), there has nevertheless been a host of accounts since that have demonstrated how policy ambivalence in the broader field of crime control was mirrored in, and simultaneously driven by, developments in cannabis and illegal drugs policy throughout this period (See Garland, 2018).

Commentators have most often focused on the reactive and punitive criminal justice-driven 'war on drugs'-style approaches that have fuelled increases in arrest and incarceration rates. This includes, inter alia: a toughening of political rhetoric, legislation and sentencing practices; greater specialization, collaboration and professionalization of local, regional, national and international agencies involved in the enforcement of illegal drug laws; and the introduction of performance management technologies that skew police action towards drug offences that are relatively easy to record. At the same time, the flourishing of developments and approaches characterized as more adaptive in nature have also been illuminated. For example, the use of risk management tools, such as drug testing; the social and political 'normalization' of recreational drug use; the emergence of multi-agency partnerships; and the rise of harm reduction schemes, such as needle exchange services and overdose prevention services (see Garland, 2001; Wacquant, 2004; Seddon, 2008; McAuley et al, 2015; Shiner, 2015).

As the most consumed illegal substance globally, cannabis has not only been at the forefront of 'war on drugs'-style strategies of control but has also assumed the position in many contexts of poster child for drug policy reform. It is particularly in this latter regard that contemporary developments in many countries across the globe appear to be shifting, with an increasing degree of fragmentation from the norm of prohibition. This has also been reflected in the orientation of research efforts. While, until recently, the overriding focus had been paid to indications of growing convergence around punitivism and approaches that fall within the (poorly defined) umbrella of a war on drugs, more recent accounts of cannabis policy have tilted towards documenting movement in the opposite direction, towards, to use Garland's term, adaptation.

Yet, in line with the earlier discussion, while there may be evidence of the manifestation of strategies of control shared across different contexts, it is not sufficient to conclude that this is indicative of *a* (that is, the same) culture of control. Thus, rather than reading off policy 'talk' or looking at the *effects* of cannabis legislation – hitherto dominant themes of criminological research (for example, Decorte et al, 2020b) – a greater understanding of why certain approaches are more or less likely to flourish in particular contexts and under what conditions can be gained through examining the processes by which policy comes into being (Jones and Newburn, 2007). While still a relatively underappreciated area, policy-making processes (rather than policy implementation) have been fruitfully explored by a number of drug policy researchers (for example, Monaghan, 2011; Stevens, 2011).

Nevertheless, as such studies have tended to use a single national case study design, the lack of empirical cross-national and intra-national comparisons means that there are limits to what they can offer to debates about control culture in comparative perspective. This is important precisely because such a research design cannot illuminate those relations and characteristics which are specific and contingent to a context or those which are necessarily shared (Edwards et al, 2013a).

It was on this basis that the research[1] underpinning this book was conducted. Using a multiple embedded comparative case study design (Yin, 2014), the project aimed to assess manifestations of control culture through an inter- and intra-national comparison of convergence and divergence in the cannabis policy-making processes of England & Wales and the Netherlands. Specifically, in order to focus the scope of empirical comparison, the policy-making processes concerning two specific policy changes were examined: the reclassification of cannabis from Class C to Class B in 2009 in England & Wales; and the amendments to the public prosecutor's guidelines for 'coffeeshops' (known as *gedoogbeleid*, 'tolerance policy') in 2012–13 in the Netherlands. Empirical fieldwork took place in 2012–13.

Given that there have been more recent and more radical developments in cannabis policy in other contexts, writing about England & Wales and the Netherlands at this juncture may come as a surprising choice. Yet, these national cases present interesting questions in respect of the theoretical and methodological points raised earlier. In both contexts, the national changes are prima facie suggestive of 'convergent divergence' (Levi-Faur and Jordana, 2005); in other words, they each represent more repressive policy responses – seemingly indicative of non-adaptive strategies – in a broader global context in which many countries are introducing liberalizing, adaptive reforms. Moreover, while there have been developments within both England & Wales and the Netherlands since the original empirical work was conducted, especially in terms of how policy is being implemented 'on the ground', it remains the case that the changes at the turn of the 2010s in these countries remain the most recent changes to national law regarding non-medical cannabis use and are thereby still deeply relevant to understanding processes of policy making. As is later argued, the road to prohibition was not an automatic or determined path and neither is the dismantling of such systems and structures of control. Thus, just as the question of how and why cannabis policy reform has been achieved is rightly an important one, so too is the question of how and why prohibitive regimes are maintained and reproduced. Nevertheless, while the substantive findings are based on empirical fieldwork from across and within England & Wales and the Netherlands, the book also draws on policy developments from other contexts across the globe. While these should not be taken as rigorous comparisons, they do nevertheless draw into sharper focus those relations and characteristics that exist within cannabis policy-making processes in England & Wales and the Netherlands, and signal important areas for future comparative research.

In line with the multiple embedded case study design, two subnational sites (local authority area/municipality) within the national jurisdictions of England & Wales (Cardiff) and the Netherlands (Utrecht) were also selected to empirically examine how policy-making processes operate at the local level of governance. These case sites were chosen on the basis that they were potentially 'deviant' cases in which assumptions of convergence could be tested.

The municipality of Utrecht, located relatively centrally in the country and having 13 operating coffeeshops at the time of the research, poses interesting questions with regards to the research agenda. One of the main justifications for the introduction of stricter measures for coffeeshops was the removal of nuisance created by drug tourism. As Utrecht is not located near where such activity is likely to occur, this begged the question of how these new regulations were accepted or resisted by local policy administrators. Furthermore, Utrecht has a strong liberal (Left-wing) political tradition and, as such, served as an interesting case to examine the relationship between a firm Left-wing municipal council and the more Right-wing national cabinet of Rutte I (2010–12),[2] which was in political office at the time the measures were introduced.

In comparing cannabis policy between national and subnational levels of governance, it is necessary to recognize the often chaotic and 'messy' realities of condensing the social world into two simplistic heuristic categories. The analysis becomes particularly tricky in relation to the United Kingdom when considering the fragmented devolution of governing powers. The coupling of England & Wales as a national polity (omitting Scotland and Northern Ireland) has been justified on the basis that these jurisdictions share the same legal system.

Although criminal justice matters remain a non-devolved aspect of Welsh governance, meaning that the 2009 changes in law and to policing guidelines applied equally across Wales, other major aspects pertaining to cannabis and 'substance misuse' have been devolved since the Government of Wales Act 2006. These include health, education, social welfare, housing and local government, and since a referendum in 2011, the Welsh Government has the capability of full legislative powers in these areas. The Welsh emphasis on substance misuse as primarily an issue of public health and not criminal justice suggests that there is potential for policy to be reworked through more adaptive strategies of control.

Cardiff offered an interesting case site for the research, as it is the capital of Wales and a centre for political activity. To understand the role of the subnational level in relation to the change in legal classification of cannabis, we have to recognize that Cardiff is a site of policy making as well as the specific local authority case site, and these were grouped together in the analysis of subnational policy streams. While this was not a perfect fit, such a definition served the purpose of exploring policy convergence and divergence from the national level of criminal justice policy making.

In order to clarify and compare the nature of control culture in different contexts, 'middle range' analytical devices were employed to capture how and why the policy changes came into being and how they were translated into the subnational sphere. However, making sense of the policy-making process is no simple task, and to date a plethora of policy-making models have been used in drugs policy research (Ritter and Bammer, 2010; Monaghan, 2011), including 'incrementalism' (Lindblom, 1959, 1979), the 'technical/rational' model (Easton, 1965; Bardach, 2005), the 'enlightenment' model (Weiss, 1977), the 'evolutionary' model (Stevens, 2007) and the 'advocacy coalition framework' (Sabatier, 1988).

In this research, a different analytical device – Kingdon's (1995) multiple streams model – was used to try and capture the processes and events by which the two policy movements[3] came into being. The selection of this model was based on an acceptance that the policy process is complex and messy, and an acknowledgement that although approaches such as incrementalism and the technical/rational model are useful in identifying a set of stages, these often fail to take into account the more ad hoc features of policy making. Moreover, while the advocacy coalition framework is useful in establishing types of policy communities and the values that drive forward policy agendas (Monaghan, 2011), with an optimal period of observation of ten years (Sabatier, 1988), there was an element of pragmatism involved in choosing the multiple streams model in that the study was premised on specific changes at particular moments in time. Moreover, set within the context of testing the culture of control, which suggests that policy making has become less rational and more prone to policy swings and incident-driven agendas, Kingdon's framework provided an apt device with which to represent the dynamic and sometimes unpredictable elements of the policy process.

According to the multiple streams model, policy change is most probable when three distinct 'streams' come together in critical windows of opportunity. First, the 'problem' stream is recognition of a problem for which a response is required. The construction of what is considered a problem is innately important, as social phenomena in themselves are not necessarily problematic. According to Kingdon (1995: 109–10), 'conditions become defined as problems when we come to believe that we should do something about them. Problems are not simply the conditions or external events themselves; there is also a perceptual, interpretative element.' Second the 'policy' stream is the formation and refining of policy proposals. Such ideas often exist independently of recognized problems, floating around in a 'primeval soup'. When policy proposals meet a set of criteria, such as fitting with dominant values, and are technically feasible, then the list of policy alternatives to recognized problems is narrowed down for selection. Finally, the 'political' stream consists of 'swings of national mood, vagaries of public opinion, election results, changes of administration, shifts in partisan or ideological distributions in [government], and interest group pressure campaigns' (Kingdon, 1995: 87). When the political dimension combines with the problem and policy streams, the possibilities for policy change are greatly enhanced.

Although this model was considered an apt device for capturing processes existing at the national level of policy change, it is important to clarify how the subnational level was incorporated into this framework for analysis. In essence, the focus was on how policy problems were perceived and constructed at a subnational level; how the measures enacted at a national level were supported, adapted or resisted in local policy arrangements; and the political factors which contributed to this process. Importantly, this allowed the research to identify structural and cultural factors and mechanisms operating at different levels of governance which led to both the genesis of policy and translation into the subnational sphere.

Data collection principally involved a series of elite semi-structured interviews with 62 policy and academic stakeholders. Participants were recruited via purposive sampling followed by a process of snowballing, which allowed for a relatively balanced mix of participants in both countries. At a national level, this included serving and former politicians, civil servants from key departments (in the Netherlands: the Ministry of Health, Welfare and Sport, the Ministry of Justice and Security, and the Public Prosecutor's Office; in England & Wales: the Home Office), policy advocates from non-governmental organizations and think tanks, expert committee members (in the Netherlands: the van de Donk Committee and the Garretsen Committee; in England & Wales: the Advisory Council on the Misuse of Drugs – ACMD) and academics who are specialists in the drugs policy field. In total at national level, there were 18 participants in England & Wales and 24 in the Netherlands (see Table 1 in the Appendix for a summary of participants).

At subnational level, reflecting the differentiated nature of 'doing' cannabis policy in each context, participants came from various backgrounds. In the Netherlands, this included representation from the police, the Public Prosecutor's Office, local politicians and an alderperson, and a member of a cannabis social club. In the Welsh setting, there were political representatives and civil servants from the Welsh Government as well as police officers, health representatives from the local council and a drugs practitioner from a third sector organization. In total at subnational level, there were 9 participants in England & Wales and 11 in the Netherlands (see Table 1 in the Appendix). It is worth adding that although participants' current or most recent former position was recorded, individuals often had many years of experience spanning multiple organizations and sectors. In the reporting of data, participants are represented using an anonymized participant key that indicates key attributes of their position (see Table 2 in the Appendix).

Interview schedules contained common themes relating to how and why the policy changes occurred, but they were also tailored according to the case site and participant (an example is given in Table 3 in the Appendix). In England & Wales, interviews ranged from 20 minutes to 1 hour 30 minutes, with an average time of around 40 minutes, while in the Netherlands, they ranged from 45 minutes to 2 hours, with an average interview lasting just over an hour. In the majority of cases (n = 51), interviews were conducted face to face, but just over a sixth (n = 11) – all at the national level in England & Wales – were conducted via telephone.

In addition to common issues associated with non-random sampling and interviewing techniques, there were considerations specific to researching policy elites, such as gaining access, power dynamics and reputational concerns (Berry, 2002; Morris, 2009). While the technique of snowball sampling may attract criticisms similar to that directed towards David Downes' classic study on post-war penal policy in the Netherlands (see Franke, 1990), with insider participants potentially referring like-minded contacts, the more purposeful aspect of the sampling strategy, to attract competing interests and actors, served to offset this. Moreover, the inclusion of participants working both inside government organizations and operating outside of it, from different perspectives, helped to ensure variation in participant characteristics. Interestingly, it was felt that this had been better achieved in the Netherlands than in England & Wales, where access to government actors proved more difficult. Moreover, the perception of researcher as 'outsider' seemed to be a distinct advantage in the Netherlands, perhaps due to my being seen as a harmless, naïve foreigner wishing to learn about Dutch cannabis policy. This was epitomized by one particularly memorable occasion when, after our interview had concluded, I was taken by a senior civil servant from the Ministry of Health, Welfare and Sport to 'experience' a coffeeshop; such an event is barely imaginable in the United Kingdom.

While I was based in Cardiff for the duration of the project, the research involved two substantive trips to the Netherlands, for three months and one month, respectively. These trips served a number of purposes. First, they allowed me to have meaningful access to contacts in a country I was not wholly familiar with. Second, punctuating the trips in this way provided an opportunity to reflect on the themes emerging from the data before returning for further fieldwork. Finally, this back-and-forth approach to conducting comparative research provided opportunity to shape the interviews and corroborate findings. As trips to the Netherlands complemented periods of research 'at home' in Wales, the data that was generated allowed for more focused lines of inquiry; also, by the final stages of data collection, I had a much clearer sense of my interpretations and was aided by participants' thoughts on these, which in turn bolstered the analysis. In addition, my second research trip to the Netherlands occurred immediately following the 2013 European Society of Criminology conference (held in Budapest), at which I had the opportunity to present with a panel of Dutch academics (Dutch academics were also present in the audience). This provided further feedback on the emerging analysis.

In addition to elite interviews, the research incorporated an analysis of key policy documents. The documents included the national drug strategies active at the time of the policy changes as well as official reports from advisory committees, such as the ACMD (England & Wales) and the van de Donk and Garretsen committees (the Netherlands) (Home Office, 1998, 2002b, 2008a; ACMD, 2002, 2006, 2008; Advisory Committee on Drugs Policy, 2009; Expert Committee on the List System of the Opium Act, 2011).

In addition, documents with specific relevance to the policy changes were examined in more depth. In England & Wales, this included the announcement of the reclassification of cannabis by the Home Secretary at the time, Jacqui Smith, in the House of Commons on 7 May 2008 (House of Commons, 2008a); the *Explanatory Memorandum to the Misuse of Drugs Act 1971 (Amendment) Order 2008*, which includes an 'Impact Assessment' (Home Office, 2008b); the *Home Office Circular 001/2009 – Controlled Drugs: Reclassification of Cannabis* (Home Office, 2009); the *Government Response to the Recommendations made by the Advisory Council on the Misuse of Drugs in its Report Cannabis: Classification and Public Health* (Home Office, 2008c); and the Association of Chief Police Officers (ACPO) *Guidance on Cannabis Possession for Personal Use* (ACPO, 2009).

In the Netherlands, documents included four 'drugs letters' which were central to the national dissemination of how and why new measures were being introduced. These were: the announcement, on 27 May 2011, of the Rutte I coalition agreement on coffeeshop policy (House of Representatives of the States General, 2011a), two drugs letters, dated 26 October and 15 December 2011, that further clarified the new measures (House of Representatives of the States General, 2011b, 2011c); and the drugs letter of 19 November 2012, which outlined the revised coalition agreement on coffeeshops under Rutte II (2012–17) (House of Representatives of the States General, 2012). In the Netherlands, the local level also publishes an explicit policy on coffeeshops (City of Utrecht, 2013), and this was also included in the analysis.

Undertaking a comparative research project that involves primary data collection in a foreign country requires careful consideration of issues relating to language comprehension, to avoid misunderstanding and misinterpretation. Owing to the widespread proficiency in the English language in the Netherlands, interviews were conducted in English. Almost all of the Dutch participants had an excellent grasp of English, and where some participants occasionally struggled, there were colleagues to assist. In addition, interviews were recorded and, to enhance validity, transcripts were provided to interviewees so that they could check their responses were as they intended. In the small minority of cases where alterations were made to transcripts, the amendments were negligible and did not affect the core content of the interview.

However, where encountering the Dutch language was unavoidable, as in the analysis of certain key documents, computer software was used to provide broad translation of the main themes. The translations were then cross-referenced with other sources to check for accuracy, and Dutch contacts confirmed that the translations were correct and provided any necessary clarification. Attention was given to the use of culturally specific concepts, as concepts constructed in the Netherlands may represent different ways of framing the cannabis problem and, thus, have implications for its governance. Most obviously, *gedoogbeleid* is a concept loaded with meaning and history alien to those outside of the Netherlands. Significant attempts were made to understand such concepts, both through a thorough reading of the literature and with the interpretation and corroboration of participants' accounts.

The main analytical framework for analysis was the multiple streams model. Data from interview transcripts were coded using the three broad categories of 'problem stream', 'policy stream' and 'political stream', and demarcated according to national and subnational levels. This framework provided a useful structure from which a more inductive style of analysis could proceed. For the policy process, smaller meta-codes were adapted from Kingdon (1995) for each stream. For the problem stream, the principal interest was in the ways cannabis had come to be defined as problematic and in need of a policy response. For the policy stream, there was an interest in 'political feasibility', use of 'research and expertise' and 'technical feasibility'. In the political stream, coding evolved around 'changes in administration', 'national mood' and 'organized political forces'. From these codes, and the broad codes of the policy level analysis, further codes were generated inductively, and these were refined iteratively as the research progressed. Regarding the documents, a looser form of analysis was conducted in which the main themes were interlaced with those generated from interview data.

Once these stages of data analysis had concluded, the findings were interpreted using the broader theoretical propositions of Garland's culture of control to assess the extent to which relevant forces have been felt in the research contexts and determine how these played out. While the research process is not without limitations given the inevitably messy realities of doing research, a logical and rigorous procedure was carried out, generating meaningful comparative data that produced a solid set of findings.

Outline of the book

Before proceeding with the substantive part of the book, a brief overview of each chapter is provided below to assist readers in navigating the contents.

Chapter 2 contextualizes the research by providing an overview of the broad currents in global cannabis policy, starting with a discussion of the international conventions, frameworks and debates that emerged from the 20th century onwards. This serves to open up questions about convergence and divergence in policy approaches, with the argument that while 'supranational' frameworks have provided the grounds for commonalities, there is space for a diverse range of approaches to emerge. From here, the chapter goes on to identify the range of response types, and their variants, that can be seen in contemporary cannabis policy – prohibition, depenalization, decriminalization and legal regulation – using case exemplars from across the globe. This draws attention to the central theme of the book: why diversity in cannabis policy exists across the globe despite an assumed convergence under globalized conditions, and how such patterns can be explained.

Chapter 3 provides a historical contextualization of sociopolitical culture and its intersection with cannabis control in respect of the two empirical cases of England & Wales and the Netherlands. Using David Garland's *The Culture of Control* as a 'theoretical scaffold', the chapter is organized around two sections: the first explores the broader conditions supporting a 'penal-welfare' state and its relationship with manifestations of cannabis control; the second discusses the social, economic and political changes associated with a transition to late modernity and how each of the cases has adapted and reacted to these conditions in respect of cannabis policy. The chapter concludes by reflecting on control culture in comparative perspective and identifies a set of components – namely, structural relations and political culture – that form an important foundation for subsequent analysis chapters.

Chapters 4, 5 and 6 are organized around the three streams of Kingdon's (1995) multiple streams model. In each chapter, the empirical cases of England & Wales and the Netherlands are discussed in turn, focusing on two national policy movements (the 2009 reclassification of cannabis in England & Wales and the 2012–13 changes to coffeeshop policy in the Netherlands), before examining other cases from across the globe. Chapter 4 engages with the problem stream, identifying the various ways in which cannabis has been constructed as a policy problem requiring political attention at the national level of policy making. Chapter 5 focuses on the policy stream, discussing the so-called primeval soup of policy ideas from which the development and selection of policy proposals emerge in relation to a given problem. Chapter 6 examines the politics stream and considers the political environment and the ways in which different social actors and groups have been able to mobilize resources and advance agendas within windows of opportunity.

Chapter 7 moves beyond the national level to examine how policy was resisted, negotiated and/or adapted at subnational level. The primary purpose of this chapter is to examine the extent of convergence and divergence between national and subnational levels of governance. Building on the national-level analysis presented in chapters 4 to 6, the chapter first explores how changes instigated at a national level unfolded at the subnational level in Cardiff/Wales and Utrecht. From there, the chapter discusses the role of the subnational level in policy negotiation, development and resistance in other contexts.

Chapter 8 goes on to critically assess the nature and extent of convergence and divergence that can be seen in cannabis policy-making processes and to explain why policy change has occurred, through the identification of a set of mechanisms and factors which condition policy-making processes. This includes discussions of policy processes in cannabis control and political institutions and relations of power. A focus on England & Wales and the Netherlands forms a substantive part of the chapter, but the global exemplars that have been woven into the preceding chapters are also brought together to compare and contrast policy-making processes in cannabis control. This allows for an articulation of factors that facilitate more punitive directions as well as those which hold the potential for a diverse range of control strategies.

Chapter 9 concludes the book, first by highlighting the core findings and propositions made in the preceding chapters in the context of their implications for cultures of control, cannabis policy making and criminological expertise. It goes on to offer a critical reflection of the study and methodology which informed these findings, and it finishes with a consideration of future directions in comparative criminology.

2

Cannabis Policy in Global Perspective

Introduction

Since the early 20th century, cannabis has been included in a series of global conventions and agreements, which continue to serve as the cornerstone of contemporary international control approaches. Ostensibly, the raisons d'être of such controls are to regulate the manufacture, distribution, supply and use of designated substances, to ensure controlled access for medical and research purposes and to prevent problems arising from drug use. Such developments at a supranational level in some respects reflect adaptation to the limitations of individual sovereign states in responding to identified problems, with increased interconnectedness and interweaving of transportation and trade across geopolitical regions under globalizing conditions necessitating the coordination of responses and collaboration with others.

However, the formation and actualization of this international drug control system is subject to varying interpretations. For some, control at this level is characterized as a rigid 'prohibition regime' (Bewley-Taylor and Jelsma, 2012: 4) in which a heavily US-influenced 'global order' of drugs control (Eligh, 2019) places pressure on nation states to strictly adhere to criminalized approaches while criticizing those who dare to 'breach' the dominant approach (Bewley-Taylor and Jelsma, 2012). However, in recent years, this perspective has faced growing criticism for failing to recognize the rather more complex role of different states in the formation of multilateral drug control agreements, as well as the considerable diversity that international regulatory systems afford to national and local policy actors in shaping cannabis control (see Mills, 2003; Windle, 2013; Collins, 2020). Consequently, it has been argued that a more appropriate way of conceptualizing control at a global level is as a 'complex regulatory system' (Collins, 2018). Thus, in considering the development and the contemporary nature of international cannabis control, it is necessary to recognize not only the asymmetrical relations of power between different actors, but also the inherent messiness and ambivalence of frameworks as well as the social agency of actors to negotiate, disrupt and subvert global governance arrangements in ways that accord with preferred agendas and goals.

This chapter maps the overall contours of cannabis control in global perspective, identifying the main actors and organizations as well as the infrastructure of international drug policy, describing the main continuities and changes over the past century and outlining the ways in which cannabis[1] is subjected to control mechanisms across different national and subnational contexts.

Governing cannabis at international level

Prior to the first set of international prohibitive controls placed on cannabis under the Second International Opium Convention of 1925, approaches to cannabis varied widely, from prohibitive regimes (in places such as Burma, Egypt and Greece) to licensed and taxed systems (such as in India) to, in the majority of cases, no controls whatsoever (Collins, 2020).

Initially in the formation of multilateral drug control agreements, cannabis was extremely marginal to issues concerning opium and cocaine. Prior to the 1925 Convention, cannabis was only fleetingly mentioned at other key international conventions and summits, with the Italian delegation first to raise concerns at the 1912 Opium Conference in relation to hashish smuggling in North Africa, and the South African delegation suggesting in 1923 that it be discussed at the next League of Nations opium conference (Kozma, 2011; Transnational Institute, 2014). At the 1925 Conference, it was the delegation from Egypt, who were for the first time represented as an independent country, that most strongly put forward the case for prohibitive controls in relation to cannabis, with claims centring around its causal role in widespread mental health problems (Mills, 2003; Kozma, 2011; Transnational Institute, 2014).[2] However, as Mills (2012: 29) intricately argues, although the evidence provided was 'questionable in origin', with most countries having little direct experience with cannabis, the pressure from Egypt, along with support from Brazil, Greece, South Africa and Turkey, ultimately led to the inclusion of cannabis under substances to be prohibited. Nevertheless, reservations from British India about the impacts on domestic trade led to a dilution of the recommendations, resulting in the 'prohibition of cannabis exportation to countries where it was illegal and the requirement of an import certificate for countries that allowed its use' (Transnational Institute, 2014: 12).

These early developments were to lay the foundations for what was to follow, but there was continuing disagreement and ambiguity about cannabis in the international community. For example, Mills (2012) notes the lack of any definitive conclusions following a lengthy period of fact-finding, from 1935 to 1940, by the League of Nations Sub-Committee on Cannabis.

Up until this point, the United States had been almost completely absent from international discussions about cannabis. The US delegation even walked out of the 1925 Convention. Nevertheless, one cannot disregard the developments in the United States given the powerful role it would come to assume in global affairs, particularly during and following the Second World War. Here, in the context of fraught race relations in the early to mid 20th century, fears emerged that cannabis use by African Americans and Mexican Americans was causing mental health problems and violence. Following the enactment of the Marijuana Tax Act 1937, a tax was introduced on the selling of cannabis, which effectively destroyed the industrial hemp industry and cemented the dominant perspective that cannabis needed to be prohibited (Transnational Institute, 2014). This sowed the seeds for the US war on drugs from the late 1960s onwards.

The international ambiguity surrounding cannabis took a clearer direction following the Second World War. In 1952, a report from the World Health Organization's (WHO's) Expert Committee on Habit Forming Drugs claimed that cannabis had no useful medical applications (WHO, 1952). Interestingly, this report drew on questionable evidence from Egypt that had been used in the earlier Opium Convention. The damning WHO position, which centred on the physical and mental effects of cannabis, was presented to, and readily accepted by, the Commission on Narcotic Drugs (CND)[3] in 1955 (see Mills, 2012). Around the same time, other key players in the international drug control community also started to become more cemented around a criminal justice-oriented position. For example, the United Nations (UN) Drug Secretariat (currently the United Nations Office on Drugs and Crime – UNODC) was important in 'agenda setting, policy dissemination and nudging towards repressive policies by suggesting they were based in best-practice evidence' (Collins, 2018: 110). This set the tone for metrics of success in the international community, with individual states seeking to 'one-up' each other in respect of law enforcement measures.

The 1961 United Nations Single Convention on Narcotic Drugs, with 73 original signatories, remains the most pivotal international treatise, as it elevated the prohibition of cannabis to a global level. At its core, the purpose of the Convention was to 'limit exclusively to medical and scientific purposes the trade in and use of controlled drugs', effectively consolidating previous international agreements on different substances under a single treatise (UN, 1973: 110). There are four schedules[4] included in the 1961 Convention, with cannabis classified as one of the most dangerous and harmful drugs (see Ballotta et al, 2008: 102). Until recently, cannabis and cannabis resin were listed in both Schedule I and Schedule IV, meaning it was considered to be a drug that poses significant dangers and has few therapeutic characteristics.

The Convention on Psychotropic Substances of 1971 and the Convention against Illicit Traffic in Narcotic Drugs and Psychotropic Substances of

1988 reinforce the principles established under the 1961 Convention. The 1971 Convention placed tetrahydrocannabinol (THC) – one of the main psychoactive constituents of cannabis – in Schedule I, with its use prohibited except for scientific and limited medical purposes (UN, 1971). The 1988 Convention focuses more on the trafficking of illicit drugs and sets in place a series of repressive standards that signatories should follow – notably, that possession with intent for trafficking and possession for personal consumption should be criminalized (UN, 1988; Ballotta et al, 2008).

One reading of the 1961 Convention, and the conventions that followed, is that they necessitate a punitive war on drugs approach to cannabis and other substances. Certainly, a core commitment of signatory states is the obligation to implement 'penal provisions' concerning cannabis-related activities. However, this masks the considerable variation that is possible, one key implication being that the 1961 Convention does not require states to introduce *criminal* sanctions for possession (Collins, 2020). In addition, as highlighted by Ballotta et al (2008), Article 2.5a states that countries should adopt 'special measures' if considered necessary (UN, 1961: 3). As this is discretionary, rather than required, it leaves countries some space to carve their own drug policies. In other words, while the 1961 Convention stipulates that cannabis should receive the most stringent control, there is also scope for countries to negotiate on the *necessity* of such control, and it is this which has allowed signatory states to diverge from the Convention while also remaining within international frameworks (Transnational Institute, 2014).

In recognizing the ambiguities that remain in this foundational treaty, the perspective of global drugs control as one based on a dichotomy between adherence to and 'breaches' of criminalized prohibition is challenged, and there is acknowledgement of the diverse ways in which the treaties have been interpreted and implemented. This further extends to global organizations such as the CND, the International Narcotics Control Board (INCB)[5] and the UNODC, whose approaches have at times been less rigid than the conceptualization of them as an 'iron triangle' defending prohibition may suggest (Sischy and Blaustein, 2018). Indicatively, as Collins (2018: 108) argues, 'drug control goals [have often been] subsumed to security, development, political stability and population welfare imperatives'.

Moreover, Collins (2018: 110) goes on to critique accounts that stress the pivotal role of the United States in devising and controlling global prohibitive frameworks (Andreas and Nadelmann, 2006; Bewley-Taylor and Jelsma, 2012), suggesting that its role has been 'vastly overstated', especially given that the US delegation initially opposed the 1961 Convention. Nevertheless, when the US government changed its position in 1967 and ratified the Convention, this marked an important moment with ramifications not only for the United States but across the world. In particular, the advancing of a punitive war on drugs, starting in the Nixon-led US administration

(1969–74) and pronounced again during the Reagan administrations (1981–89), was a key domestic and foreign policy agenda. Certainly, there is evidence that indicates the influence of this on policy negotiations with other countries; for example, Friman (1991) demonstrates how Japan's adoption of tougher measures against the illegal drug activities of organized crime groups (*yakuza*) came about as a concession for trade arrangements concerning the Japanese automobile industry.

Of course, we should be careful not to downplay the fact that the Japanese government's position on illegal drugs had hitherto shared many points of alignment with the United States – the introduction of more punitive measures was hardly oppositional to the political ideology of Japan's Liberal Democratic Party, or counter to other domestic public policy aims. The point here is that in considering the development and maintenance of a prohibitive global regulatory order, one cannot ignore the asymmetrical power relations between different political actors and entities at international level which enable the use of governing resources to pursue preferred goals.

Since the formation of the conventions, there has not been any major movement in international cannabis control, but this is not to imply that no change has taken place. At the United Nations General Assembly Special Session on Drugs (UNGASS) in 1990 and 1998, commitments to drug eradication were reaffirmed by member states. Nevertheless, in 1991, a recommendation from WHO to reschedule dronabinol – a synthetic version of THC – from Schedule I to Schedule II in the 1971 Convention was adopted by the CND, thereby cautiously ceding that components of cannabis have useful therapeutic applications (Transnational Institute, 2014). In some ways, this marked the beginning of a steady shift in position by WHO, which gradually came to acknowledge the medical benefits of cannabis and recommended further changes in international control scheduling during the 2000s (WHO, 2003, 2006). However, during this period, these recommendations were consistently kept off the voting agenda at CND meetings, stalling any further reform.

By the end of the 2000s, creaks in the dominant position of the international community were becoming more evident. In the context of failures to stop rising levels of consumption, incarceration and conflict, new approaches to drugs control were called for at the 2008 UNGASS, openly challenging the dominant rhetoric that had hitherto dominated discussions. However, the impact of this was not immediately apparent, with the 2009 Political Declaration and Plan of Action on International Cooperation towards an Integrated and Balanced Strategy to Counter the World Drug Problem regurgitating previous discourse to urge members to 'eliminate or reduce significantly and measurably' supply and demand for illicit drugs by 2019 (UNODC, 2009: 14).

In spite of this, momentum for reform continued, and by 2014 a bloc of Latin American countries along with influential former leaders and drug reform advocates from across the globe asserted the need to rethink punitive global systems of control and instead approach drugs control from perspectives of harm reduction and treatment (Global Commission on Drug Policy, 2011, 2014; Collins, 2018).

By the 2016 UNGASS, clear contradictions and fragmentations in policy positions on cannabis had become apparent among international bodies as well as across and within regions and nation states. Although some countries had for some time been using approaches based on depenalization and decriminalization, in 2013 Uruguay became the first signatory member of the UN conventions to legalize cannabis, drawing condemnation from the INCB (INCB, 2013). Certain developments in North America were also confronting the strict prohibitive approach that was advocated by the UNODC, the INCB and the CND; several US states had legalized medical cannabis and/or were pushing for legalization of 'recreational' cannabis, and Canada was moving in the same direction. For the United States, who, at national level, had for decades been at the forefront of advocating a 'war on drugs'-style approach, these developments highlighted the significant degree of hypocrisy that had emerged between federal and state levels, arguably eroding influence in the international arena. Moreover, international bodies such as WHO, the Joint United Nations Programme on HIV/AIDS (UNAIDS) and the United Nations Development Programme (UNDP) were coalescing around agendas of harm reduction, human rights, social justice, criminal justice reform and sustainable development (WHO, 2014; UNAIDS, 2015; UNDP, 2015).

These movements contributed to what Sischy and Blaustein (2018: 74) describe as a 'critical moment' for global drug policy at the 2016 UNGASS, revealing a 'broken consensus' in international control, with deep and clear contradictions being brought to the surface. However, while there was growing noise around drug policy reform, these voices were still relatively marginal, with a range of other influential international actors and UN member states, such as China and Russia, seeking either to downplay reform debates or to continue to affirm commitment to the goal of eradication through punitive sanctions (Collins, 2018). As such, this resulted in little substantive movement, and in respect of cannabis specifically, questions of legalization were distanced from proceedings.

Nevertheless, the 2016 UNGASS did lead – at least rhetorically – to an adopting of public health and human rights positions (Collins, 2018). Indicatively, in 2017, a joint statement by all UN agencies and WHO called for a 'reviewing and repealing of punitive laws that have been proven to have negative health outcomes and that counter established public health evidence … [including] drug use or possession of drugs for personal use' (WHO,

2017). Moreover, while the CND continues to reaffirm a 'determination to address and counter the world drug problem and to actively promote a society free of drug abuse', it has somewhat softened its position in respect of punishment, promoting 'alternatives' that are consistent with international conventions and domestic law (CND, 2019: 1, 3).

Most recently, in 2020, following many delayed and postponed voting opportunities, cannabis and cannabis resin were removed from Schedule IV of the 1961 Convention (CND, 2020). However, rather than indicating a significant tangible shift in international control frameworks, this represents a largely symbolic move, as cannabis remains in the highest schedule of control. Nevertheless, this move, almost 70 years since cannabis was denounced by WHO for having no medical benefits, has solidified and legitimized the opposite position, providing greater scope for medical regulation and research.

Notwithstanding the move away from advocating punitive sanctions for individual users and the recognition of medical applications of cannabis that is now shared across UN bodies and affiliated supranational drug control bodies, it is clear that international cannabis control is more fragmented than has been the case since the 1961 UN Convention. This has resulted from the influence of individual key players on the global stage but is also reflected in the positions of regional blocs, which, as political and economic units, have the potential to play a powerful role in shaping international drug policy agendas and voting on proposals. The Latin American bloc has already been mentioned in relation to its role in advocating reform, but it is also worth briefly considering how other regions – such as the African Union, the Association of Southeast Asian Nations (ASEAN) and the European Union (EU) – have been approaching cannabis and illegal drug control in recent years.

In Africa, while there has traditionally been support for approaches based on criminalization, recent statements and plans of the African Union – an intergovernmental organization comprising 55 countries and representing almost 1.3 billion of the world's population – have embraced a position in accordance with the *Outcome Document of the United Nations General Assembly Special Session on the World Drug Problem* (UNODC, 2016). Indicatively, the African Union's most recent *Plan of Action on Drug Control and Crime Prevention* affirms that: 'People who use drugs must be offered support, treatment and protection, rather than be faced with punishment and a criminal record. This includes the provision of alternatives to arrest, sentencing and incarceration' (African Union, 2019: 15). In relation to cannabis, this has translated into 11 member states having liberalized policies either in law or in practice in the 18 months after the 2016 UNGASS. Nevertheless, this should not diminish the fact that a large majority of countries in the African Union continue to support criminalized approaches (Eligh, 2019).

In Europe, many countries have, to varying degrees, liberalized cannabis policy. However, as a regional bloc, the EU has lacked a definitive overall position in reform debates. As with other policy issues at the European level, cannabis – and, by extension, drug policy – reflects a careful balancing act between policy harmonization envisaged under the Treaty of Maastricht and the granting of autonomy to member states (Chatwin, 2013). As such, EU drug strategies have not sought to impose particular approaches, but are instead framed as 'add[ing] value to national strategies' (EU, 2013: 5). Given the considerable diversity that has emerged within European states as well as the current challenges facing the integrity of the European project, there has been little political impetus to challenge the position of cannabis in global control frameworks. It is nevertheless noteworthy that all member states have now adopted harm reduction measures with increasing experimentation in cannabis control, which in itself illuminates the flexible application of drug control conventions and the tacit tolerance of this by the EU (Chatwin, 2007; Hughes and Stevens, 2010, 2012).

In East Asia and South Asia, the position on cannabis and other illegal drugs has largely been one of adhering to a 'drug-free' vision, with ASEAN consistently reaffirming this commitment (ASEAN, 2017). Often, this involves the use of extremely punitive measures: 16 countries in Asia retain the death penalty for drug-related activities, and forced detention of drug users is common in several countries (International Drug Policy Consortium, 2019). Yet here too there are signs of fragmentation in respect of cannabis control, with some countries, such as South Korea and Thailand, revising drug laws to regulate the cultivation and/or use of cannabis for medical purposes.

In summary so far, the formation and development of international cannabis control throughout the 20th century resulted in the emergence of a dominant paradigm centred around criminalized prohibition. In considering why this came to be, one cannot ignore the asymmetrical relations of power between different actors on the global stage. It is difficult to dismiss the immense resources and political capital spent by the United States throughout the latter half of the 20th century in advocating a war on drugs. Yet key moments in the development of international cannabis control have been shaped by other players too, whether that be Egypt in the 1920s or Latin American countries at the end of the 2000s. What the discussion so far alerts us to are the complex processes and constantly evolving power struggles between different actors, who have used available resources to advance and maintain preferred agendas or challenge established orders that often coexist with broader social, economic and security concerns.

Thus, contrary to a perspective which sees international conventions and bodies as being the instigating and policing agents of a strict prohibitive agenda, it is more useful to consider these as providing 'a useful enabling mechanism to coalesce member states around' (Collins, 2018: 111). A prohibitive approach came to fit with the sorts of narratives and policies that dominant political actors, faced with various domestic and foreign policy problems, sought to pursue in response to a multitude of threats to social stability and power. As Collins (2018: 111) further notes, 'a global regulatory framework matured alongside and was co-opted by the "war on drugs", but it was not a determining factor'. Thus, global cannabis policy reflects the political choices of member states, which have been legitimized by, and simultaneously served to further cement, a dominant international paradigm.

Moreover, it is apparent that international controls are not as rigid as one might assume prima facie. Owing to the inherent ambiguity of global agreements that has featured since their emergence, strictly enforced prohibition is but one of many different possible interpretations of the cornerstone conventions. As more and more jurisdictions across the globe continue to embrace a range of control approaches, this serves to further fragment global cannabis control (Collins, 2018). Commenting on the ambivalent array of governing arrangements and policy positions which have contributed to an 'impasse' in international policy debates, Sischy and Blaustein (2018: 80) argue that this will 'likely foster greater opportunities for state and non-state actors to openly contest or simply ignore the international drug control conventions'.

Governing cannabis at national and subnational levels

The discussion in the previous section has alerted us to the importance of 'passage points' at an international level in how the governance of cannabis is performed (Edwards, 2016). However, recent trends towards policy liberalization across the globe have been driven less by coordinated global or regional agreement and action than by unilateral political decision-making at national and, arguably even more so, local levels. Tellingly, in a European context, Decorte et al (2020a: 3) note that 'until very recently, the national governments of Europe seemed to be either inert or in denial about the changing policy landscape'.

Recognizing the 'bottom-up' nature of many of the changes that have occurred in cannabis policy in recent years brings to the fore the differences which already existed and those that have emerged *within* national jurisdictions – for example, between federal and state levels in the United States, or between national and municipal governments in countries such as the Netherlands. This reflects one of the main themes that later chapters of this book engage with – the types of relations which exist between social actors that enable political power to be executed, negotiated and resisted. Having canvassed the broad strokes of international policy developments, we now turn to look at specific contemporary manifestations of cannabis control within differing governable spaces across the globe.

Yet what exactly has emerged and how different approaches can be typified remains hazy, with no clear consensus on classification of different types of control regime. Even a cursory search of the literature reveals a wide array of categories that fall between the extremes of prohibition and regulation. Often, similar terminology and categories are used, but their precise meanings and rules for inclusion differ depending on the author(s). For example, Room et al (2008) include 'diversion' within the category of 'depenalization', while Stevens et al (2019) designate 'diversion' as its own category; Belackova et al's (2020) conception of 'depenalization' is inclusive of criminal sanctions up to custodial sentences, whereas others define it as the removal of all criminal sanctions (Stevens et al, 2019); and Eligh (2019) uses categories of 'prohibition (hybrid)' and 'decriminalisation (hybrid)', which are not used by others.

These definitional issues become further complicated when considering the different sorts of cannabis-related activities that are subject to regulation and control, such as 'use', 'possession', 'supply', 'trafficking' and 'cultivation' (see Belackova et al, 2020). While a single legal jurisdiction may operate a strict prohibitive approach to cultivation and trafficking, it may simultaneously have a regulated system for the cultivation and possession of cannabis for medical purposes as well as a depenalized approach to non-medical users.

Even where different jurisdictions share a similar approach to the same type of act, what constitutes an act subject to control in one context may not necessarily be the same in another. A good example relates to cultivation; in some contexts, possessing seeds from a cannabis plant is enough to transgress the law, while in others, it is only once a seed has germinated that possession is legally determined to constitute an offence.

It is not the aim here to attempt to resolve the considerable complexity in classifying different types of cannabis control, but for the sake of clarity, the following four categories are distinguished: prohibition, depenalization, decriminalization and legal regulation. An overview and examples of each category is given in turn.

Prohibition

On first appearances, the most straightforward type of cannabis control is prohibition. This refers to the drug control law(s) of a jurisdiction that prohibit cannabis-related activities – including, inter alia, use and possession (including for both medical and non-medical purposes), supply and production – and the enforcement of these statutes with criminal sanctions. Despite the flourishing of alternative approaches, prohibition remains the most widely adopted model of control across the globe, particularly in the regions of Africa, Asia and the Middle East (see, for example, Al-Shazly and Tinasti, 2016).

However, the prohibition model is not as straightforward as it may first appear, as even those asserting to be its staunchest advocates may actually have approaches which effectively lessen the potential punitiveness. Rather than this being expressly applicable to cannabis offences, such outcomes often result from the general nature and functioning of the criminal justice system in that context.

Indicatively, Japanese authorities have consistently advocated for a tough application of criminal sanctions for violations of the country's Cannabis Control Act 1948, through aggressive enforcement of the law (see National Police Agency, 2021). Moreover, where there are grounds to arrest a suspect and pursue an investigation, such efforts are seemingly made. Given the lack of alternative disposals, arrest represents a crucial stage, with 98.6 per cent of arrestees being subsequently detained for up to 23 days in what has been described as a 'substitute prison' while an investigation is undertaken (Croydon, 2016).

Yet even in the case of Japan, which is often perceived to exemplify a prohibitive approach, the picture is muddied when considering the various processes that serve to sift and sort individuals from receiving formal sanctions. In 2019, out of the total number of suspects for Cannabis Control Act violations, 62.6 per cent were arrested, and among those arrested, only 50.6 per cent were prosecuted (Ministry of Justice, 2020). However, the high rate of convictions in the Japanese criminal justice system is infamous (see Johnson, 2002), and those charged under suspicion of contravening the Cannabis Control Act are no exception, with only one person found innocent in 2019. Nevertheless, in the same year, among those found guilty in the court of first instance, 85.9 per cent were given a suspended sentence and a further 2.1 per cent were given a partially suspended sentence (Ministry of Justice, 2020). Thus, the actual outcomes from the criminal justice system suggest that most of those arrested are either not prosecuted or do not serve custodial time – a far cry from the sentence of five years' imprisonment that is possible for possession offences.

Depenalization (de facto)

The gap between prohibitive statutes and how they are enforced is wider in contexts where there is a de facto depenalized approach. Stevens et al (2019: 3) define this as a 'reduction of the use of existing criminal sanctions'; in other words, cannabis-related activities are legally prohibited but laws are actively unenforced.

In some cases, such as England & Wales, the 'grey zone' between what the law says on paper and the discretion afforded to policing agencies in how it is enforced leaves a large space for discretion as to what is enforced and to what degree. Police discretion has long featured in how cannabis laws are applied in this context (May et al, 2002; Warburton et al, 2005), but this approach became more formalized following the introduction of cannabis warnings in 2004 and penalty notices for disorder in 2009, which allowed officers to 'dispose' of simple possession cases without needing to arrest and charge the individuals involved (ACPO, 2003, 2009). Since then, depenalization practices have further shifted and become more localized owing to the removal of centralized performance indicators along with the introduction of local democratically elected police and crime commissioners (PCCs). These developments provide police force chief constables and PCCs greater freedoms to set priorities and allocate resources. Consequently, while some police forces may pursue criminal sanctions for cannabis offences, a growing number are choosing to deprioritize cannabis possession (and in some cases also low-scale cultivation offences) and to build on the suite of out-of-court disposals through the introduction of diversion schemes (Gayle, 2015; Transform Drug Policy Foundation, 2022).

In other cases, while still attracting formal sanctions, more systematized de facto depenalization approaches can be found. These involve the use of instruments which direct agencies not to enforce applicable laws, such as prosecutorial guidelines that stipulate a specific set of conditions under which a prosecution for a cannabis offence should or should not be pursued. For example, in Belgium the cultivation of one cannabis plant is given the lowest prosecutorial priority, meaning that ordinarily prosecutions will not be sought in such instances. This mechanism has effectively enabled the growth of cannabis social clubs (CSCs). These grassroots user groups have been able to take advantage of 'the flexibility and ambiguity within the domestic drugs legislation' afforded to individual cultivation to collectively cultivate and distribute cannabis to their members (Decorte et al, 2017: 46). Prosecutorial guidelines in the Netherlands go even further; in addition to rules concerning home cultivation and possession for personal use, the selling and purchasing of cannabis at designated coffeeshops is also 'tolerated' if certain conditions are met (see Chapter 3). Given the power conferred to the Public Prosecutor's Office in directing the enforcement activities of the police, cases which meet the non-prosecution criteria are not brought to the attention of authorities in the first place – regardless of the number of transgressions of a given individual – making depenalization more systematic and certain.

Decriminalization (de jure)

While de facto depenalization approaches leave legally proscribed criminal sanctions intact, de jure decriminalization approaches involve the 'removal of criminal sanctions' (Stevens et al, 2019: 3). Within this category, three main variations in policy approaches have been observed: the replacement of criminal sanctions with civil sanctions; the diversion of users to health and/or social support services; and the lack of any sanction at all.

The first variation can be seen in the case of the Czechia, where the personal use of illegal drugs was decriminalized in 1990, being later criminalized where the amount found was considered 'greater than small' (see Mravcik, 2015). The difficulties of interpretation of the 'greater than small' definition led to revisions in 2010 and 2013 that set threshold amounts. Under the current legislation, individuals who are caught in possession of up to 10 grams of herbal cannabis or 5 grams of cannabis resin will receive a fine of up to approximately €580 (around £500), representing a civil – rather than criminal – sanction (Mravcik, 2015; Eastwood, 2020).

The second variation, diverting users to support services, has been discussed most frequently in relation to Portugal, which, since 2001, has pursued a policy of decriminalizing personal drug use for all illegal drugs. At the same time as removing criminal penalties for possession offences, regionally based Commissions for the Dissuasion of Drug Addiction (CDTs) – panels involving lawyers, social workers and medical professionals – were established. In addition to being able to proscribe administrative sanctions – such as fines, bans and community service – CDTs can order individuals to enter treatment and education programmes in lieu of sanctions. This is particularly the case for those identified as dependent users; for those identified as non-dependent drug users, CDTs can also 'suspend' proceedings, resulting in no further action – whether it be sanction, treatment or education – being taken (Hughes and Stevens, 2010).

This aspect is akin to the third variation of decriminalization, which involves replacing criminal sanctions with no sanction at all, as seen in Germany and South Africa. In the latter case, the Constitutional Court of South Africa ruled in 2018 that the use and growth of cannabis in private spaces would no longer be a criminal offence. Importantly, however, this has not resulted in any form of new regulation, but simply removed criminal sanctions in the law (Parry et al, 2019).

Thus, in all three variations, prohibitive legislation remains, but this is supplemented by other legislation and directives which remove the legal capacity of criminal justice agencies to enforce criminal sanctions.

Legal regulation

Finally, there is also a range of policy approaches that can be broadly categorized under legal regulation. The approaches range from partial regulation, usually in respect of medical prescriptions, to full regulation. Across partial and full regulatory approaches, a variety of models exist, involving different governing actors, such as national, regional and local state agencies, medical practices and pharmacies, cooperative CSCs and licensed for-profit businesses (see Caulkins et al, 2015).

While drawing a lot of international attention, full regulatory approaches are still comparatively rare, with, at the time of writing, only the national governments of Canada and Uruguay having legalized the entire cannabis market. Uruguay was the first to do so, with the passing of Law 19.172 in 2013 and the establishment of the Institute of Regulation and Control of Cannabis. The Uruguayan approach is comprised of three modes by which the cultivation and selling of cannabis is regulated: cultivation for personal consumption (since 2014), CSCs (since 2015) and sales at pharmacies (since 2017).

Individual cultivators are required to be registered, and once they are, it is permissible to grow six in-flower plants and have an annual harvest of up to 480 grams per household (Pardo, 2014). An alternative means by which cannabis can be obtained is through CSCs. By 2018, 110 CSCs had been established. These registered civil associations are comprised of 15–45 members, who must be citizens or permanent residents. CSCs are responsible for cultivating and distributing the cannabis to members, but they are subject to tight regulations: each CSC is permitted to cultivate a maximum of 99 plants, with members able to obtain up to 40 grams of cannabis per month; they must define opening hours and not operate activities beyond that schedule; they are prohibited from advertising; they must submit a crop and distribution plan; they must secure a non-visible crop preparation site and storage space; and they must have a security system (see Pardal et al, 2019; Queirolo, 2020). The third way cannabis can be obtained in Uruguay is through sales at licensed pharmacies, of which there were 14 in 2018 (Pardal et al, 2019). In this model, there is a strict separation of production and supply, with two national companies granted licences to sell cannabis to the pharmacies. At the supply end, cannabis is sold at a fixed price (as of 2019, US$1.30, equivalent to £1.06, per gram). However, with just two brands and five varieties, which contain relatively low THC content (6–9 per cent), the selection of products is quite limited in comparison to the overall cannabis market (Obradovic, 2021). Similar to CSCs, consumers are able to purchase up to 40 grams per month or up to 10 grams per week (Pardo, 2014).

In the current landscape of cannabis control, much more common than approaches involving full legal regulation are those with partial regulation, particularly in respect of cannabis for medical purposes. One of the most recent entrants to this rapidly growing club is Thailand. Following an amendment to the Narcotics Act in 2019 along with subsequent legal notifications, Thailand has established a tightly regulated system for the cultivation, distribution and use of cannabis for medical purposes.

Under the Thai approach, practitioners of both modern and traditional medicine are able to acquire government-approved licences. As of November 2020, there were 339 medical cannabis clinics and 419 traditional cannabis clinics. In these settings, cannabis products can be prescribed for medical conditions in accordance with one of the following criteria: there are studies approving its use; they are used to control symptoms of diseases; or they are used as a 'last resort' medicine at the discretion of the physician. Moreover, patients can acquire a licence to grow up to six plants (of government-authorized strains) per household. Cultivation of cannabis intended for medical purposes is similarly controlled under a licensing system; farmers are required to have a signed contract from a hospital or medical practitioner, to whom they will sell their product, or the Thai government will purchase the product at a set price (approximately US$2,200, equivalent to £1,797, per kilo). In addition, the recent legal reforms also removed cannabis materials/products containing less than 0.2 per cent THC from legal statutes, creating a legal pathway to use hemp and cannabidiol (CBD) in agriculture, cosmetics, food and so on, which was previously prohibited under Thai law.

Frequently, as is the case in Thailand, in settings where medical cannabis has become regulated, acts relating to non-medical use remain illegal and are dealt with through prohibition, depenalization or decriminalization. There is also an increasing number of countries where, despite regulations permitting cultivation for medical purposes, possession and/or use for medical purposes remains illegal. For example, with the passing of the Dangerous Drugs (Production of Cannabis for Medical and Scientific Use) Regulations 2018, Zimbabwe opened the door for state-approved licences for domestic cannabis cultivation intended for the medical cannabis market. By the end of 2020, 44 such licences had been issued. Nevertheless, with all use in Zimbabwe remaining strictly prohibited, the cannabis that is being grown is aimed for export markets (Ndlovu, 2020), a pattern that can be observed elsewhere on the African continent (El-Khoury et al, 2020).

Beyond the national level of policy and legislation, differences exist between and across the local spheres of governance within a national jurisdiction. Arguably, nowhere is this seen more starkly than in the United States, where, in recent decades, a range of regulatory approaches have flourished. As of May 2021, 36 states and 4 territories had active legislation permitting individuals to be prescribed medical cannabis, while a growing number of states and territories – 18 and 2, respectively, at the time of writing – have gone further, passing legislation that regulates the sale, possession and use of non-medical cannabis. There are also 12 states with legislation permitting, to some extent, cannabis products containing CBD and/or low THC. Three states have no public cannabis access programme in force (National Conference of State Legislatures, 2021).

Notwithstanding the obvious raft of differences *between* partial and full regulation, there are also some considerable differences in how approaches have manifested in subnational governable spaces that have introduced *either* partial *or* full regulation. In respect of the latter, this includes, inter alia: the limit on the quantity allowed for personal public possession; whether retail outlets can sell cannabis; licensing, taxation, advertising, packaging, product and zoning regulations for retail outlets; whether home cultivation is permitted and, if so, the number of plants permitted per household; and the limits for driving under the influence of THC (Pardo, 2014; Caulkins et al, 2015; Lancione et al, 2020; Obradovic, 2021).

Summary

The contemporary landscape of cannabis control across international, regional, national and subnational contexts is incredibly diverse, with different themes and variations in control approaches and governing actors. As more polities come to embrace alternatives to the prototypical prohibitive model that had become coded into international drugs control throughout the 20th century, this has made the policy sphere more animated and more complex. Returning to questions of context-independency and context-dependency, it is evidently difficult to explain policy manifestations as being *either* indicative of globalizing convergence around the same culture of control *or* a series of hermetically sealed exceptions at national or subnational levels of governance. It is precisely in trying to unpack and make sense of how cannabis control has manifested and continues to evolve that the importance of understanding and explaining how different governing actors at local, national and international levels have negotiated the policy landscape and its structured boundaries within particular settings is drawn into focus. It is in these regards that we turn next to consider two cases – England & Wales and the Netherlands – in further depth to elicit the dispositions and policy agendas of policy actors and how these are situated within their respective sociopolitical and cultural contexts.

3

Sociopolitical Change and Cannabis Control

Introduction

Contemporary manifestations of cannabis control represent a complex milieu of responses both across and within countries. Understanding how this variation is possible, and where it has arisen from, requires us to examine historical patterns of political institutional cultures. Focusing on England & Wales and the Netherlands, which constitute the main empirical cases of this book, this chapter charts the development of domestic cannabis control from the 20th century within the broader sociopolitical context of each country. In some ways, the trajectories of governing crime and illegal drug problems appear to share remarkable similarities, with both countries evidencing a broad shift from a penal-welfare system to one fitting the characteristics of an ambivalent culture of control. At the same time, however, there are crucial differences in respect of foundational aspects of political institutional cultures as well as how political actors have reacted to endogenous and exogenous shocks that continue to produce different opportunities and restraints for policy manoeuvring in cannabis control.

The chapter is structured in two sections, organized chronologically, to allow for a critical exposition of the extent to which there has been a similar transition in each case from a system of control based on penal-welfarism to one characterized by a culture of control. Each section is framed around a comparison of the broader social and political environments and how these relate to developments in cannabis control.

Cannabis control and the penal-welfare state

Up to the middle of the 20th century, the issue of cannabis as a domestic political concern in both England & Wales and the Netherlands was fairly insignificant, rarely featuring in the thoughts of politicians. Yet, broader developments in the control of substances and crime, and how these responses were located within the respective social and political contexts, provided an important foregrounding for how cannabis would be responded to once it became more politically pertinent in the 1950s and 1960s.

Political culture and cannabis control in England & Wales

From the early 20th century until around the 1970s, and particularly in the post-war period, it has been asserted that the broader culture of crime control in England & Wales[1] was predominantly oriented around penal-welfarism (Garland, 1996, 2001) (see Chapter 1). Loader and Sparks (2007: 79) outline three interlocking axioms of this paradigm: first, that crime is conceptually unproblematic and geographically and socially delimited; second, that policy and practice are informed by causal theories that understand crime as a presenting symptom of deep-seated social problems; and finally, that crime control is the province of 'experts' and expert knowledge.

The emergence of this control culture was shaped by the political architecture of this context, which is structured around an adversarial 'first past the post' system and that, since the end of the First World War, has witnessed the growth and dominance of two main political parties – the Conservative Party and the Labour Party – split traditionally along the cleavage of social class.[2] Moreover, although the British constitution as a whole is largely 'uncodified', and 'depends heavily on constitutional understandings' (Moran, 2005: 71), two striking characteristics often attributed to the British constitution are parliamentary supremacy and the rule of law (Bogdanor, 1999). The 'Westminster system' tends to favour one party holding office with the other main party forming the 'opposition', and it grants considerable power to the dominant party and to the prime minister, who has a pivotal role in the direction and management of the executive branch, the coordination of policy across the different departments and the spearheading of the government. These aspects have contributed to a 'deferential civic culture', with policy processes heavily shaped by experts, civil servants and elected representatives rather than the public (Almond and Verba, 1989: 315; see also Ryan, 2003).

In addition, although this political system is inherently conflictual, conditions of the Second World War and immediately thereafter facilitated a shared recognition of the need for collective social responsibility and state intervention. This culminated in the nationalization and centralization of services, while also leading to the end of the 'golden age' of local government and a growing 'culture of disdain' towards the local sphere (Thomson, 1965; Pugh, 1994; Cole and John, 2001; Wilson and Game, 2011).

It was within this context that national welfare provisions grew substantially, with the concept of welfare changing from one based on provisions made to those unable to care for themselves to one based on the principle of 'unified universal contributory insurance to ensure at all times to all men a subsistence income for themselves and their families as of right … without any form of means test or inquiry about what means they had' (House of Lords, 1953). One of the most influential moments which solidified the 'welfare state' was the publishing of the Beveridge Report in 1942 which proposed the introduction of insurance to provide universal protection against unemployment, poverty and illness (Moran, 2005). This was further bolstered by a growing economy, which reaped the rewards of the post-war economic boom and improved living conditions. As a result, this period enjoyed high employment, relatively stable social conditions and a broad political consensus shared between the two dominant parties, centred on the notion that the state had a significant role in providing universal welfare to its citizens (Thomson, 1965).

Owing to the deferential top-down nature of governance (Almond and Verba, 1989), elites – such as practitioners, and academics, working within and around government – had substantial room for manoeuvre in advancing programmes for social reform without being questioned by citizens (Ryan, 2003). Thus, much decision-making was done behind closed doors by liberal 'platonic guardians', hidden away from public scrutiny (Loader, 2006). Thus, in respect of crime control, and paralleling the broader sociopolitical environment, the leading experts at this time broadly agreed on the basic principles of 'modern' criminology, 'with its faith in instrumental reason, its vision of the technocratic state and its commitment to social progress and social engineering' (Garland and Sparks, 2000: 194). The dominant paradigm in this period was based on a rehabilitative ideal, and responses aimed to reduce crime through identifying the cause of the criminal behaviour and treating it through individualized programmes of reform. A dominant belief was that through social reform and treatment, criminality could be reduced and ultimately eradicated. Such correctionalist criminology 'assumed without question the possibility and desirability of reintegrating delinquents and deviant individuals' (Garland, 2001: 44). Thus, the use of imprisonment in a retributive sense was viewed as counterproductive to the hegemonic principles of penal-welfarism.

The emergence of a broader penal-welfare infrastructure appears to have also shaped developments in the sphere of illegal drugs policy, particularly in respect of opiates. However, it is also important to consider the United Kingdom's history of being large producers and exporters of opium from the 17th century to the 19th century, and its monopolization of the market following the end of the Opium Wars. This contributed to the establishment of opium as the dominant solution to many medical problems within the United Kingdom, and as opiates became firmly established in physician practices, this also led to the creation of a small population of dependent users, existing largely in professional circles (Beeching, 1977).

Such contingent conditions relating to drugs and health policy, economic affairs and foreign affairs, as well as the broader welfare-oriented features of control systems, allowed illegal drugs policy, at least in respect of some substances, to be marked by 'medicalization' (Shiner, 2003). This 'British system' was affirmed in the 1926 Rolleston Report – which defined the contexts in which prescription should be advocated, primarily for heroin and morphine, to enable gradual withdrawal or to prevent serious disruptions to people's lives – and continued largely unchanged until the 1960s (Ministry of Health, 1926; Measham and South, 2012).

However, cannabis was largely absent from this broader approach of medicalization. While the use of cannabis as a medicine in Britain can be traced to the 19th century and was also bound together with economic interests of the British Empire (Reynolds, 1890; Booth, 2003; Mills, 2013), the extent of its use in domestic medical practices during this period was very limited and can be attributed to the dominance of opiates in treatment, a lack of regular supply and uncertainty over its action in different patients (Berridge, 1981; Taylor, 2008). With minimal knowledge and experience of cannabis domestically, there was little resistance or willingness to object to pressures from the international community when cannabis was included in the Second International Opium Convention in 1925 and ratified under an amendment to the 1928 Dangerous Drugs Act.

Following this, domestic expertise about cannabis remained limited, being shaped by conflicting accounts emanating from across the British Empire and the international community that portrayed cannabis as either an 'exotic pleasure or a foreign poison' (Mills, 2013: 61). Up until the end of the Second World War, non-medical consumption of cannabis appears to have been limited to small numbers of seafarers of mainly Arab and Asian origin. While, on the whole, this was not deemed to be a significant problem by authorities, cases involving the supply of cannabis from these foreigners to young white women began to sprout concerns that tied together issues of 'race' and cannabis (Mills, 2013). Moreover, the formation and expansion of the Drugs Branch within the Home Office during the 1920s and 1930s meant that the control infrastructure was well organized to respond when consumption came to be seen as more of a problem following the Second World War. As a result, the control of cannabis in the first half of the 20th century became largely separated from a dominant medical framework and lay dormant within a system of control and restriction tainted by colonial perspectives of the 'other' along with a politics of ignorance, fear and moral indignation towards drug consumption.

In the immediate post-war period, cannabis remained relatively low-key, with small numbers of cases continuing to be concentrated in port areas and among seafarers. However, in the context of the United Kingdom's declining position in the world and the migration of half a million people from former colonial countries such as Jamaica, where cannabis consumption had long been present, ideas circulating officialdom about cannabis became more firmly embedded with broader underlying racial tensions, prejudice and discrimination. As Mills (2013: 79) carefully illustrates, concerns grew about the use of cannabis and connection to violence, particularly among Caribbean populations, with cannabis serving as 'a useful pretext for the authorities to keep an eye on and to interfere with groups considered problematic largely because of the colour of their skin'.

These early racialized discourses and experiences of cannabis became further interwoven and more complex from the 1960s onwards with the acceleration of a vast range of shifts in social, economic and political conditions tied to processes of globalization and a questioning of modern structures and institutions. These developments are explored in far more depth elsewhere (see Friedman, 1986; Bauman, 1998; Giddens, 1998; Beck, 2000; Castells, 2001; Garland, 2001), but alongside postcolonial migration, they include: changes to family life and identity; shifts in work patterns and organization; developments in communications and transport technologies; the uprooting of traditional communities and the rise of the urban 'metropolis'; greater 'democratization' and empowerment of oppressed groups; organized civil disobedience; and, relatedly, particularly in the late 1960s, a rejection of 'traditional' norms and values, with accelerated secularization.

At the start of the decade, recorded cases were still low and political responses to cannabis maintained a wary disinterest, with the Interdepartmental Committee on Drug Addiction arguing in 1961 that 'cannabis is not a drug of addiction; it is an intoxicant' (quoted in Booth, 2003: 370). Nevertheless, changes in society became enmeshed with increased ability to import cannabis, and opportunities arose for new consumers to have contact with the substance (Mills, 2013). As the decade wore on, cannabis use began to be reported more in celebrity circles and the growing counter-culture movement, coming to be highly symbolic of a zeitgeist centred on individuality, liberty and resistance, as well as stretching to working-class youths who were having more encounters and associations with settled migrant populations (Young, 1971; Shiner, 2009; Mills, 2013; Seddon, 2020).

It was this fear that patterns of consumption were spreading beyond ethnic minority groups and into white populations that heightened official concerns. In this sense, problematizations of cannabis saw a fusing of historical underlying racialized discourses and emergence of new narratives, with political elites constructing the substance, its users and those responsible for its trafficking and supply as threats to the social and moral order.

The 1965 Dangerous Drugs Act ratified the 1961 Convention and consolidated the previous Dangerous Drugs Acts (Measham and South, 2012). As was the case in the UN scheduling, cannabis was treated the same as opiates, with no distinction between possession and trafficking of the drug. Following this piece of legislation, also in 1965, the reconvened Interdepartmental Committee on Drug Addiction reported similar findings to its report of four years prior, but added that there was a 'risk that young people may be persuaded to turn to cannabis' (quoted in Booth, 2003: 370). The reaction from law enforcement bodies was initially one of hostility, with the expansion of drugs squads and more rigorous enforcement practices contributing to an increase in convictions for cannabis offences from 4 in 1945 to 2,393 in 1967 (Advisory Committee on Drug Dependency, 1968; Young, 1971).

However, in reaction to the perceived overzealous actions of law enforcement, a campaign was initiated in 1967 by the Society of Mental Awareness and backed by publicly influential individuals. Moreover, in reaction to criticism of the government for its stance on cannabis, an Advisory Committee on Drug Dependency was established in 1967 with a sub-committee, headed by Baroness Wootton, to investigate the position of cannabis within the legal framework (see Seddon, 2020).

The Wootton Report questioned the approach the government had taken with regards to criminal sanctions for cannabis offences and suggested that 'the long-term consumption of cannabis in moderate doses has no harmful effects' (Advisory Committee on Drug Dependency, 1968: 9). The report went on to argue that 'the present penalties for possession and supply are altogether too high' (Advisory Committee on Drug Dependency, 1968: 27) and suggested that prison terms for possession should be very limited. In some ways the dispositions of the Wootton Committee typified those of the liberal 'platonic guardians' seeking to provide freedom and protection *from* the state. Furthermore, with expertise having an influential role in policy making during this period, the committee was in a good position to shape changes to legislation (Seddon, 2020).

Nevertheless, the recommendations were largely rejected by the government, with the Home Secretary, James Callaghan, noting that it would be 'sheer masochism' to facilitate the growth of this 'social evil' through legal lenience (The Times, 1969). Yet despite this initial hostility, the Wootton Report was to have a lasting influence, shaping the Misuse of Drugs Act of 1971, which remains the foundational framework for contemporary illegal drugs control in the United Kingdom. This Act split illegal substances into three categories – A, B and C – based on 'the social harm attributable to a drug when it is misused' (House of Commons, 2000: 13). Also telling of the report's influence is the cementing of the role of expertise in policy processes by making a permanent feature of the ACMD, whose purpose was to review the situation of drugs and make recommendations to government based on research (Mills, 2013). At this time, cannabis was placed in the Class B category, which carried with it a maximum of 5 years' imprisonment and/or an unlimited fine for possession, and up to 14 years' imprisonment and/or an unlimited fine for production or supply.

Political culture and cannabis control in the Netherlands

Responses to cannabis and its relation to political institutions and culture becomes more evident once we consider the case of the Netherlands. Here, the political architecture is based on a system of proportional representation in which coalitions of two or more political parties form a ruling government. For most of the 20th century, it was characterized as a 'consociational democracy' in which the elite actors belonging to different social 'blocs' or *zuilen* (pillars), distinguished along religious and class cleavages, engaged in a 'politics of accommodation' (Lijphart, 1968; see also Andeweg and Irwin, 2005). Up until the mid-1960s, most people's lives existed almost entirely within the pillar with which they were associated (see Bryant, 1981: 57; van Mierlo, 1986). For Lijphart (1968), 'pillarization' was made possible due to a political consensus and culture generated through abidance to the 'rules of the game'.

First, there was a duty of 'proportionality', which allowed all groups to be represented in coalition rule and required parties to share power and work together. Moreover, the power and role of the prime minister in the Dutch setting was much more limited than under a majoritarian regime, with ministers serving *with*, rather than *under*, the leader (Daalder, 1955) This also accords with the fact that the prime minister could only come from one pillar and, therefore, could not fairly represent the interests of all (Andeweg and Irwin, 2005). Furthermore, the 'agreement to disagree' required acceptance of fundamental ideological differences between opposing political actors, while 'depoliticization' meant that the state could refrain from engaging in conflictual politics by relying on constitutional and legal principles. The need to work together facilitated the role of expertise in informing judgements, with a high proportion of cabinet ministers being policy specialists (Bakema and Secker, 1988). Moreover, serious problems had to be resolved through 'summit diplomacy', involving inter-elite bargaining between the leaders of each pillar. This also tied into the 'business of politics', which prioritized clinical, results-orientated decision-making. Expert committees were the modus operandi of this approach, which developed pragmatic and non-partisan ideas that could further stabilize coalitions. Additionally, 'secrecy' aided the overall process, as the compromising decisions made by elite leaders were shielded from publicity. This allowed elites to make pragmatic decisions without the burden of external pressures. This was supported by lengthy negotiation processes, which put even greater distance between the preferences of voters and what was eventually decided as government policy, thereby insulating the policy process from crude populism. Finally, there was an ingraining of the 'government's right to govern', which allowed the core executive to govern without harassment from parliament.

While national state infrastructure grew considerably during this period, as was also the case in England & Wales, an important point of difference related to central–local relations of governance. Indeed, the Netherlands has a long history of refraining from over-centralized authoritarian control, whether in respect of the 'polder model',[3] cultural and religious tolerance, or the 'regent' mentality that developed in the region (Buruma, 2007; see also Daalder, 1966). These historical residues can be detected in the foundational House of Thorbecke framework, which granted considerable autonomy to municipalities and provinces (Daalder, 1955). This, Blom (2000: 159) asserts, played an important role in pillarized society, through 'conflict control, looking for compromises, damping down the inclination towards conflict and channelling it into moderate paths'.

The political stability generated by the politics of accommodation facilitated the growth of a generous welfare state. Initially, the Dutch welfare system was rather limited and consisted of a patchwork of uneven welfare programmes based within the different pillars. However, following the Second World War, systems of national welfare expanded substantially, taking inspiration from the van Rhijn Report, which suggested that the state ought to take responsibility for protecting its members by providing social security (van Oorschot, 2006). As a result, the post-war period saw vast increases in public expenditure on pensions, widows and orphans, child benefits, medical insurance and disability programmes, arguably culminating in a process of collectivization and solidarization, and further reinforcing the politics of accommodation (Andeweg and Irwin, 2005; van Oorschot, 2006).

Developments in crime and illegal drugs control paralleled the rise and dominance of a penal-welfare state. While it is important not to 'mythologize' the Dutch experience (see Franke, 1990), it is possible to argue that a distinct paradigm came to dominate crime control in the post-war period. Rising economic prosperity along with the stable pillarized political environment, in which there was a high level of elite consensus around welfare provision, enabled crime policy to be largely shaped by liberal practitioners and academics. The influence of such experts facilitated a process of decarceration premised on an ideal of 'resocialization', which suggested that punishment should be orientated towards the successful reintegration of the individual back into society (see Downes, 1982, 1988; Boone, 2011). An important component of why the ideal of resocialization took hold must be placed within the context of the 'trauma' of the war and occupation by Nazi Germany (Withuis and Mooij, 2010). Post-war liberation gave reformers an ideal opportunity to inscribe long-lasting change on penal institutions, based on notions of freedom and humanism. This was shaped by the moral entrepreneurship of a group of elites from the Utrecht School, comprised of criminologists, lawyers and psychiatrists (van Swaaningen, 2006; Junger-Tas and Junger, 2007).

In the sphere of drugs policy, similar to the United Kingdom, the Netherlands took advantage of its global geopolitical position during its colonial years, prioritizing economic interests in the trading of opium, where, until 1942, it maintained a monopoly in what was the Dutch Indies. Moreover, even in the early years of international illegal drugs control, there was a pragmatic recognition of the limitations enforcing a prohibitive regime (de Kort, 1994). In light of such sentiments, opium users were not typically prosecuted; a medical approach to illegal drug use was preferred instead. While trade interests formed an important aspect of this early approach, de Kort (1994) also points to the size of the dependent user population, which existed in similar proportions to that of the United Kingdom. In addition, the role of the medical profession was influential in policy development and implementation, with the task of enforcing the 1919 Opium Act balanced between the health and justice departments. Health was focused on allowing doctors to prescribe drugs to dependent users, while justice was focused on illegal trafficking and smuggling.

In respect of cannabis, its use in the Netherlands during the early 20th century was limited, located primarily within small circles of artists and writers who would access it through the major port cities (de Kort, 1994). After the Second World War, cannabis use became associated with jazz musicians in some of the more cosmopolitan areas of Amsterdam and Rotterdam. Although trade in cannabis cigarettes increased after the war, the police were unable to do anything about this, as possession was not made illegal under the Opium Act until 1953, and it was not until 1955 that the first arrests took place among smugglers and users (de Kort, 1994). From the 1960s onwards, cannabis started to become more available and was consumed in an underground market, mainly by well-educated individuals involved in a youth subculture movement (Korf, 2008). Cannabis use came to symbolize a counterculture in which a new generation were keen to make a *doorbraak* (breakthrough) (Andeweg, 2008). At first, the police would rigorously enforce the laws on cannabis, searching for those in possession of small amounts, but following scenes of violence between the police and youth groups, an informal system of tolerated cannabis consumption and sales through 'house dealers' located predominantly in youth centres began to take shape (de Kort, 1994; Korf, 2008).

In attempting to account for why the Netherlands started to adopt a different position on cannabis at this time, there are several important contributory factors. In comparison with the United States, de Kort (1994: 17) argues that '[t]he Netherlands … lacked a specific ideology associated with marihuana … [and] also lacked a moral entrepreneur' willing to criminalize the drug. In other words, the dominant disposition oriented around moral conservativism that was found elsewhere did not exist in the Netherlands. When cannabis use spread throughout society, this was framed predominantly as a youth counterculture issue, and as such was treated with the same permissive approach granted to other 'deviant' practices at the time, such as sexual diversity and abortion (Leuw, 1994).

Importantly, Uitermark (2004) argues that a significant factor in why the Netherlands followed a different route in cannabis policy is the way the religious and other established mainstream parties responded to growing divisions across society. From around the late 1960s, there began to be serious challenges to the pillarized structure. Along with similar processes in the United Kingdom, detailed in the previous section, the post-war 'baby boom' created a new generation who were tired of the formal controls of the *zuilen* (Bryant, 1981). With the process of secularization accelerating the urge for reform in the shape of voter mobility, Dutch society was becoming more heterogeneous and, as a result, the rules of the game were changing to become more politicized, more open to public scrutiny, and the relationship between the elites and the mass public had become increasingly strained (Lijphart, 1977, 1989; Daalder, 1987).

As new political parties emerged, the pillar parties (particularly the religious ones) lost their stranglehold on voters, which allowed a *doorbraak* of the pillar monopoly in government (Andeweg, 2008; Pennings and Keman, 2008). Moreover, with support for the mainstream political parties waning in the initial stages of depillarization, changing elite behaviour also resulted in recognition of the need to concede issues to the younger groups in society so as not to exacerbate the generational conflict (van Schendelen, 1978; van Mierlo, 1986; Uitermark, 2004).

Free from a moralistic ideological perspective on cannabis, and in the spirit of an expertise-led and compromise-based approach to policy making at a national level, two commissions were established to look at the issue of illegal drugs, specifically cannabis. The first was in 1969, initiated by the National Federation of Mental Health Organisations and led by the penal abolitionist Professor Hulsman. This commission suggested that cannabis was less addictive than tobacco, and it dismissed the 'gateway theory', arguing that criminalization of the drug would be one of the most important factors in users turning to harder drugs, making it more difficult to return to socially accepted lifestyles (Leuw, 1994; Buruma, 2007). The spirit of the report was very much based in the zeitgeist of the time, drawing on the ideals inscribed in the Utrecht School and other established liberal philosophies. As Leuw (1994: 29) argues, it was 'based on the principle that the state should refrain as much as possible from interference with behaviors that have consequences for the individual person only'.

Furthermore, the history of empowered subnational authorities and the recent experience of war trauma was also relevant. These dynamics allowed for a flourishing of autonomy from overzealous state intervention and the promotion of individual freedoms, which contributed to the articulation of alternative paradigms to cannabis policy (Pakes, 2003). This liberal perspective was especially prevalent in the larger, more urbanized cities. As illustration, the colloquial name 'Amsterdam Republic' referred to that city's status as independent from national rule. The liberal perspective contributed to political normalization of cannabis through the application of liberal expertise, a key component of the penal-welfare paradigm.

While the Hulsman Report may have been viewed as having a more radical perspective on drugs and prohibition, it provided an influential context to the second committee, which was sponsored by government and headed by Professor Baan, a key member of the Utrecht School. The findings of this commission were communicated in much more pragmatic terms, discussing the legal framework surrounding illegal drugs and suggesting that cannabis should not be included in the same classification as drugs that pose 'unacceptable' risks (Buruma, 2007). There was an acceptance that individuals will use cannabis, and it was proposed that integration of the drug into society was possible, though this did 'not mean that no risks are involved, but that those risks could be acceptable' (Working Group on Narcotic Drugs, 1972: 66). Given the changing political context at the time, the findings of this report were almost all accepted by the centre-Right government.

While the Hulsman and Baan commissions were clearly significant in granting legitimacy to the political normalization of cannabis, it is perhaps more telling that these were indicative of a range of practices that were already apparent in Dutch society and which had sprouted from the local level of policy making. It is at this level that practitioners found pragmatic solutions to accommodate what was considered a relatively harmless substance. Thus, existing practices formed a base from which scientific expertise via respected commissions legitimized and shifted cannabis into a health-driven national framework and away from more reactive and repressive criminal justice responses.

Following a de facto depenalization experiment with house dealers, the state formalized its approach to cannabis control through the revised Opium Act 1976, which distinguished between Schedule 1 (hard) and Schedule 2 (soft) drugs. Although the revised Opium Act was officially established in 1976, it had been drafted three years earlier. During this time, premises were able to adjust their practices to fall in line with the new legislation. The idea of experimentation was also evident in the Baan report, which suggested that this should form an important part of drugs policy evaluation so that 'when sufficient faith in the safety of new positions exists, then the old ones can be left' (Working Group on Narcotic Drugs, 1972: 74). As will be seen, this notion has left an important impression on contemporary policy making.

The government proposed a 30-gram limit on cannabis possession, above which it would be considered a prosecutable offence. While the 1976 Opium Act officially incorporated a policy of *gedogen* (tolerance) towards house dealers, the rules concerning their operation did not come into force until 1980 (Jansen, 1994), having grown out of practices that many youth centres had been using over the previous decade with those selling cannabis.

The *Guidelines for Investigation and Prosecution* were based on the expediency principle, meaning that prosecution would be waived for certain offences under certain circumstances if it was in the public's interest (see Korf et al, 1999). Notably, Buruma (2007) argues, there was an important reframing of this principle in 1970, which shifted it from 'prosecution, unless' that is not in the public interest to 'prosecution only if' it is in the public interest. The implication is that law enforcement agencies should prosecute cannabis offences only if they contravene the dominant underlying principles of the health-driven policy. Thus, although the revised Opium Act ratified the 1961 Convention, the unique policy regarding cannabis was made possible on the basis that it was 'necessary' to protect public health through a separation of markets.

The guidelines stipulated that the selling of cannabis would be tolerated (it would be a low priority for prosecution) if the house dealers abided by a set of criteria, which became known as the AHOJ-G criteria in 1991: *geen affichering* (no overt advertising); *geen harddrugs* (no hard drugs); *geen overlast* (no nuisance); *geen verkoop aan jeugdigen* (no sales to underage clients[4]); and *geen verkoop van grote hoeveelheden per transactie* (no sales of large stocks) (Korf, 2002; Buruma, 2007; van der Stel et al, 2009).

Moreover, and quite significantly, in 1977 it was established that local 'triangles' – tripartite consultations between the mayor, chief of police and chief prosecutor – would determine the approach to cannabis retailers in municipalities. This formally empowered local practitioners to tolerate the selling and consumption of cannabis (van der Stel et al, 2009). This reiterates the implicit notion in Dutch politics that local municipalities should have the authority to determine policies that fit the local context. By the end of the 1970s, the house dealer became a powerful force in the cannabis scene, overtaking street dealers and the underground market (Korf, 2008).

Summary: cannabis control and the penal-welfare state

Throughout the early to mid 20th century, both England & Wales and the Netherlands embraced the formation of a large penal-welfare state. Particularly in the immediate post-war period, this was supported by a relatively stable political environment, liberal elitism, and commitment to a rehabilitative ideal. Yet throughout this time, cannabis was not a major domestic political concern and was rather alienated from this penal-welfare framework, being quietly sidelined into prohibitive frameworks and shaped by racialized narratives.

After the war, and particularly from the 1960s, both countries started to experience similar social and economic changes associated with globalization and the shift to late modernity, such as changes in the family and work, secularization, postcolonial migration and the growth of youth counterculture. It was from this time onwards that cannabis became more prevalent in society and political questions about whether to reform punitive laws emerged on policy agendas.

The establishment of core pieces of legislation in both countries occurred at the zenith of penal-welfarism, and the use of, and recommendations by, expert committees were strikingly similar. However, the outcome of these policy debates resulted in quite different policy approaches, and this appears to have been mediated by the political institutions and relations found within the respective cultural contexts.

In England & Wales, the adversarial political system and history of the Westminster system encourages competition between two major parties and favours a 'strong' government. Where one political party commands a parliamentary majority and a small group of its elected members run the core executive, the need to give consideration to others is limited. In response to the growing 'problem' of cannabis consumption and social change in the 1960s, ruling national political actors in England & Wales were able to readily reject expert advice and translate their moral preferences – based on perceived dangers of ethnic minority populations and youth immorality – into policy decisions, which maintained an approach of criminalized prohibition. It is argued that even though expertise had a significant degree of legitimacy in guiding policy in the broader climate, its use was shaped by the dynamics of governing generated by the political system in this context.

This is contrasted with the consociational democracy which came to characterize Dutch politics. Embedded within, and shaped by, a history of pragmatism and power-sharing, this resulted in coalition governments that represented all blocs in society. The structure of governing through coalition produces a dynamic whereby consensus is needed to rule. It is in this regard that expert committees play an important pragmatic role by finding the middle ground for conflicting parties. This was arguably more accentuated at a time when the pillarized system was being severely weakened by growing divides between younger and older generations. Driven by both a pragmatic need and a normative desire to negotiate and find compromise, the formal response to cannabis drew heavily on the recommendations of experts and attempted to inclusively accommodate the younger generation.

A further key difference between England & Wales and the Netherlands concerns the relations between national and local authorities. In England & Wales, notions of 'parliamentary supremacy' and a growing nation state were accompanied by the withering of the power of local authorities, which were gradually becoming delivery agents for central government. In the Netherlands, and not least in the context of the trauma of the Second World War, municipalities were afforded greater freedoms and powers to inform and participate in the development of policy. This aversion to perceptions of authoritarianism coupled with empowerment of local actors facilitated a flourishing of alternative responses to criminalization, and this further shaped the depenalization of the sale and consumption of cannabis at a national level.

Convergence around a common culture of control?

Since the early 1970s, both countries have witnessed considerable changes in the social, economic and political landscape which have intimately affected and reshaped responses to crime, deviance and disorder. Cannabis was no exception in this regard, but though both countries experienced similar 'exogenous shocks' that made the politics of cannabis control more politicized, polarized and ambivalent, the continued existence of core differences in policies and policy-making processes remains. This brings into question the extent to which each country has converged around a common culture of control under late modern conditions.

Political culture and cannabis control in England & Wales

In England & Wales, after the Misuse of Drugs Act was introduced in 1971, core legislation and policy specifically concerning the classification of cannabis remained untouched for 33 years until the reclassification to Class C in 2004. However, the broad environment in which responses to criminality and illegal drugs were formulated underwent considerable change.

In combination with the vast social changes of the 1960s already discussed (see also Garland, 2001: 81–9), the economic recession of the 1970s triggered the collapse of the post-war political consensus. The Conservative Party's vision of how best to counter the economic and social problems was explicitly anti-welfarist, focused on a backlash against 'big government' and the 'permissive culture' of the 1960s. This proved to be appealing to a majority of the electorate (Newburn, 1991; Garland, 2001). The election of Margaret Thatcher as prime minister in 1979 heralded, inter alia, sweeping deregulation and privatization reforms, the decommissioning of British manufacturing industries and the promotion of individual ownership and entrepreneurship. From this period on, UK politics has been increasingly penetrated by neoliberal and neoconservative principles. As Garland notes: 'If the watchwords of post-war social democracy had been *economic control and social liberation*, the new politics of the 1980s put in place a quite different framework of *economic freedom and social control*' (2001: 100, emphasis in original).

The politics of 'law and order' became a crucial political battleground, not least because this period witnessed a steady increase in the recorded prevalence of both crime and fear of crime. Connected to this was the increase in illegal substance use by 'respectable' middle-class youth, by individuals in lower social strata and by ethnic minorities. The aftermath of the hippie counterculture, which embraced cannabis and other psychoactive drugs such as LSD, saw the rise of a new zeitgeist in the late 1970s and 1980s with greater availability of heroin and cocaine. While prior to this, heroin was used in small circles of professionals, mostly dependent users, in the context of increased flows of people and goods, heroin became more widely available and appealed not only to the hippie generation, but also, and more worryingly for government authorities, to lower social classes and ethnic minorities in urban communities already experiencing social problems associated with deindustrialization (Seddon, 2006, 2008). It was at this point that the link between drugs, community degradation, violence and antisocial behaviour became especially heightened (see Parker and Newcombe, 1987; Jarvis and Parker, 1989) and contributed to a broader questioning of the penal-welfare system and the ability to maintain a medicalized system.

The rise of heroin and other forms of illegal drug use align with Garland's broader arguments about the perceived ineffectiveness of traditional responses to issues of crime and disorder. These trends challenged the ability of a penal-welfare framework to successfully tackle crime and drug use. More specifically, prohibitive approaches appeared to be doing little to stem the increases in drug use, and as a result, alarming new challenges surfaced. These were evident in public health, with the spread of AIDs and other blood-borne viruses among injecting drug users, as well as in the arena of crime control, with the upsurge in criminal activity connected to the new wave of drug users. As such, it has been argued that this produced a drug policy predicament in which the state needed to adapt, due to the failure of traditional approaches, but was also wary of the political ramifications of withdrawing the projection of sovereignty in the provision of law and order (Garland, 2001; Seddon, 2008).

On the one hand, responses assumed non-adaptive forms in which illegal drug users came to be seen as 'dangerous others' who posed threats to the core of society. Marginalizing and punitive measures were imposed to manage such risky populations. This is intimately connected to the rise of politically tough rhetoric from the New Right. As Seddon (2006, 2008) suggests, heroin, and later crack cocaine, became associated with an 'undeserving' and socio-economically deprived group of individuals and links were made to acquisitive crime. Tougher measures were introduced through several pieces of legislation, notably the Controlled Drugs (Penalties) Act 1985 and the Drug Trafficking Offences Act 1986, which increased maximum penalties for Class A trafficking to life imprisonment and allowed the police to seize assets. In addition, law enforcement became more specialized, through, for example, employing intelligence-led and problem-oriented models and establishing 'drugs wings' in the regional crime squads (Lee and South, 2008: 501).

On the other hand, systems of illegal drugs control adapted to the perceived crisis. In one prominent sense, there was a departure from the dominant view that the eradication of drug use is a viable goal, with moves towards drug use management and harm reduction. Thus, rather than seeking to stop the use of illegal substances through traditional law enforcement methods, there was a growing acceptance that individuals will use illegal drugs, and so measures were introduced which sought to minimize the harms. One of the most important responses was the introduction of needle exchange programmes and public health campaigns, which effectively reduced the transmission of blood-borne viruses. A further notable example of the adaptive and preventative shift in drugs and crime policy can be seen in relation to the development of local multi-agency partnerships in the 1980s, further culminating in the establishment, by the 1995 drug strategy, of Drug Action Teams to look at problems created by illegal drugs (Home Office, 1995; MacGregor, 2006). Nevertheless, while this is suggestive of responsibilization, it is important to bear in mind that local government was being squeezed, with authorities 'expected to be the agents of central government' (Baker, 1993: 111).

With political attention drawn to heroin and crack cocaine during the 1980s and early 1990s, the issue of cannabis appeared to drop down the policy agenda. Nevertheless, cannabis use continued to grow and, through the popular gateway theory, came to be seen as a key factor in the use of 'harder' substances (Kandel, 1975). Moreover, the increasingly punitive approach to law enforcement in relation to illegal drugs had an impact on relations between subsections of cannabis users and the police, who had a large degree of discretion in dealing with cannabis offences, not least owing to the availability of stop-and-search powers for suspected drug offences, which were first made possible under the Dangerous Drugs Act 1967. This contributed to varied styles of policing, with ethnic minorities living in urban settings being key targets of increased enforcement activity (Scarman, 1982; Lea and Young, 1984). This was particularly pertinent given the tense race relations, but also since convictions and cautions for cannabis offences accounted for 90 per cent of all drug arrests by 1990 (Booth, 2003). Notwithstanding the variation in enforcement practices across the country, it is important to note that the Wootton Report's recommendation to avoid incarceration for cannabis users had largely found its way into practice, with most users dealt with through police cautions and non-custodial sentences (Mills, 2013).

By 2000, estimates of cannabis use over the lifetime had reached 29.5 per cent, and the proportion of 16- to 24-year-olds reporting lifetime use was 46.2 per cent (Ramsay et al, 2001). For some, this indicated the normalisation of youth recreational drug use (Parker et al, 1998). While this interpretation was deeply contested on the basis of more frequent trends of use and the number of individuals who 'just say no' (see Shiner and Newburn, 1997, 1999; Wibberley and Price, 2000; Measham and Shiner, 2009), it is fairly undisputed that the policing of cannabis possession offences became burdensome for law enforcement agencies.

These changing patterns of drug use and responses to illegal drug markets in the 1990s occurred at an important point in the political environment. With the Conservatives in power from 1979 to 1997, the need for the Labour Party to reformulate itself and adapt to the contemporary landscape led to a rebranding of the party under the leadership of Tony Blair. The watchword of this 'New Labour' project was the quest to find a 'third way' between Labour and the success of the New Right and its traditional allegiances (Giddens, 1998). This opened up a critique of 'Old Labour', which was judged to have 'marginalised individual empowerment and local control' through a commitment to a centralized state as a means of emancipation (Hain, 1999). The New Labour project attempted to reconstruct a new 'governmentality' that responsibilized citizens and communities in the construction of identity and values and aimed to reinvigorate the moral civic duty of citizens (Rose, 2000).

As part of this shift, New Labour advanced the agenda of 'modernising government', which attempted to increase government efficiency and effectiveness through managerialist reforms (Cabinet Office, 1999). A dual process became evident, with increasing powers given to local authorities, multi-agency partnerships and private entities, and a simultaneous renewal of centralized control through national performance management targets. This relationship, while premised on ideals of local governance and democratic frameworks, seemingly further confirmed the role of local authorities as service delivery organizations within a hyper-centralized model of control (Chandler, 2001).

However, owing to New Labour's emphasis on 'decentralisation, democracy and popular sovereignty', along with the pressure mounting within the United Kingdom's polities, historic devolution settlements were agreed for Scotland, Northern Ireland and Wales (see Hain, 1999: 25, see also Chaney et al, 2001; Deacon and Sandry, 2007). In Wales, for example, the establishment of the Welsh Assembly under the Government of Wales Act 1998 resulted in the transferral of powers in education, health, local government, cultural matters, public transport and agriculture (Tomaney, 2000). These coexisted within a complex legislative arrangement whereby Westminster still had the possibility of legislating in them, though under the Sewel Convention it was agreed that Westminster would not normally legislate without consent from the Welsh Assembly (Trench, 2008). Since this initial devolution package, further powers have steadily been granted to Wales, under the Government of Wales Act 2006 and the devolution referendum in 2011. This has created a distinct executive branch (Welsh Government) separate from the legislature (Welsh Assembly) and allows for full lawmaking powers in 20 fields, as proscribed in the 2006 Act (see Evans et al, 2021).

Alongside these changes, the political sphere in England & Wales became more politicized, competitive and scrutinized, challenging the status of professionals and experts. As a result, there appeared to be an ambivalent mix of populist and pragmatic strategies within New Labour. On one hand, there were desires to please the electorate and demonstrate the departure from Old Labour philosophies on issues such as welfare and crime. For example, the drive to address problems of antisocial behaviour effectively led to the criminalization of a whole plethora of behaviours previously hidden from the criminal justice sphere, thereby amplifying problems of deviant youth behaviour (see Squires, 2008). On the other hand, pragmatic 'what works' strategies were employed in policy development, cementing the economic and managerial reasoning that had come to the fore in Conservative governments in the 1980s (Powell, 2000).

In respect of drug policy, one of the primary goals of the early Blair administration was to tackle the vast increase in crime that had occurred over several decades. Central to this was the connection between 'problematic' Class A drug users and acquisitive crime. Significant investments were made to deal with these problems, for instance through methadone maintenance programmes and tough criminal justice interventions as envisaged in the drug strategy *Tackling Drugs to Build a Better Britain* (Home Office, 1998; see also Home Office, 2002b, 2004). This included the introduction of legislation that placed more stringent conditions on drug offenders, such as mandatory treatment and monitoring (for example, via the Crime and Disorder Act 1998 and the Drugs Act 2005).

Moreover, the early incarnations of drug-related multi-agency arrangements (Drug Action Teams) were given more prominence under the New Labour government, which established statutory Crime and Disorder Reduction Partnerships in England and Community Safety Partnerships in Wales. The premise for these partnerships was to bring together all relevant agencies who deal with substance misuse (most notably health and criminal justice) to find more effective solutions and to promote joined-up working. In this respect, devolution has created an interesting dynamic between the two governments in the field of drug policy. While criminal justice remains a non-devolved issue, related policy spheres such as health and education have been fully devolved. This marks a significant point of departure from previous relations of governance – especially given the strong social democratic political tradition and 'internal political solidarity' – with opportunities to generate more tailored policy responses and resist unfavourable shifts at the broader UK level of policy making (Osmond, 2007; Drakeford and Gregory, 2011; Brewster and Jones, 2019; Jones, 2020).

The manifestation of ambivalent strategies of control in response to a drug policy predicament was reflected in policy on cannabis. By the end of the 1990s, the policing of cannabis had become a serious task, with 93,190 officially recorded seizures in 1998, most of which were for low-level possession offences (Mwenda et al, 2005). According to Warburton et al (2005) one in seven offenders were cautioned or convicted for cannabis possession in 1999, and May et al (2002) estimated that the policing of cannabis equated to the time of 500 full-time police officers and cost £50 million per year. However, pointing to discretionary behaviour in law enforcement practices, Warburton et al (2005) interviewed 150 police officers and found that two thirds had turned a 'blind eye' to possession offences. In addition, based on case study sites, May et al (2002) found that 3 per cent of police officers who had made arrests for possession of cannabis accounted for 20 per cent of the arrests. This suggests that there were not only considerable differences between de jure and de facto policy, but also uneven practices within law enforcement.

As recorded cannabis use rose significantly throughout the 1990s, pressure mounted on the government to reconsider its position on the drug. In 1997, the British newspaper *The Independent on Sunday* launched a media campaign to decriminalize cannabis, and this was followed by an independent inquiry into drugs legislation led by Dame Ruth Runciman (Police Foundation, 2000). The Runciman Report proposed several recommendations concerning cannabis, including reclassification to Class C, which would make possession a non-arrestable offence, and the use of out-of-court disposals for law transgressors.[5] The Runciman Report initially received a mixed response in political networks but was broadly accepted across different segments of the media, creating the sense that the government had been caught out of tune with public sentiment.

Alongside these developments, a pilot project was introduced by the Metropolitan Police Service in 2001. The Lambeth Cannabis Warning Pilot Scheme introduced on-the-spot warnings for cannabis offences under the rationale of alleviating time which could be spent on policing Class A drugs and related offences, such as burglary. The results showed improvements in police efficiency and resource deployment, and the scheme received broad support by both local residents and the general population (Metropolitan Police Authority, 2002; MORI, 2002).

As the debate continued, Home Secretary David Blunkett, new in post, asked the ACMD to review the scientific evidence on cannabis. The ACMD recommended that cannabis be reclassified to Class C, and this view was cemented by the findings of the Home Affairs Committee (ACMD, 2002;

Home Affairs Committee, 2002). Notwithstanding individual political goals, David Blunkett announced in July 2003 that on the basis of support for reform and the penetration of expert evidence in a rare window of opportunity, cannabis would be reclassified to Class C (Monaghan, 2011). Although the reclassification progressed, eventually coming into force in January 2004, there was widespread confusion over how it would be policed (see May et al, 2007). In response to media and police concerns, a compromise was made to keep the arrestable element for possession where 'aggravating factors' were present, but 'street warnings' (later termed 'cannabis warnings') were introduced as an out-of-court disposal (Home Office, 2002a; ACPO, 2003). Additionally, sentences for production and supply were retained at the same levels as Class B drugs, with a maximum of 14 years' imprisonment, further dissolving the divide between the classification of cannabis and other drugs.

For its advocates, the reclassification marked an enlightened, rational and evidence-based response to cannabis (Monaghan, 2011), an adaptation to the drugs policy predicament that allowed police officers to deal with cannabis in a more informal way and reduce pressure on resources throughout the whole criminal justice system (Garland, 2001; Seddon, 2008). However, owing to a central performance indicator – offences brought to justice – police forces were perversely incentivized to target low-level cannabis offences as easy sanction detections, resulting in a significant increase in the number of possession offences recorded (see Sosa, 2012; Home Office, 2013; Shiner, 2015). Indicative of this, cannabis warnings increased from 40,138 in 2004–05 to 107,241 in 2008–09 (Home Office, 2012a). Given long-standing patterns in many police forces, it is not surprising that this also intensified the policing of ethnic minorities, with such populations increasingly targeted for stop-and-search on suspected drug offences (Eastwood et al, 2013).

Following the 2004 reclassification, there was sustained pressure on the government, largely by the Right-wing press and the Conservative Party, which sought to discredit and problematize the reclassification decision. In this critical climate, the same New Labour government twice sought advice from the ACMD on whether the classification was suitable. On both occasions, the ACMD reported that cannabis should remain a Class C drug (ACMD, 2006, 2008). Despite the recommendations, the decision was made under the new leadership of Gordon Brown to reclassify cannabis back to Class B, and this came into effect in January 2009.

However, as the distinction between policing Class B and Class C substances had all but been dissolved under earlier legal reforms, the actual changes made in 2009 were relatively few. The cannabis warning was retained as an out-of-court disposal, but a penalty notice for disorder was added, to be employed within a tiered approach to possession cases (see ACPO, 2009). The only other tangible change was to the maximum court penalties available for adult possession offences, which increased from two to five years' imprisonment. However, as already noted, given that the vast majority of those caught do not receive a custodial sentence, this can be interpreted as having a more symbolic than tangible impact.

The 2009 reclassification demonstrated a clear tension between the role of expertise and political drivers in drugs policy, and this was confirmed by the controversial sacking of Professor David Nutt as chair of the ACMD and the subsequent resignation of eight ACMD members in protest of ministerial influence (Laurance, 2010). A further development in 2012 saw the revision of the drugs sentencing framework – despite the upgraded classification, this has relaxed certain guidelines, particularly regarding medicinal users and low-level cultivation offences (see Sentencing Council, 2012).

A further sign of support for alternatives to criminalization, and arguably the most significant change at national level, was in respect of medical cannabis, with prescriptions of cannabis-based medicines – at least technically– being made available from the National Health Service from 2018. This was spurred on by prominent incidents highlighting the plight of young children suffering from severe diseases but unable to legitimately access medical cannabis, which would alleviate their symptoms (Schlag et al, 2020). Additionally, numerous high-profile reports were published, from both parliament and external sources, alongside growing awareness of international developments embracing alternatives to blanket prohibition of cannabis. These moved debates away from the negative mental health effects of cannabis use and towards the injustices of criminalization (Home Office, 2014; Global Commission on Drug Policy, 2014; WHO, 2017).

Yet it was at a local level, in police forces, where the most significant movement took place. With the removal of centralized key performance indicators and the introduction of directly elected PCCs in 2012, variation in local policing strategies flourished again. In a period marked by significant cuts to public service budgets, this latter development was particularly important given that PCCs oversee police forces, having responsibility for appointing chief constables and setting policing objectives and force budgets. Within this context, several PCCs openly criticized cannabis laws and called for reforms (Gayle, 2015). In addition, a significant proportion of police forces headed by PCCs favourable to reform either deprioritized the policing of cannabis or introduced diversion schemes that minimize criminal justice contact for cannabis possession offences. At the time of writing, 14 police forces in England & Wales have introduced such schemes, and more are considering available options (see Transform Drug Policy Foundation, 2022). Alongside this, the notable rise in CSCs, with 65 local clubs officially registered in the United Kingdom, has drawn the attention of senior police figures (Kelsey, 2018; UK Cannabis Social Clubs, 2022).

Nevertheless, it is worth stressing that such indications of liberalization are not evenly spread, with some police forces continuing to use local performance indicators that perversely incentivize police officers to target cannabis offences, (HM Inspectorate of Constabulary, 2013). Moreover, despite a curtailment of 'stop-and-search' for most of the 2010s, there has been a recent growth in this practice, particularly on the grounds of suspected drug offences. Ethnic minorities continue to be targeted in an overwhelmingly disproportionate way, and given that over 60 per cent of stop-and-search events in 2020 were for drugs, the effects of cannabis criminalization and law enforcement differ sharply depending on one's individual background and location (Shiner et al, 2018; Allen and Tunnicliffe, 2021).

Further concrete policy developments at a national level have also been limited in recent years, and it appears that the current Conservative-led government will not consider any approach beyond the model of prohibition with regards to non-medical cannabis (HM Government, 2017; BBC News, 2021). Indeed, with other 'drug scares', such as the 'county lines' phenomenon[6], rising in political importance, there are continuing calls to toughen control strategies and a reluctance to consider other reforms in drug policy (Spicer, 2021). Finally, considering broader exogenous conditions such as Brexit and COVID-19, the issue of cannabis policy reform currently occupies a far less important position than it did during the 2000s, and there is little indication that there will be significant policy movement at the national level in the near future.

Political culture and cannabis control in the Netherlands

At the time the (landmark) revised Opium Act was introduced in 1976, the Netherlands was already in the midst of social upheaval and transformation facilitated by the raft of social and economic forces associated with processes of globalization and a transition to late modernity. Broader social processes of secularization, individualization and democratization all served to weaken the pillar system, and with a blurring of the lines between 'us' and 'them', voting behaviour was less predictable (van Mierlo, 1986). Other factors further disintegrated the consensual and collectivist spirit of the political system; in particular, the effect of the 'Dutch disease'[7] on the welfare system, with the cost of welfare provision outstripping the capacity of the government to pay, was further exacerbated by increased unemployment and government borrowing in the 1980s (Andeweg and Irwin, 2005; van Oorschot, 2006). The effect of these macro relations has shifted the rules of the game in different periods, demonstrated by the 'pendulum consociationalism' which has reflexively weakened, strengthened and then further weakened the consensus model over the past few decades (Pennings and Keman, 2008: 175).

In the early stages of depillarization, the confessional parties reacted by merging together under the Christian Democratic Appeal (Christen Democratisch Appel – CDA) party in 1977, and by fusing confessional trade unions with secular ones. It is argued that these moves prevented further destabilization and provided some balance during the 1980s (Pennings and Keman, 2008). The economic downturn after the oil crisis in the 1980s facilitated the return of a depolarizing type of politics, and from the mid-1980s to the late 1990s, CDA and Labour Party (PvdA) elites came together substantially on social welfare (Jones, 2002; Adams et al, 2011). In response, neoliberal philosophies came to the fore in government attempts to reduce welfare spending and increase competitiveness in the global marketplace (Andeweg and Irwin, 2005). Moreover, and somewhat in contrast to the United Kingdom during this period, neoliberal influences drove the responsibilization of subnational authorities, with reforms from the 1980s onwards favouring decentralization of national tasks to local municipalities (Andeweg and Irwin, 2005).

However, political actors reacted to the changing environment not only through institutional consolidation and adaptation but also through conflict, with a shift towards a more Anglo-American model of polarization and politicization (Jones, 2002; Pennings and Kema, 2008). This was evidenced by several proxy indicators, such as: the concentration of executive power vs power-sharing; the inclusivity of coalitions; the politicization of ministers (in respect of the proportion of ministers with 'political experience'); and the types of coalitions that were formed (see Andeweg, 2008).

These increasingly ambivalent features of governance became extremely evident in the sphere of crime and illegal drugs control, with severe strain placed on the penal-welfare paradigm and elitist ideals of resocialization. From around the mid-1970s, cracks began to appear in the surface of a largely successful decarceration project. From 1980 to 1985 alone, recorded crime increased rapidly from approximately 4,500 to around 7,000 incidents per 100,000 population (Downes and van Swanningen, 2007) The rise in crime has largely been attributed to processes of depillarization, social and economic expansion and failure to integrate the increasing number of settlers from Morocco, Turkey and the former Dutch colony of Surinam. In relation to this latter aspect, Downes and van Swaaningen (2007: 45) suggest that owing to language barriers, these mainly unskilled groups became excluded from Dutch society and 'often ended up unemployed, living in their own "ghettos" ... many [ending] up as problematic heroin users'. Alongside the advent of heroin importation, growing public and political insecurity concerning drug-related crimes committed by these socially and economically marginalized populations posed problems for a country still coming to terms with a postcolonial, post-pillarized social order. These came to 'symbolize newly emergent problems, which began to test the penal consensus to destruction' (Downes and van Swaaningen, 2007: 45).

Downes and Swaaningen (2007: 57) suggest that 'crime was implicitly portrayed as a problem outside of Dutch society rather than as a problem rooted in social and economic relations, as was hitherto the common vision'. This served to challenge traditional views about resocialization and culminated in a distinctive point in Dutch criminal justice policy with the 1985 *Society and Crime* report (Ministry of Justice, 1985). The main purpose of this report was to restore credibility to the criminal justice system through distinctively managerialist measures to improve the efficiency and coordination of the system. Moreover, it signalled a shift towards crime prevention measures led by local municipalities, highlighting responsibilizing strategies in crime control (Jones, 1995; van Swaaningen, 2005). It was from this point on, proponents of a culture of control suggest, that the core of Dutch criminal justice policy started to shift from an emphasis on the values of resocialization and penal-welfarism to a focus on balancing managerial and retributive goals (Pakes, 2000; van Swaaningen, 2005).

In this latter respect, there was a more than doubling of the custodial capacity between the early 1990s and early 2000s and a rapid expansion in custodial sentences up until 2005 (Pakes, 2004; Downes and van Swaaningen, 2007). At one point, the Netherlands was, proportionately, expanding its prison population faster than the United States (Tak and van Kalmthout, 1998). This was driven by hard drugs offences as well as violent crime and sex offences. Such offences were treated more severely, with the judiciary under pressure to sentence more heavily in these cases (Grapendaal et al, 1997). Yet, in respect of hard drugs, it is important to acknowledge the existence of more adaptive responses by organizations such as the Drug Advisory Foundation, which advanced innovative harm reduction practices, such as needle exchange services and drug checking services, that would come to be the foundation of contemporary national policy.

Alongside the tough justice system, there was a distinct change in attitudes to crime and punishment following the publication of the 1989 International Crime Survey, which showed that the Netherlands had the highest crime rate of the 14 countries involved (van Dijk et al, 1990: 41). While the survey methods were critiqued, the effect on public opinion further tipped the politics of crime control in a more punitive direction and shaped the *Law in Motion* report of 1990, which emphasized greater managerial instrumentalism (Ministry of Justice, 1990; see also van Swaaningen, 2005; Downes and van Swaaningen, 2007). By the early 1990s, crime and immigration was a central political issue, met with tough, risk-oriented political rhetoric as well as punitive detention (van Swaaningen, 2005).

The tendency to read off national crime policy talk as evidence for the emergence of a shift to punitiveness does not capture alternative manifestations in specific fields and spaces that challenge this assumption. Developments in cannabis policy illuminate a different set of dynamics. Since the 1980s, there has been a major shift away from house dealers to commercial outlets known as coffeeshops, which have become the focal point for cannabis *gedogen* in Dutch society. The establishment of cannabis coffeeshops was a rather happenstance and unforeseen development. Rather than this being an invention of national policy makers, coffeeshops started at a grassroots level in the major cities, most notably Amsterdam.

While the revisions to laws on cannabis primarily saw house dealers performing the social function of separating markets, in the late 1970s, café-style outlets began to tolerate the selling of cannabis. As the income from this source became more important to proprietors, and in combination with the publishing of the prosecutor's guidelines, local governance triangles recognized these outlets as a viable way of maintaining the policy of market separation. As a result, the number of coffeeshops rose exponentially during the 1980s.

However, there are other important factors to consider when looking at the rapid growth of coffeeshops. Even before the legislation of 1976 was established, heroin was a prominent issue in Dutch society. As public health concerns became more pressing with the spread of AIDs, more attention was given to heroin and how best to combat its negative effects. Thus, attempts to separate cannabis from hard drugs became a pertinent policy goal. While heroin was seen as a major threat, cannabis use offences were tolerated, drawing on the distinction made in the Opium Act between hard and soft drugs. While a hardened tone began to take hold in some areas, this was not experienced evenly across all policy areas, and low-level cannabis offences were tolerated at a local level.

With AIDs and heroin use both declining in the early 1990s, law enforcement agencies took this as a sign that their tough enforcement had been successful (despite the existence of a widely accredited harm reduction programme). As concerns about heroin receded, and in the broader context of heightened fears surrounding immigration and crime, drugs such as ecstasy and cannabis came back into the frame as problematic phenomena requiring policy intervention (Ossebaard and van der Wijngaart, 1998).

A fundamental issue was that while the 'front door' of sales and consumption was formally tolerated, the 'back door' of production and supply remained unregulated. Alongside domestic concerns about the back door problem and the widespread growth of coffeeshops – which, in media reporting, were increasingly linked to supply of hard drugs and ethnic minority populations – the approach to cannabis attracted widespread international criticism. Indeed, from the enactment of the revised Opium Act in 1976, the market separation policy had angered the INCB and proponents of more prohibitive regimes, particularly those from France, Sweden and the United States (see Transnational Institute, 2014: 50). Moreover, with state borders becoming practically invisible following the Schengen Agreement of 1985 and the creation of the EU in 1993, neighbouring countries also had cause for concern, as there was evidence that the Netherlands had become a hub for drug trafficking across Europe as well as a centre for drug tourism (MacCoun and Reuter, 2001). Claims that 90 per cent of illegal drugs in France arrived through the Netherlands led to the accusation by a French senate commission member that the Netherlands had become a 'narco-state' (Ossebaard and van der Wijngaart, 1998:267).

It was in this rather testing context that the myth of the polder model emerged during the mid-1990s as a way to reconstitute consensus politics in a positive way. This paved the way for two successive 'purple cabinets' – comprised of social democrats (the PvdA), conservative liberals, the People's Party for Freedom and Democracy (Volkspartij voor Vrijheid en Democratie – VVD) and progressive democrats (Democrats '66 – D'66) – between 1994 and 2002 (Jones, 2002). These governments offered a distinct policy window for a more progressive and liberal approach to cannabis policy, not least owing to the constellation of philosophical ideologies in this coalition, but due also to the fact that both the PvdA and D'66 had openly called for legalization prior to winning the elections (Boekhout van Solinge, 1999).

The culmination of these internal political shifts and external pressures was the 1995 policy paper *Drugs Policy in the Netherlands: Continuity and Change* (House of Representatives of the States General, 1995). For advocates of the coffeeshop policy, this represented a reaffirmation of the original goals of the drugs policy which solidified the *gedoogbeleid* (Pakes, 2003). For example, the total stock that coffeeshops were allowed to hold at any one time was increased from the impractical limit of 30 grams to a more feasible 500 grams. Further measures that would have regulated the back door were ultimately abandoned due to international pressures (Boekhout van Solinge, 1999), but by focusing on large-scale production and tolerating small-scale individual activities (individuals could grow up to five plants), the policy advanced the notion of coffeeshops as low-key local facilities serving local customers.

Nevertheless, for other commentators, the 1995 changes were indicative of the failure of tolerance and the resultant tightening of controls surrounding cannabis regulation (Boekhout van Solinge, 1999). This included: consolidation of local practices according to a national guideline prohibiting individuals under 18 years of age from entering coffeeshops; a reduction in the maximum amount coffeeshops could sell to a single customer, from 30 grams to 5 grams daily; and greater monitoring of organized cannabis cultivation to prevent importation from and exportation to neighbouring countries. Perhaps indicative of this more aggressive stance, seizures of cannabis in the Netherlands accounted for 44 per cent of the total for the EU in 1995 (MacCoun and Reuter, 1997, 2001).

Moreover, in keeping with a broader pattern of decentralization in the Netherlands, local municipalities were given considerable powers to decide whether to permit coffeeshops, how many could be established, where they could operate and if they should be closed due to causing 'nuisance'[8] (Pakes, 2005; van der Gouwe et al, 2009; Wouters et al, 2010). These measures had a marked effect on the total number of coffeeshops in the Netherlands. The number declined significantly, from around 1,500 in the early 1990s to 846 in 1999. By 2009, 77 per cent of municipalities had chosen not to have a single coffeeshop (Bieleman and Goeree, 2001; Bieleman et al, 2012).

Although the purple governments signalled a return to consensus-building, this period also witnessed polarization on emerging issues that the traditional parties were not well equipped to deal with (Adams et al, 2011). A similar set of forces that had punctured the politics of accommodation in the 1970s re-emerged in a heightened form at the end of the 1990s, and this led to a questioning of all the major parties while new parties gained support (Jones, 2002; Pennings and Keman, 2008; Adams et al, 2011). Whereas the attack on the political system in the 1970s was from the political Left, the attack in the late 1990s came predominantly from the political Right, who were 'able to mobilize voters on issues that are linked to (the loss of) national identity and outside "threats" like immigrants and the EU' (Pennings and Keman, 2008: 158; see also Keman and Krouwel, 2007). Nestled together with accusations of government indifference to major disasters, there was growing discomfort with 'grey' policy responses, such as the *gedoogbeleid*, and calls for clearer policies (Pakes, 2004; Uitermark, 2004).

In a growing political vacuum, new populist challengers arose, seeking to challenge the political elite. The notorious Pim Fortuyn emerged in 2001 as part of Liveable Netherlands before breaking off to form his own party, List Pim Fortuyn (LPF). Fortuyn positioned himself as anti-establishment and against the perceived threat of Islam and immigration for Dutch social life. His success was rooted in a section of White working-class voters, particularly from Rotterdam, who had become disaffected with the political establishment and the perceived threats of immigration and were bolstered by Fortuyn's blistering attacks on the larger established parties in the run-up to the election.

These developments occurred around the same time as the 9/11 terrorist attacks in the United States, which only served to heighten tensions associated with Muslim ethnic minorities. Yet another catalyst in the highly toxic political arena came when Pim Fortuyn was assassinated by an environmental activist shortly before the 2002 elections. Despite Fortuyn's assassination, the LPF successfully broke through into government, becoming the second-largest party (Irwin and van Holsteyn, 2004). However, the turbulence surrounding the 2002 elections continued into the following year, which saw the collapse of the coalition between the CDA, the LPF and the VVD in the Balkenende I cabinet (2002–03) due to growing internal conflicts in the LPF.

Although Pim Fortuyn and the LPF were only briefly part of the political landscape, their legacy was substantial, with tensions over European integration and immigration remaining at the forefront of political debate. These were fuelled even more by the murder of the film-maker Theo van Gogh by a Dutch-Moroccan Islamic activist in 2004 (Aarts and van der Kolk, 2007). In the space left by Fortuyn, a new populist Right-wing party emerged in the form of the Party for Freedom (Partij voor de Vrijheid – PVV), which grew to become the third-largest party (with 15.4 per cent of the vote) in the 2010 elections. As a result, the party was reluctantly included in the Rutte I government in a parliamentary support capacity to the main coalition partners – the CDA and the VVD (Aarts and van der Kolk, 2011).

These wider developments within Dutch society and the growing influence of populist parties starting at the end of the 1990s and continuing throughout the 2000s also shaped policy debates and measures regarding cannabis, with a particular focus on nuisance and cultivation. Further powers were granted to local municipalities, allowing them to impose sanctions on, or to close down, coffeeshops that transgressed the tolerance criteria – an example is the Damocles Act 1999 (Article 13b of the Opium Act) (Ministry of Health, Welfare and Sport, 2003; van der Gouwe et al, 2009). Additionally, a raft of measures were granted to municipal councils to aid in the detection and prosecution process with regards to financial rewards in the drug trade. For example, the Criminal Confiscation Measure (also known as the *pluk ze* (squeeze 'em) law) allowed for the confiscation of criminal assets, and under the Disclosure of Unusual Transactions (Financial Services) Act and the Identification (Financial Services) Act, more powers were granted to investigate monetary irregularities (van der Gouwe et al, 2009).

From the early 2000s on, developments in cannabis policy continued to demonstrate ambivalent features, with the toughening of approaches to coffeeshop nuisance and organized crime occurring alongside the reaffirmation of the market separation philosophy. In 2003 an interdepartmental policy paper advocated a stricter and more criminal justice-oriented approach with integration of different agencies, such as the police, prosecution service, housing associations and tax authorities (see House of Representatives of the States General, 2006). While aiming to restrict cannabis regulation further, this also restated the primary goal of coffeeshops to provide a useful social and public health function in Dutch society. An important theme running throughout the policy paper is the importance of local municipalities in ensuring that policy is aligned with local circumstances.

This can be seen with responses to cannabis-related nuisance. There have been numerous attempts, particularly in the south of the country, to deal pragmatically with this problem – by, for example, relocating coffeeshops from the inner city to the borders (Snippe et al, 2005). However, the success of such experiments was largely marred by local and national politics and negotiations both within the Netherlands and with the neighbouring countries of Belgium and Germany (MacCoun and Reuter, 2001). In 2007, under the Balkenende IV cabinet (2007–10), comprised of the CDA, the PvdA and the Christian Union (ChristenUnie – CU)], municipalities were given the power to close coffeeshops located within 250 metres of schools (van der Gouwe et al, 2009). While this is not a mandatory rule, after discussions within the Association of Netherlands Municipalities (Vereniging van Nederlandse Gemeenten), most municipalities with coffeeshops have integrated this policy into existing practices (Bieleman et al, 2012). Thus, while policy innovations at a local level are an important and fundamental part of policy evolution with regards to cannabis, it is important to remember that such experiments are constrained by multidimensional forces at local, national and international levels.

Alongside developments that have placed more responsibility and power in the hands of municipalities, there have also been firmer centralized responses. For instance, the unresolved problem of the back door has been met with increasing recourse to criminal justice-led approaches. In response to growing evidence of large-scale cultivation, the Taskforce on Organized Cannabis Cultivation was established in 2008 (see van Ooyen-Houben, 2006; van Ooyen-Houben et al, 2009).

Despite numerous attempts, over two decades, to counter the negative effects of cannabis policy, the perception and reality of problems remained, and in 2009 the Balkenende IV government established an expert committee, chaired by van de Donk, to examine ways to proceed with illegal drugs, and specifically, cannabis. Following this commission, three new measures were announced in 2011 under the Rutte I government (discussed in greater depth in Chapters 4–7): restricting entrance to coffeeshops to residents of the Netherlands (the residency criterion); requiring coffeeshops to become private member clubs with a maximum membership of 2,000 per club (the closed club criterion); and closing all coffeeshops within 350 metres of secondary schools (the school distance criterion). The first two of these measures were to be trialled in the three southern provinces from May 2012 and introduced nationally from January 2013; the third measure was to be applied nationally from January 2014.

However, in 2012, as the trials were proceeding, a shift of government to Rutte II – comprised of the VVD and the PvdA – and considerable resistance to the new measures led to their revision. This removed the closed club and school distance criteria from the prosecutor's guidelines, leaving only the residency criterion intact. The latter was given greater flexibility in its enforcement. Moreover, following a further health-led expert commission, chaired by Professor Garretsen, a further proposed measure was announced: the reclassification of cannabis with a THC content of over 15 per cent as a 'hard drug' following continued concerns relating to high-strength cannabis and mental health problems (Expert Committee on the List System of the Opium Act, 2011; House of Representatives of the States General, 2012). However, this did not materialize into policy.

Following the 2012–13 reforms to the coffeeshop criteria, further movements in cannabis policy and practice have unfolded at both national and subnational levels. Increasingly strict policies have led to further closure of coffeeshops, with the total number declining by almost 100, to 564, by 2020, though this number has remained about the same since then (Mennes et al, 2021). At the same time, however, in response to the perceived inadequacies of the reforms initiated under Rutte I, a number of municipalities have sought to introduce their own methods of regulating the back door. The municipality of Utrecht – the subnational empirical case explored in depth in Chapter 7 – has been one of the main proponents of this. Together with other municipalities, it called on the national government to allow municipalities to engage in cultivation experiments. By 2017, this Manifest Joint Regulation had gained the signatures of over 60 mayors, many of whom were from municipalities that have coffeeshops (Korf, 2020).

Although any form of regulated cannabis cultivation was fiercely rejected under the Rutte I and Rutte II governments, a bill submitted by a D'66 politician that would exempt cannabis growers from prosecution under certain conditions was narrowly adopted by the Dutch parliament in early 2017. Shortly thereafter, a new coalition government, Rutte III (2017–22) – comprised of the VVD, the CDA, D'66 and the CU – came to power, and while three of the parties in this coalition have been traditionally aligned against further liberalization of cannabis policy, they agreed to start a national experiment on a 'closed coffeeshop chain'. An expert committee was established to provide advice on how the experiment should be run (see Advisory Committee Experiment Closed Cannabis Chain, 2018; Korf, 2020). In 2019, after further negotiations, the House of Representatives approved the Controlled Cannabis Supply Chain Experiment Act, and in 2020 the law came into force, followed by a call for applications from municipalities who wished to participate. Intriguingly, though, some of the larger municipalities who had made their own attempts to introduce back door regulations opposed these national plans, largely on the grounds that they are too restrictive. Thus, the tensions and struggles between national and subnational political actors in cannabis policy continues, but after 30 years it appears that a solution to the back door problem finally appears to be working its way into policy.

Summary: convergence around a common culture of control?

Following a similar pattern, the political environments of both England & Wales and the Netherlands have changed considerably since the 1970s, becoming more insecure and volatile in response to the acceleration of social and economic pressures. In the broader sphere of crime and illegal drugs control, with increases in recorded crime and heroin use, as well fears over safety, community degradation and immigration, political processes appeared to mark growing convergence around a culture of control in which both adaptive and non-adaptive control strategies replaced the rehabilitative ideal. Arguably, this shift was more severe in the Netherlands, where a politics of accommodation and consensus was purportedly replaced by more adversarial and politicized modes of governance.

These broader dynamics were also reflected to varying degrees in cannabis control in both countries. In England & Wales, growing rates of use coupled with the increased burdens on enforcing criminal legislation in the 1990s provided the 'fertile ground' for an adaptive policy change in 2004, with the reclassification of cannabis to Class C. At the same time, in the broader political environment, issues of crime and drugs control were fiercely contested and politicized policy agenda items. What then transpired was a quick policy reversal, within five years, by the same political party. Since then, notwithstanding some modest changes in provision of medical cannabis, successive Conservative-led governments have shown very little appetite to discuss any further reforms. Nevertheless, in the current landscape, a substantial gap exists between the worlds of policy making and policy implementation, with considerable variations in terms of targets and scope of local law enforcement.

In the Netherlands, the emergence and rapid growth of coffeeshops in the 1980s is an important counter to assumptions of a punitive turn, but developments from the early 1990s reflect an acceleration of pressures which have put cannabis policy under strain. The continued decline of coffeeshops, coupled with stricter enforcement against cultivators and traffickers, has shifted the emphasis away from public health and towards criminal justice. With a volatile political environment in which new perceived threats and new populist parties have emerged, cannabis policy has not been an exception to overall tendencies towards tougher, and less tolerant, approaches. In one sense, this may be indicative of convergence towards response strategies that attempt to affirm – to both internal and, perhaps more importantly, external audiences – the myth that governors are capable of controlling and managing undesirable social behaviours and populations. Yet, despite warnings of the potential end of coffeeshops (Garretsen, 2010), there is still a pervasive belief among policy actors that the coffeeshops are beneficial for public health and are a desirable alternative to criminalization and marginalization. This is particularly strong at a municipal level, where actors have attempted to protect the coffeeshop system.

While developments in England & Wales reflect the rapidity by which policy change can occur, those in the Netherlands demonstrate a much slower and more incremental approach to reforming cannabis policy. In some respects, it is possible to assert that a common culture of control has penetrated both settings, but this downplays and masks the ways political decision-making takes place and how this may lead to very different outcomes in manifestations of policy.

Summary

This chapter has attempted to cover a lot of ground, tracing the development of cannabis policy and how this has been located within social and political spheres in England & Wales and the Netherlands. What emerges from this historical and comparative overview is that while similar social, economic and political conditions may have been present over the past century, reactions to issues concerning cannabis have not followed a neat trajectory of convergence.

It has been suggested here that an important reason for the variegated movements in cannabis control relates to the dispositions of political actors and their ability to enact change within the structured relations of political institutions in different cultural contexts. The contexts discussed here reflect the adversarial political system and history of the Westminster system in England & Wales, which favours strong government by one party, and the system of proportional representation in the Netherlands, which necessarily results in coalition government.

While the social, economic and political conditions have changed considerably over past decades, it is important to remember that the historically shaped structures of formal institutions have changed very little. For example, would-be governors in the Netherlands still need to find points of common ground to form a coalition, and this generates constant negotiation to find mutually acceptable positions on policy issues among diverse parties. Given the constant coming and going of political parties in ruling coalitions, this makes definitive breaks with previous policy more difficult to realize, resulting in more piecemeal reform. In contrast, the Westminster system does not have this same dynamic. Where a ruling party commands a parliamentary majority, it is not necessary to find compromise, and this grants considerable power to introduce sweeping reforms and initiate policy reversals.

In the context of political environments becoming more politicized, volatile and shaped by the 'noise' of populist demands, the role and place of expertise has been called into question, and this experience has been shared to some degree across both countries. Yet a key hypothesis is that under adversarial 'first past the post' political systems, this dynamic is particularly accentuated, with expertise seemingly utilized in cannabis policy only when it suits political goals, whereas in proportional representative systems such as that of the Netherlands, there is value in expertise as it can be used to identify neutral positions that are largely acceptable to different parties.

A further contrast concerns the relations between actors involved in cannabis policy processes, particularly in national and local spheres of governance. Overall – again shaped by historical, cultural and political contexts – the local sphere in the Netherlands has significantly more powers than that of England & Wales. Notably, in the Netherlands, local relations contribute to governing based on compromise while also providing a powerful space in which policy can be developed, resisted or subverted.

However, unlike national political structures, local relations have not remained fairly static. In some ways, changes have only reinforced and enhanced prior dynamics; local authorities in the Netherlands have become stronger, and those of England & Wales have been progressively weakened. However, it is important to note that the reality is vastly more complex than this simplistic rendering, especially given the changes to police governance and the processes of devolution in the United Kingdom since the turn of the millennium, which have led to greater empowerment at subnational level. One of the questions that emerges is whether, and to what extent, this influences national processes of policy making relating to cannabis.

Chapters 4–7 dissect these mechanisms and dynamics, exploring in more depth the processes of cannabis policy making relating to specific policy changes in England & Wales and the Netherlands, as well considering other cases from across the globe.

4

Problematizing Cannabis

Introduction

This chapter examines the ways in which cannabis has come to be problematized across different contemporary societies. What social phenomena are considered to be problems and how these are projected as such at particular moments in time are central elements in the policy-making process (Peters, 2005). Making sense of problem definition requires us to recognize the influence of immediate factors, such as 'focusing events, crises and symbols' (Kingdon, 1995) as well as more long-standing perceptions and dispositions towards cannabis and other illegal drugs. Here, our concern is less with the historical origin of problematization, but more on the ways in which particular discourses are used to frame social issues by those who have the resources to enact change. This allows us to understand the sorts of values that underlie problem recognition and how this is connected to the selection of policy alternatives, and the political parameters and forces that enable or hinder favoured solutions to be realized (Kingdon, 1995).

Recognizing the interwoven nature of problems in particular contexts, the chapter examines exemplars from different countries in turn. First, in-depth findings from an analysis of empirical and secondary data are drawn on in relation to the 2009 reclassification of cannabis in England & Wales and the 2012–13 changes to coffeeshop criteria in the Netherlands. These findings are then contrasted with an interpretation of recent policy movements in two further contexts: Canada's Cannabis Act 2018 and Jamaica's Dangerous Drugs (Amendment) Act 2015.

England & Wales: political insecurity and the emergence of a threat

In England & Wales, the construction of cannabis as a policy problem was centred around three main areas: social order, health and morality. Each of these themes emerged in relation to the perceived failure of the earlier reclassification to Class C in 2004. While interlinked in this respect, these themes also stood independently. These problematizations are discussed in turn.

Cannabis as a threat to social order

Cannabis first became problematized as creating a sense of a threat to social order, with the legacy of the 2004 reclassification leaving the public and police largely confused about its legal status. This fed into a wider perception that the reclassification was a mistake and had failed. To better understand the reasons for this confusion, it is worth examining some of the dynamics that shaped the political decision to reclassify cannabis to Class C and the implications of this decision.

As noted in Chapter 3, the 'Lambeth experiment' was influential in terms of lending support for the downwards reclassification. However, it was noted that the responsible commander, Brian Paddick, conducted this experiment "gun-ho" and like "a bull in a china shop",[1] without the full support of senior officers in the Metropolitan Police and without consulting with the ACPO. Nevertheless, evidence from the Lambeth experiment was quickly picked up by Home Secretary David Blunkett and used as a justification to reclassify to Class C.

> 'We are sitting outside the Home Office waiting to be pulled in there … we hadn't had much part to play, and it was basically told, right tomorrow we don't want to embarrass you, tomorrow there is going to be an announcement in the House about the reclassification of cannabis … I remember saying to the minister, look we haven't really been engaged on this, is it really worth me trying to challenge that? And he was like, no it's not. We were in and out of that meeting in five minutes.' (EW-POL1: Former Chief Constable and ACPO Lead on Drugs)

The political urgency to reclassify within a suitable window of opportunity led to major oversights in the process. The exclusion of senior police officers and the immediacy with which they had to respond with guidelines ultimately contributed to widespread confusion over how the reclassification was to be operationally managed: "I think it was an absolute dog's dinner … I'm pretty convinced that actually, sadly, the operational side got itself in a right mess. So, what practical operational cops do when policy doesn't help them on the street, they just ignore it."[2]

Fears that cannabis possession would cease to be an arrestable offence caused concern within the police that this would lead to a loss of respect[3] and eliminate a useful tool that can be used as a gateway for detecting other offences. Nevertheless, the resulting measures meant that officers could still arrest individuals for possession under certain circumstances (ACPO, 2003), and this contributed to the view that police officers could do whatever they saw fit, as opposed to following a prescribed route of sanctions.

> 'If I'm a cop who loves enforcement of cannabis possession, nothing changes for me, because they will make the circumstances fit if they want to, providing the evidence is there. On the other hand, if you are someone who is much more liberal in your outlook on cannabis ... you could make [the individual's] alleged actions fall outside of the aggravating factors and therefore you don't have to do anything.' (EW-POL1: Former Chief Constable and ACPO Lead on Drugs)

However, owing to a perverse incentive structure connected to national performance indicators (see May et al, 2007; Sosa, 2012; Shiner, 2015), there was a rapid increase, across police forces, in police detections for possession offences. Moreover, this appeared to legitimize a significant growth in the use of stop-and-search, and notwithstanding some local variation in enforcement practices, disproportionate targeting of ethnic minority populations became extremely evident (Eastwood et al, 2013). Indicatively, in 2009–10, across all police forces, Black populations were subject to stop-and-search for drug offences at 6.3 times the rate of White populations. Such racial disparities were not just in respect of out-of-court sanctions, but existed at all stages of the criminal justice system. For example, in the same year, Black people were charged with cannabis offences at five times the rate of White people (Eastwood et al, 2013).

The significance of these enforcement activities is that they fed into a wider set of police-driven fears about cannabis, with substantial disparities illuminating the continuation of historical connections made between 'race' and cannabis (see Chapter 3). Further, there was concern around a perceived change in cannabis cultivation, whereby reported increases in the scale, nature and prevalence of intensive large-scale cultivation sites – so-called 'cannabis factories' – became linked with foreign organized crime networks. This was solidified in 2008 following the emergence of police data from a national baseline assessment and the establishment of a National Co-ordinator for Cannabis Cultivation (ACPO, 2010). Data suggested that there had been an increase in cannabis factories found per year, from an average of 800 between 2004 and 2007 to over 3,000 per year in 2007–08 (ACPO, 2010). This police intelligence highlighted the link between these activities and organized crime networks, particularly Vietnamese groups, who were capable of supplying the investment required to establish high-tech large-scale cannabis plantations.[4]

Thus, the prevailing image emerging from police activities was that cannabis was not as harmless as it was once thought, and from around

2007, it was increasingly portrayed by the police and media outlets as being underpinned by illicit networks run by "foreigners who are exploiting a lax situation growing a vast amount of cannabis".[5] A narrative grew among those who opposed policy liberalization that the 2004 downgrading had signalled a laissez-faire attitude towards the policing of cannabis which encouraged the growth of production in the United Kingdom. This added to the wider critique that the 2004 reclassification had failed and caused more problems to occur. "It was part of a creation of a completely new industry … not only did it not save police time, it increased [the problem] because the cannabis industry in the UK is now massive."[6]

However, this is not to suggest that there was a dearth of counter-perspectives, as more critical participants alluded to the simultaneous processes of international law enforcement activity, technological changes and market competition as factors shaping changing market conditions.[7] Importantly, though, these types of narrative did not have any tangible influence on key policy stakeholders. Rather, police-generated evidence was used selectively by opponents of the 2004 reclassification to legitimize the perception of worsening conditions connected to an 'external threat' that required state intervention.

Cannabis as a threat to health

Projected threats to social order became intertwined with growing concerns about the health risks of cannabis consumption. This is of course by no means a new problem (see Chapter 2), but the renewed interest in the links between cannabis and health issues from the turn of the millennium was shaped by several factors: first, the emergence of new research evidence linking cannabis to the onset and triggering of mental health conditions; second, the reconstruction of cannabis as 'skunk' (a colloquial term used to describe high-potency herbal cannabis); and, third, the problematization of cannabis use among young people.

A series of research studies, particularly in the field of psychiatry, emerged throughout the 2000s, with increasing claims of a causal link between cannabis and the onset of schizophrenia (see Arseneault et al, 2002; van Os et al, 2002; Zammit et al, 2002). However, the link was downplayed in the decision to reclassify in 2004, with both the Home Affairs Committee and the ACMD concluding that such a link could not be comprehensively established (ACMD, 2002; Home Affairs Committee, 2002). Moreover, there were conflicting perspectives among participants about the evidence base and what it suggested about the problem, with some critical participants questioning the causal link to mental health problems.

However, more studies surfaced, and were reported in the media, with the discovery of high-strength cannabis, which became linked to the purported surge in domestic cannabis cultivation. By the time cannabis was reclassified in 2004, media outlets such as the *Daily Telegraph* and the *Daily Mail* questioned the decision to reclassify, with a "huge media hysteria"[8] and "full-blown moral panic about the relationship between cannabis and schizophrenia".[9] The use of the construct skunk allowed for cannabis to be reconstructed as a new type of cannabis that was much more dangerous and pervasive in society. Such discourses infiltrated the political talk, with Home Secretary Jacqui Smith stating: 'I am concerned to ensure that the classification of cannabis reflects the alarming fact that a much stronger drug, known as skunk, now dominates the cannabis market' (House of Commons, 2008a).

This problem was further legitimized through a Home Office-funded research study that suggested cannabis containing higher levels of THC constituted as much as 81 per cent of the market (Hardwick and King, 2008). This study became an important source for legitimizing the existence of a policy problem, as it indicated that high-strength cannabis was a widespread issue in need of a policy response. Moreover, the dangers of skunk became particularly associated with young people's use of this 'new' type of cannabis, the perception being that it was an acute medical threat to the still-developing brains of young people. Several participants alluded to political perceptions being shaped by high-profile tabloid media campaigns and the relaying of personal experiences by constituents. In both instances, the accounts were "individual stories of young men who'd taken cannabis and had a terrible psychotic breakdown".[10] In this way, a sense of impending crisis was constructed, based on the potential for previously unknown risks of cannabis to destroy lives – especially those of young, vulnerable individuals.

Interestingly, the role of 'concerned mothers' played a central role in these debates, and they, rather than the young people involved, were often depicted as the victims.

> 'If you look at the examples of cannabis users who have got lots of press attention, the mothers of cannabis users, the Mary Bretts of this world, it was the idea of victims … people that the *Daily Mail* readers could aspire to be like, and they were the ones who were suffering most from their children's use of cannabis. It was very rarely the users who were interviewed, it was the mothers.' (EW-A1: Academic Expert in Criminology)

Such depictions of cannabis as a threat are further conditioned by the prevailing framework of control. The criminalization of cannabis activities serves as a reference point to justify and legitimize its harmfulness and the subsequent need for greater control. In this sense, critical participants argued that illegality shapes how cannabis is constructed as a health problem in the political realm. "It's illegal because it's harmful, and then you say, well, alcohol is harmful but isn't illegal. And then the politician says you can't compare alcohol to cannabis, and then the scientist says why, and the answer by the politician is, because it's illegal."[11]

Depictions of harm (and lack of medical benefit) were, at that point, heavily ingrained in the international conventions on illegal substances, and so in terms of constraints on official conceptualizations of cannabis, it is important to consider that narratives reproduced at a national level are not wholly separate from those found above the nation state. Thus, cannabis was implicitly as a problem by virtue of its criminalization, but specific health issues were elevated due to the (re)emergence of research indicating links to mental health problems. Moreover, this fed into the idea that cannabis had transformed into a different substance, distinct from the cannabis considered in the 2004 reclassification, and that the effects of its use on young people were causing significant problems. Taken together, these ideas became prominent in the policy debate, and alternative perspectives were marginalized. Negative stories were used by the media and opponents of the 2004 decision, and felt in the common lived realities of concerned parents. This put pressure on the government to be seen to be doing something about an apparent epidemic problem.

Cannabis as a threat to moral order

The construction of cannabis as a threat to social order and health were also shaped by, and shaped, the perception of cannabis as a moral problem. Such perceptions have been conditioned by sociohistorical residues of conservative and religious moral dispositions that view forms of drug taking as corrupting to the mind and body. Over time, this has served to solidify a legal distinction between culturally tolerated and legal substances and illegal substances.[12] In this sense, there is a grouping of substances into dichotomous categories that are loaded with meanings of both safety and morality.

> 'The Misuse of Drugs Act is not about harms, it's about some other morality which says that alcohol is acceptable and cannabis isn't. And that would be a much more difficult break for [the government] because they would have to admit that there is no science in the Misuse of Drugs Act. It's all about morals, or bias or prejudice.' (EW-A-AC-H1: Former Chair of the ACMD)

Cannabis remained marginal to the dominant schema of New Labour politicians, with key figures holding a "puritanical view"[13] in relation to illegal drugs. The reported increased dangers of cannabis helped reconfirm and reconstruct prevailing views that the use of cannabis was a moral evil.

Within this context, and following the arguments above that the use of cannabis by young people became problematic, the focus on young people became embroiled in a wider critique of New Labour. One 'conservative'-leaning participant claimed that "Blair's feral youth" were creating vast problems, with cannabis seen to be playing a key role in this social antipathy: "We had a whole generation of kids quite seriously damaged ... there were social problems created by this vast number of kids not getting into employment at a time of a booming economy."[14]

While there was some evidence of increasing admissions for treatment for cannabis-related mental health problems (see Department of Health, 2011), the attention brought by the media may have aggravated the perception of cannabis as a driver of unruly behaviour and other social ills; it was easy for parents to point to cannabis as the reason why their teenage children were behaving in undesirable ways. This further contributed to the growing perception that the reclassification had been a political mistake, with the government being careless over its young citizens' health. Given that cannabis was the most widely used illegal substance in England & Wales (Home Office, 2013), fears about its increasing harms became coupled with the idea that "the place is awash with drugs [and] everybody has ready access to them".[15] In this way, a 'moral panic' emerged, centred on the view that cannabis was more dangerous than in the past and particularly problematic given its widespread use (Cohen, 1972).

These views helped reconstruct cannabis as a problem at the national level and reinforced the idea that the 2004 reclassification had transgressed acceptable political and moral boundaries and was fuelling a widespread crisis. Notions that cannabis had since transformed and had become more dangerous fed into this view, which was conflated by perceptions of harm and criminality and was driven by law enforcement activities which disproportionately targeted ethnic minority populations.

The Netherlands: coming to terms with unintended, unforeseen and uncontrolled consequences

The construction of cannabis as a problem preceding the 2012–13 changes to coffeeshop policy in the Netherlands shares features of the 2009 reclassification of cannabis in England & Wales, being viewed in terms of threats to social order, health and morality. Nevertheless, in 2012, with the trial of the closed club and residency measures put forward by Rutte I and the change in government, to Rutte II, problem definition shifted. It was the policy changes themselves that were seen as the source of a series of problems – the tougher measures were viewed as exacerbating existing social order issues as well as threatening individual liberties and the valued existence of tolerated coffeeshops.

Cannabis as a threat to social order

The construction of cannabis as a threat to social order in the Netherlands at the end of the 2000s centred around problems of public nuisance and organized crime. These issues were shaped by experiences from the 1990s onwards, including the exceptional existence of de facto legal selling points, the easing of movement across European borders, significant demand for cannabis and the entrepreneurial spirit of coffeeshop owners looking to maximize profits.

While coffeeshops were not seen to produce much nuisance overall, due to the tight regulations and possible sanctions if coffeeshops were to transgress proscribed rules, some southern municipalities with coffeeshops experienced problems caused by large numbers of visitors. Indicatively, in Limburg, it was estimated that there were almost four million visits to coffeeshops in one year.[16] In accounting for the stark concentration of public order problems in a small minority of areas, it is relevant to take into consideration the cross-border issues in the Maas-Rijn region of Western Europe, a densely populated area sharing three state borders. The compact nature of the area, coupled with ease of mobility across borders following the Schengen Convention of 1990, created a hub of migratory movement that was a key factor in worsening public order issues. However, the numbers of foreign visitors were not seen as problematic until the turn of the millennium, when there was a rapid increase. "Before that [2008], let's say 2001, 2000, there were only hundreds of people … you see in those beginning years that there were 10,000 people, 100,000, and now in the millions."[17]

The "burden"[18] of accommodating increased numbers of visitors to the coffeeshops, which were often located in inner cities, mainly concerned traffic and parking issues. Although the severity of this problem was dismissed by liberal-leaning individuals,[19] for others, this was a significant problem for mayors of affected municipalities. "In these border cities here, Roosendaal, Bergen op Zoom, small cities, the mayors came here [and said] 'we can't sustain this anymore … all these Belgians and French foreigners who come to our small cities, they are really burdening us in many ways.'"[20]

The increase in foreign visitors to coffeeshops was also connected to concerns about other forms of criminality, particularly dealing of cannabis and other substances around coffeeshops, which was not a tolerated practice. "Of course, the dealers and the pushers around these coffeeshops, they try to sell everything, they are market people."[21] Also of concern were 'drugs runners' operating between the Netherlands and bordering countries.

The increase in demand in southern border municipalities meant that coffeeshops – such as Checkpoint in Terneuzen, which according to some reports had approximately 3,000 customers daily (Volkskrant, 2008) – "became an illegal criminal paradise".[22] There was a consensus among interviewees that organized crime had become a dominant force in cannabis cultivation since the late 1990s. This view was also reflected in the findings of the van de Donk Committee. 'Drug tourism in the border areas and in large towns and cities … has risen sharply, fostering large-scale cannabis production and trafficking in this country. Such operations have also developed into major, innovative enterprises' (Advisory Committee on Drugs Policy, 2009: 19, official translation).

With the unavoidable and intimate connections between some coffeeshops and large-scale growers, the image of the coffeeshop became tainted – what were once considered normalized, tolerated outlets came to be seen as intrinsically criminal organizations. Moreover, stemming from the unresolved issue of how coffeeshops acquire products to sell, and with the proscribed stock limit being 500 grams per shop, the visitor numbers led to difficulties of supply. In turn, this often led to the creation of stashes as well as the need for regular topping up of supplies. Having to restock often contributed to nuisance and criminality around coffeeshops, including robberies by rival criminal gangs.

To some extent the involvement of organized crime was not a new problem, given the historical importation of hashish, but domestic cultivation was previously believed to be on a small scale, conducted by the stereotypical peaceful hippie, with most cannabis, and harms, coming from abroad. With the transition to greater domestic cultivation, the internal threat grew. The Netherlands was encountering a significant internal challenge, with police estimating that 60–90 percent of domestically produced cannabis was being exported (van der Giessen et al, 2014). Moreover, in some cases, these activities were seen to be conducted by social 'undesirables', such as Roma and travellers as well as foreign crime groups,[23] with prominent incidents emerging in the public sphere. This new form of back-end activity in the cannabis industry was characterized by "tough criminality",[24] commonly associated with violence and other illicit activities, such as human trafficking and the hard drugs trade.

> 'We have a lot of murders, we have a lot of torturing, we have a lot of assaults just around cannabis … organized crime isn't only cannabis plantations, it is also synthetic drugs, ecstasy, cocaine, human trafficking. But all these facts are together in organized crime, and cannabis plantations are most [of the] time used to earn money to support the other organized crime.' (NL-POL2: Police Officer, Organized Cannabis Cultivation Taskforce)

One factor influencing the construction of a problem of organized crime was the more explicit labelling and reaction to the issue. Evidence of the rising threat to security posed by cannabis cultivation was generated by the Taskforce on Organized Cannabis Cultivation in combination with the activities of the National Police Services Agency (Korps Landelijke Politiediensten – KLPD) (National Police Services Agency, 2008, 2012a, 2012b). From a critical perspective, it was suggested that the police focus on small-scale growers had led to more opportunities for organized crime to develop. "The individual growers of small plantations in their attics or in their cellars became a very specific point of danger for police and the Public Prosecutor's Office."[25]

Moreover, the relative ease of cannabis cultivation led to the perception that the threat could exist anywhere and everywhere. The problem of small-scale cultivation was framed to citizens as a safety issue. This practice was often carried out in houses or apartments, and there were potential safety hazards (for example, fire hazards) for other citizens. This concern was particularly pertinent in the context of the Netherlands' relatively high ratio of population to living space.

It was suggested that these issues encouraged a shift towards a tougher approach to all scales of cannabis cultivation. There was a degree of conflation between coffeeshops, small-scale cannabis cultivation and organized crime. While problems of drug-related public nuisance and organized crime have existed for some time, they took on new meanings and 'focusing effects' (Kingdon, 1995) that captured the attention of national government. The political importance of cannabis grew at national level during the 2000s due municipal lobbying, increased law enforcement efforts and negative media and public opinion, and this served to shatter the 'innocence' of cannabis and cast problems through the lens of law enforcement. These threats became further entangled with a deeper and broader set of public and political anxieties concerning cannabis and coffeeshops.

Cannabis as a threat to health

The development of advanced growing techniques and knowledge of selective breeding of cannabis strains, combined with financial investment from organized crime groups, reduced risks in domestic cultivation and the entrepreneurial spirit of growers and coffeeshop owners, has led to the growth of stronger cannabis domestically. While, as several interviewees[26] noted, cultivation of *nederwiet* (Dutch weed) started in the early 1990s, policy concerns arose with indications that the potency – particularly in respect of THC content – increased rapidly at the end of the 1990s and in the early 2000s (see Niesink and Rigter, 2013: 22–5). The perceived problem was very similar to that in England & Wales and occurred at around the same time. This is perhaps not all that surprising given the exportation of not only cannabis itself but also growing techniques and knowledge.

Research studies linked the use of more THC-potent cannabis to low educational attainment and poor mental health, particularly among young people. There was increasing evidence of cannabis users seeking treatment (Arseneault et al, 2002; van Os et al, 2002; Zammit et al, 2002; Wisselink et al, 2012; Verweij et al, 2013). The mounting evidence of the risks associated with cannabis challenged a fundamental aspect of Dutch drugs policy: that cannabis is a soft drug, one whose harms are relatively benign. This significantly infiltrated a range of perspectives internal and external to the policy machinery with the sense that cannabis was "not [as] innocent as we thought it was".[27]

> 'When you blow [smoke/consume] and you think you are blowing soft drugs and it has a high THC amount, then it has almost the effect of hard drugs … they say this is very dangerous stuff, you must not misuse it.' (NL-PP2: Public Prosecutor, Limburg)

> 'We concluded, point one, cannabis is not so innocent as once had been thought. There have been several studies that say if you use cannabis at a very young age, it is damaging to the brain.' (NL-CS-AC-CJ: Senior Civil Servant in Ministry of Justice and Security and Member of van de Donk Committee)

> 'Public opinion changed also because of the constant stories about how bad marijuana is for young people and that it is stronger than what it was … it is not your parents' weed any more, now it is really a hard drug.' (NL-NGO1: Drugs Policy Reform Organization and Psychiatrist)

> 'The Ministry of Health was always leading in the drug debate, but now there were more negative aspects of health in the debate, so the Ministry of Health was also changing its attitude towards cannabis and thinking about more repressive measures.' (NL-CS-AC-H2: Senior Civil Servant in the Ministry of Health, Welfare and Sport and Member of the van de Donk Committee)

> 'Soft drugs must stay soft. … Hard drugs do not belong in coffeeshops, and in future these establishments will only be permitted to sell cannabis with a THC content of under 15 per cent.' (House of Representatives of the States General, 2012: 4)

However, among participants there were countervailing views concerning the extent to which cannabis had become increasingly harmful, and whether harms could be legitimately associated with cannabis. For example, one interviewee pointed out that high-strength cannabis existed prior to the introduction of *nederwiet* to the market, thus challenging the notion that this is a new problem: "I said to the government, if that is true, this warning [needed] to be started in the 1960s, because when the foreign hashish came into the market, it was already stronger than the *nederwiet* of 1994, so fuck off."[28]

Indeed, THC levels in *nederwiet* are not wildly different to those in imported hashish, which has had an average THC content of 12–20 per cent; and since the high point of 2004, trends have indicated a longer-term decline of THC levels in cannabis consumed in the Netherlands (see Niesink and Rigter, 2013: 22–5). Critical participants suggested that the problematization of cannabis was in part due to a medicalizing of deviance by psychiatric professionals, which in combination with greater public awareness and the labelling of cannabis as a problem, caused people – particularly concerned parents – to associate deviant or undesirable characteristics of youth with the use of cannabis.

> 'From the moment you make cannabis that dangerous by such public campaigns, what happens is that parents don't start talking any more about cannabis … they [go] to the clinic, yes, my child, something is wrong.' (NL-A-NGO1: Independent Research Organization and Drugs Worker)

> 'It has been reframed by, I would say, a new generation of researchers, typically from the clinical and medical field … all the issues in the cannabis debate are readdressed with new evidence, so the cannabis psychosis, schizophrenia, those terms, shift over time.' (NL-A2: Academic Expert in Criminology)

Even though clear changes in the nature of cannabis occurred over the past couple of decades, the relationship to health issues was deeply contested. Nevertheless, the construction of cannabis as a hard drug had clear symbolic appeal that challenged the traditional image of cannabis as a relatively safe and innocent substance, and it was this narrative of the problem that became dominant in policy debates.

Cannabis as a threat to moral order

In the political context at the end of the millennium (see Chapter 3), there was growing dissatisfaction with *gedoogbeleid*, not only because it created practical difficulties but also in the sense that it allowed coffeeshops to become too normalized in Dutch society and challenged the moral tolerance of cannabis. This was driven mainly by the religious parties and their belief that coffeeshops are "bad examples"[29], whose visibility encourages cannabis use among young people.

> 'They see it, they see other people going in and out so probably they get more enthusiastic towards trying to find a way to get a joint from somewhere and to try it themselves.' (NL-CS-CJ: Civil Servant in the Ministry of Justice and Security)

> 'People say this is an innocent thing, this is nice, why shouldn't we go there? ... They do everything to accommodate to the normal world.' (NL-A-AC-CJ: Academic Expert in Criminology and Member of the van de Donk Committee)

Links were made between young people, health concerns and the presence of coffeeshops, and a perception grew that "young pupils … need to be protected from the sight of coffeeshops".[30] Cannabis was also linked to youth delinquency and exclusion, as intimated by the van de Donk Committee (Advisory Committee on Drugs Policy, 2009: 18). As one critical participant suggested:

> 'In the mid-1990s it became more and more popular among the lower level of the society … young people with the "monkey on their [back]", young people with no future, the poor people, no school, no job … so the cannabis use [is an escape]. … But they connected that with coffeeshops and with the Dutch weed, and that started from the second part of the 1990s … wow the soft drugs are not soft drugs any more, and the dealer is the coffeeshop.' (NL-A-NGO1: Independent Research Organization and Drugs Worker)

Similar to England & Wales, where cannabis was associated with "Blair's feral youth", a moralistic framing was attributed to cannabis use, with political actors employing "vengeful rhetoric"[31] to protect 'vulnerable youth' (House of Representatives of the States General, 2011b: 1, author's translation). There was a sense that problematizations of cannabis were "more of a moral discussion and … fed by more stories than facts and figures I think … there are politicians who think that cannabis is the worst of all. I think that is more a moral point."[32] This framing supported an emphasis on tougher measures and stricter law enforcement as means of instilling values.

Cannabis policy as a threat to order (again) and liberty

The definition of cannabis as a problem was also affected by the trials of the residency and closed club measures in May 2012. The trial of these measures in three southern provinces occurred in a rapidly changing context with widespread criticism of the new and planned coffeeshop measures. The problematization centred around the closed-club measure, particularly the *wietpas* (weed pass), requiring users to register at a particular coffeeshop, and the apparent increases in criminality and nuisance as well as threats to individual human rights.

An evaluation of the measures found that while there had been serious declines in the number of foreign visitors to coffeeshops, this was accompanied by increased purchasing of cannabis from non-tolerated outlets, such as '06' (telephone) dealers, street dealers and home networks (Research and Documentation Centre, 2013: 157). Significantly, it was felt that the new measures had created a "shadow economy" with serious negative side effects.

> 'Suddenly there is this *wietpas* and that has had some terrible effects in the south where you see now that there is a shadow economy that didn't exist before. And after three or four months of this pass situation, people start looking outside the coffeeshop … so there were people on motorbikes from Rotterdam going to the cities in the south and just starting to sell, and there is an instant market. And they became very aggressive against foreigners, very aggressive against people living there, so it actually took three or four months at most to destroy 30 years of good practice.' (NL-CS-AC-H1: Senior Civil Servant in Ministry of Health, Welfare and Sport and Member of Garretsen Committee)

> 'When you talk to the mayors of the eight cities who have coffeeshops, they say altogether that there is a lot of increased dealing activity with criminality, and the public experienced a lot of bad effects of those aggressive dealing activities.' (NL-PP2: Public Prosecutor, Limburg)

The perceived increase in "aggressive dealing activities" was linked not only to the diversion of foreign users to non-tolerated sources, but also to the number of Dutch cannabis consumers who chose not to register at a coffeeshop (see House of Representatives of the States General, 2012: 3). Given that cannabis remained legally prohibited, and occurring at a time when the government was facing data security issues related to passports, the need to register at a coffeeshop created significant resistance and distrust due to fears over what would happen to people's personal information.

In addition to these issues, the new measures had significant resistance from municipalities across the Netherlands. The problem was that the new measures lacked policy legitimacy, as powerful local mayors, particularly in areas that did not have problems with foreign visitors, rejected the need for the measures. Thus, the introduction of stricter measures for coffeeshops caused an immediate negative backlash against the government, leading to a re-problematization of cannabis policy and protests against a perceived threat to the idealized 'separation of markets' philosophy underpinning Dutch drugs policy.

Problematizations of cannabis in global perspective

From the discussion in this chapter so far, it is possible to detect some strong similarities in the underlying problematizations of cannabis that shaped policy debates in England & Wales and the Netherlands. Nevertheless, there were also some key differences – not least, the influence of a counter liberal perspective in the Netherlands, which demonstrated that there was space available for a range of possible problematizations to emerge. Such a space is even more evident in other contexts where there have been more 'liberal' reforms. This final section of the chapter contains a brief exploration of how cannabis came to be problematized in relation to Canada's Cannabis Act 2018 and Jamaica's Dangerous Drugs (Amendment) Act 2015.

Canada

In 2018, Canada became the second country, after Uruguay, to legally regulate, in its entirety, the use, supply and cultivation of cannabis. Under the provisions of the Cannabis Act, federal and provincial governments hold considerable powers in respect of issuing licences, controlling distribution and regulating the contents of cannabis products and how they are sold, representing a firm grip over the newly established legal market (Shanahan and Cyrenne, 2021).

The nature of this regulatory approach is connected to the sorts of dominant problematizations that emerged preceding the policy shift. Interesting in this respect is that although there were a number of policy problems which appeared similar to social phenomena experienced in England & Wales and the Netherlands – particularly concerning crime, safety and health – the prevailing narrative to emerge was nevertheless shaped by differing values and interpretations.

In Canada, as in many other Western liberal democracies, cannabis use is relatively prevalent, especially among young people. In the 2017 Canadian Tobacco, Alcohol and Drugs Survey, 14.8 per cent of the general population (aged 15 and over) and 26.9 per cent of young people (aged 15–24) reported cannabis use in the past year (Canadian Centre on Substance Use and Addiction, 2020). Related to this purported normalization of cannabis use (see Osborne and Fogel, 2017), narratives of children and young people being at risk from cannabis – owing to its psychopharmacological effects on mental health and cognitive development, as well as the involvement of nefarious actors and organizations in the production and supply of cannabis – became a strong theme present in political discourse prior to the policy change (Cox, 2018). Indeed, the expert Taskforce on Cannabis Legalization and Regulation – established to examine the feasibility of regulating the cannabis market – recognized the existence of a 'widespread and deep rooted network' in society (Taskforce on Cannabis Legalization and Regulation, 2016: 9).

However, in Garland's (2001) terms, if the sorts of strategies adopted in England & Wales and the Netherlands, especially during the late 2000s and early 2010s, could be described as non-adaptive, then developments in Canada appeared to embrace adaptation. In this respect, the desire to 'save the children' was grounded in the discourse of protecting children's rights (Webster, 2018; Barrett 2019). However, while Article 33 of the Convention on the Rights of the Child – 'to protect children from the illicit use of narcotic drugs and psychotropic substances' (Office of the High Commissioner for Human Rights, 1989) – is often used as a rationale to reinforce criminalizing legislation and policy, this took on an alternative interpretation in the Canadian context. As Barrett (2019) suggests, policy reform advocates sought to advance an interpretation based on how to pragmatically protect young people in the face of perceived failures of prohibitive modes of cannabis control.

In this vein, the problem was the legally prohibitive control system itself, which was seen as contributing to, rather than preventing, public health harms (Cox, 2018); in other words, it was an 'ineffective strategy' that provided little protection to young people's health and future, because the drugs market was unregulated and controlled by black market actors (Taskforce on Cannabis Legalization and Regulation, 2016: 10; see also Crépault et al, 2016; Fischer et al, 2016; Shanahan and Cyrenne, 2021).

This 'failures of prohibition' narrative was not just framed in relation to young people, but had a wider scope, with new policies targeting broad public health and safety concerns, such as public consumption, workplace safety and driving under the influence of cannabis (Shanahan and Cyrene, 2021). According to the Department of Justice (2021), the Cannabis Act had three goals: to 'keep cannabis out of the hands of youth'; to 'keep profits out of the pockets of criminals'; and to 'protect public health and safety by allowing adults access to legal cannabis'.

This is not to disregard the existence of other ways in which cannabis was represented as a problem; there were certainly actors and organizations whose normative standpoints on cannabis were less aligned or antithetical to a framework of legal regulation (Kalant, 2016; Kelsall, 2017). Moreover, it is important to stress that the notion of the criminal justice system as a source of harm was by no means a new problematization; attempts to advance policy reforms aiming to dampen the impact of such harms have a relatively long history in Canada, as evidenced by the 1969–72 Commission of Inquiry into the Non-Medical Use of Drugs (which recommended non-criminalizing provisions), the implementation of the Controlled Drugs and Substances Act of 1996 (which separated cannabis from other substances) and the decriminalizing reform efforts of the early 2000s (Fischer et al, 1996; Fischer et al, 2003; Fischer et al, 2020).

Nevertheless, legal provisions for medical cannabis were in place since 2001, and the political acceptance and expansion of this programme – even by political actors opposed to non-medical cannabis – arguably 'paved the way and pre-shaped key features of foundations towards the general legalization of non-medical cannabis use and supply to come' (Fischer et al, 2020: 94; see also Fischer et al, 2015). Also, the 2018 reforms cannot be separated from the influence and widespread reporting of legalization developments in the United States, the election in 2015 of the Liberal Party and its charismatic leader Justin Trudeau, who strongly favoured legalization, and the favourable position of the influential Centre for Addiction and Mental Health towards legal regulation (Fischer et al, 2020).

Thus, in Kingdon's (1995) terms, such historical residues and focusing events provided a fertile ground for problematizations – premised on the inadequacies of criminal justice-led approaches – that rationalized the move to a firmly controlled legal regulatory framework, within a suitable window of opportunity.

Jamaica

In Jamaica, possession of cannabis for personal use was decriminalized under the Dangerous Drug Amendment Act 2015, with possession and use in public spaces becoming an administrative offence with a fine as a sanction. Additionally, cultivation of cannabis on personal property was legalized and legal regulations were put in place for domestic medical and scientific use (Rychert et al, 2020).

These legislative revisions represent a significant sea change from nearly a century of prohibitive statues and law enforcement introduced under British colonial rule and continued in postcolonial Jamaica (Davenport and Pardo, 2016; Hanson, 2020). This history of criminalization was positioned in a context where the use of cannabis – also called ganja – is 'embedded in the unique culture and fabric of the Jamaican society' (Hanson, 2020: 376), having a high level of cultural acceptance as well as being used in traditional medicinal practices and by religious groups. In the latter case, the use of cannabis is not only intrinsic to Rastafari spirituality but also considered as a means of economic survival and rebellion against Western-imposed norms and culture (Jones et al, 2017; Hanson, 2020). Yet it was arguably owing to these aspects that minority groups, such as the Maroons and Rastafari, who have been most associated with cannabis, faced a high degree of social ostracism and criminalization throughout the 20th century.

However, from around the 1970s, political discourse on cannabis and the treatment of the Rastafari community opened up considerably, with the global platform of hugely popular reggae music artists such as Peter Tosh and Bob Marley providing a strong voice to policy reform and the legalization movement. The gradual political recognition of the problems that punitive cannabis legislation posed for particular communities was also connected to structural inequalities and tensions in Jamaican society, with young men from poorer communities being more likely to use cannabis and be subject to sanctions. By the end of the 1990s, notwithstanding broader sociocultural currents, the problem of criminalization of these populations for cannabis offences became more politically pertinent, as political parties began to recognize the voting potential of this large section of the electorate (Hanson, 2020).

Yet despite greater incentives and more efforts to act on these recognized problems, notably through the establishment of the National Commission on Ganja by the People's National Party in 2000, these ultimately did not lead to any policy reform. This was due partly, as Hanson (2020) suggests, to the commission lacking representation from the very communities who were most affected by law enforcement of cannabis laws. Moreover, it was influenced by alternative problematizations and movements in the political stream, and there were fears about the political ramifications of reforming policy concerning a moralized social issue as well as the potential impact this could have on Jamaica's international reputation.

Nevertheless, while no changes were enacted at the turn of the millennium, the identification of problems with existing control structures had attained a significant degree of political legitimacy, laying the groundwork for future reform. In this sense, pro-reform narratives and possible policy alternatives did not disappear from the political landscape but remained dormant until they became politically viable. This window of opportunity for political action came with a focusing event – the murder in 2014 of a young man in jail after being arrested for possessing a small amount of cannabis. This provided the fertile ground for political and public sympathy to surface, acting as an impetus for activists, lobbyists and politicians to mobilize for reform (Hanson, 2020). According to the Jamaican government, the change in law, towards decriminalization, in 2015 had a number of aims relating to long-standing problems in Jamaican society: to reduce 'corrosive antagonism' between police and young men from disadvantaged communities; to reduce corruption and violence as well as the burdens on the criminal justice system; and to recognize the constitutional rights of the Rastafari community (Wilson, 2015; Davenport and Pardo, 2016; Gordon, 2016; Rychert et al, 2020).

Along with prior problematizations concerning the discrimination of religious communities and criminalization of disadvantaged communities, a further key problematization became evident, highlighted by civic and business communities. This was the problem of (missed) opportunities for economic growth through cannabis cultivation and research. This problematization can be understood in the context of greater global liberalization of regulations for medical cannabis by the time of the reforms, with one of the key strands of the Jamaican government's political vision being to 'increase foreign exchange earnings via exports of cannabis and cannabis tourism' (Rychert et al, 2020; see also Gordon, 2016). This represents a rather different problem to that which has been discussed thus far. Feeding into a 'market-oriented approach', the problem is one of prohibitive cannabis policy blocking opportunities for economic development (Davenport and Pardo, 2016: 61). Thus, in Jamaica, the problematization of cannabis in the context of the shift to decriminalization in 2015 centred around three main issues: rights of minority religious communities; criminal justice harms; and (missed) economic opportunities.

Summary

The chapter has illuminated a diverse range of problematizations that were influential in shaping cannabis policy debates across differing contexts. These included issues of public safety and social order, morality, health, liberty and human rights, and economic development. Such problems are not a direct representation of an objective state, but instead reflect how social actors assign meaning to a constantly metamorphosing phenomenon.

These aspects are explored further in Chapters 5 and 6, but such processes of meaning-making often draw on a variety of sources and bodies of knowledge to represent a problem, including, inter alia, police and medical agencies, government departments, and researchers as well as popular opinion, civil advocacy and interest groups, and media outlets. Nevertheless, what comes to be projected, represented and taken seriously as a political problem cannot be disconnected from the sorts of 'expressive' and 'instrumental' dispositions which drive interpretations of what can be observed and sensed (Edwards and Hughes, 2012), and the legitimacy of a problem ebbs and flows with social, cultural, economic and political currents and events.

It appears to be rarely the case that problematizations are entirely unique to a given context, even if their precise manifestations are attuned to contingently shaped conditions of existence; arguments about the restrictions or harms that criminalization poses to individual liberty are very much present in England & Wales, just as notions of the immorality of cannabis use exists in Jamaica or Canada. However, certain ideas proliferate at certain times in certain contexts. Thus, while in England & Wales and the Netherlands issues of organized crime and health risks were projected in ways that aligned with a strengthening of existing control frameworks, in Canada very similar phenomena resulted in an entirely different interpretation that problematized a criminal justice model of control. What this alludes to is the constant competition over defining a problem requiring political action, and how these definitions become aligned with the normative positioning of those actors with the resources to advance their preferred views of the problem and solution to it.

Thus, we can understand that even where cannabis policy exists in turbulent and politicized environments, it is possible for problematizations to emerge not only in policy narratives that are aligned with non-adaptive responses, but also those which are more adaptive and/or progressive. To further comprehend the sorts of constellations that are made possible in policy formation, we turn next to consider how some of the problematizations identified here became aligned with particular policy proposals.

5

The 'Primeval Soup' of Policy Proposals

Introduction

As discussed in the previous chapter, the identification of something as a problem that requires a policy response is not an objective process. Even in very similar contexts, problems can take different forms. According to the multiple streams model, those problematizations that make it onto the policy agenda then become attached to ideas and proposals in the policy stream (Kingdon, 1995). Problems and policies cannot be said to be inherently connected, nor is it the case that a problem necessarily predates its corresponding proposal. Some policy proposals that have remained dormant for years or decades can suddenly arise and mesh with policy problems when a suitable window of opportunity presents itself. A good example here is that of cannabis legalization, which, as a policy idea, has existed for a considerable period of time but has only recently been taken up as a serious policy option in some contexts across the globe. The sense is that a number of policy alternatives exist relatively independently of problems at any given time in what Kingdon (1995) describes as the 'primeval soup' of policy. Which proposals are taken seriously in relation to a problem deemed to warrant a response is based on a number of considerations, such as: the expressive and instrumental dispositions of political parties and politicians; the perceived palatability to voters and stakeholders; the alignment with research and expertise; and the legal, financial and organizational feasibility.

This chapter concentrates first on aspects of the policy stream – grouped here as political feasibility, research and expertise and technical feasibility – in the main cases of England & Wales and the Netherlands. Then the dynamics of these three aspects are elucidated in two further cases: Australia and Spain.

Returning cannabis to its 'rightful position' in England & Wales

In England & Wales in the mid to late 2000s, the process of selecting policy options in response to a recognized set of problems related to cannabis appeared to counter the rational model of policy making, whereby a plethora of possible alternatives are considered logically and systematically before being narrowed down.

Cannabis had been reclassified as a Class C drug in 2004, but as soon as this happened, the option to reverse the decision was placed in the primeval soup, where it became attached to concerns in the problem stream. In 2009, in response to the problematization of cannabis, reclassification of the drug from Class C to Class B was advocated as the only acceptable change, returning cannabis to its rightful position. Nevertheless, the reclassification needed to meet a set of criteria before it would come into force. Importantly, as shown here, the 2009 reclassification was politically feasible and chimed with dominant political values, it was supported through the selective 'marshalling' of research and expertise, and it was technically feasible.

Political feasibility

The political feasibility of changing drugs policy at national level in England & Wales is conditioned by a series of interlinking factors which, on the whole, more readily facilitate punitive responses to problems surrounding illegal substances. One of the major themes arising from interview data in the current study concerns the notion of 'political currency'. In the political sphere, particularly at the time of the 2009 reclassification, drugs policy was viewed as a "toxic third rail issue",[1] as it was seen to offer "no obvious gain".[2]

Reflecting on this, a senior political figure noted that for many, drugs policy is an area in which it is not worth "sticking your head above the parapet".[3] The types of favoured responses are largely influenced by perceived public attitudes. Liberal reforms are purportedly difficult due to the "culture and background of the country",[4] with the two main parties, Labour and the Conservatives, very resistant to change in the drugs policy sphere. However, this is not to overemphasize the lack of counter-doxic perspectives in England & Wales, and it is important to note that since the completion of fieldwork for this study, the toxicity surrounding drug and cannabis policy has somewhat lessened for these major parties, as indicated by the emergence of the Labour Campaign for Drug Policy Reform and the Conservative Drug Policy Reform Group. Nevertheless, the number of senior politicians willing to take a public position outside of the political norm remains low, with prominent politicians explicitly rejecting reforms that would dismantle criminalized systems of control (Forsyth, 2021; Hatton, 2022).

This alludes to an important condition in the selection of policy alternatives, that of the historical basis of criminalization. The treatment of cannabis as a criminal justice matter, led by the Home Office, has reinforced the notion that cannabis is a criminal problem (rather than a social or a health problem, for example) and that "the way we can influence behaviour is through legislation, control".[5] In a broader political context favouring punitive reaction, problems are given ready-made labels and solutions (for example, being weak on crime, must punish more). As suggested in Chapter 4, the status of illegality serves as a referential indicator of its harmfulness, which marginalizes alternative paradigms. Thus, appropriate policy responses to the problems emerging in the mid-2000s became aligned within an existing criminal justice template, as corroborated in the policy talk of Home Secretary Jacqui Smith: 'My decision to reclassify cannabis is part of the relentless drive to tackle drugs and the harm they bring to families and communities. … This is the right action to protect the public, particularly the future health of young people and the most vulnerable' (House of Commons, 2008a).

For Smith, part of the justification for the 2009 reclassification was the 'consequences for policing priorities' (House of Commons, 2008a). She stated in relation to the purported growth in commercial cultivation: 'This cannot be tolerated. … Reclassifying cannabis will help to drive enforcement priorities in shutting those farms down' (House of Commons, 2008a). In this sense, the option of reclassification back to Class B became a politically feasible way to respond to the perceived failures and criticisms levelled at the 2004 reclassification which construed New Labour as being weak on crime. Given the political sensitivities of policy making in this area at this time, this blocked alternative options from being considered.

The problematization of cannabis resonated with a set of instrumental and moral values that guided the selection of a policy alternative. As one academic noted, policy selection is "based on this combination of morality and power, with people donating their own moral preferences with the benefit of the power they have to back them up with".[6] In this way, the particular moral preferences of key decision makers in the process allowed the option of reclassification to Class B to become a plausible response to the set of concerns that had emerged. In particular, the preferences of Prime Minister Gordon Brown were particularly salient, given his powerful and influential position. Brown became prime minister with a strong religiously guided view on morally contested activities, and he sought to make an impression on a number of policy areas (for example, super casinos and alcohol licensing). Cannabis came to be part of these concerns, reinforced by its problematization in the public sphere.[7]

> 'I suspect with Gordon Brown that he was making a break from the past ... there was lots about gambling and mega casinos. This was seen as a liberal elite in the Labour Party ... the new leader of the Labour Party willing to exert some of his Presbyterian philosophies.' (EW-NGO-AC: Independent Drugs Policy Organization and Former ACMD Member)

Thus, the individual preferences of key decision makers were important in shaping what policies were advocated as possible responses to a recognized problem. This is not to suggest that Brown's Presbyterian beliefs were widespread or dominant, but that they paralleled a set of public anxieties on the issue of cannabis at that time. Thus, reclassification was not only preferable in terms of Brown's own value system, but it was congruent in terms of other criteria, such as satisfying public and political pressures. As such, it became the only politically realistic 'choice'. The conditions of doing cannabis policy during this period highlighted the "three 'p's of political decision-making: perception, prejudice and pressure".[8] These seemingly placed greater emphasis on populist and media-driven fears, facilitated by the power and ability of political leaders.

Research and expertise

Another factor in why the reclassification to Class B became the preferred policy option is research and expertise. This is of interest precisely because the key recommendation of the ACMD, not to reclassify cannabis, was rejected. The relationship between the ACMD and the government was tested several times during the 2000s, culminating in the eventual dismissal of its chair, Professor David Nutt, and the simultaneous resignation of several members in the aftermath of the reclassification.

Indicative of the political urgency attributed to cannabis throughout the 2000s, the ACMD were asked to review cannabis classification three times in a six-year period (ACMD, 2002, 2006, 2008). Pressure mounted to revisit the classification of cannabis almost immediately following the 2004 reclassification, with then Home Secretary Charles Clarke requesting a second review. In its report, the ACMD concluded that it 'does not advise the reclassification of cannabis products to Class B' (ACMD, 2006: 1). The advice was accepted by Clarke, and for political reasons (detailed in Chapter 6) the issue was "kicked into the long grass".[9]

Despite Clarke accepting the ACMD's report and using it to justify keeping cannabis as a Class C substance, the issue remained on the political agenda. By 2007, the third review was called for by the newest Home Secretary, Jacqui Smith. By this time, the ACMD had slightly shifted its position on the link between cannabis and mental health, but it still concluded that cannabis should remain a Class C drug, stating that since the last review 'the evidence has become more, rather than less confused', and suggesting that 'cannabis – in the population as a whole – plays only a modest role in the development of [psychotic illnesses]' (ACMD, 2008: 33). According to interviewees who were ACMD members at the time, their decisions surrounding cannabis classification were largely supported by a broad consensus within the Council.

Despite the recommendations of the ACMD, the government ultimately chose to ignore its advice and reclassified cannabis to Class B. Even so, the ACMD report was used alongside the Home Office study on cannabis potency to justify the political decision. As Jacqui Smith's announcement in the House of Commons stated:

> Today I am publishing the results of a study undertaken with 23 police forces across England and Wales. This provides *clear evidence* that skunk now makes up 80 per cent of street-seized cannabis, compared with 30 per cent in 2002. ... The advisory council's report confirms that cannabis use poses a *real threat* to health. The council is concerned about its use among young people, and points to growing evidence of a causal link, albeit a weak one, between cannabis use and psychotic illness. ...
>
> There is a compelling case for us to act now rather than risk the future health of young people. Where there is a *clear and serious problem*, but doubt about the potential harm that will be caused, *we must err on the side of caution and protect the public.* I make no apology for that. I am not prepared to wait and see. (House of Commons, 2008a, emphasis added)

It is contended that the decision to reclassify was already at the forefront of the minds of those in power at the time. In 2007, Gordon Brown stated that the Home Secretary would 'consult on whether it is right that cannabis should be moved from Class C to Class B' (House of Commons, 2007). Thus, the announcement of the government's intent to reclassify was made in the House of Commons even before the advice of the ACMD was sought, immediately closing off alternative policy solutions.

The problematization of cannabis had put pressure on the government to respond to its own earlier decision to reclassify downwards. Supporters were waiting with a suitable response, and evidence was used to legitimize their chosen policy response, which fitted more with political desires than evidence-based expert advice.

> 'At the time he asked us to reclassify, or the Home Secretary did ask to have a look at it again, he sent his minders out on the street saying he is going to reclassify to B, even before we told him what the evidence was … I did actually write to the home secretary and I wrote to the

> prime minister and said if you have already made your mind up, what's the point of asking our advice?' (EW-A-AC-H2: Former Chair of the ACMD)

In the midst of conflicting evidence, it would appear, then, that policy decisions became tied to politically instrumental and moralistic rationalities. The unwillingness of politicians to 'think outside the box' due to deeply held beliefs and/or consideration of the political ramifications of appearing soft meant that evidence was used in a self-serving manner to justify the accepted 'fact' that a more punitive display of policy was the most appropriate measure to 'protect the public'. The political currency of adopting a law and order approach was valued much more within drugs policy, and as a result, this had a trickle-down effect on the types of evidence used and the policies civil servants and ministers could propose. "There is not much political benefit. … People get marginalized. Young politicians in their rising career are not going to do anything to upset their future career prospects and put themselves on a huge collision course with their whips and leaders."[10]

Corroborating the findings of Stevens (2007), one interviewee noted that civil servants wishing to please their political masters needed to marshal evidence to suit policy initiatives and give them a label of scientific legitimacy:

> 'Sometimes, dare I say, you might have to marshal the evidence in such a way that it supports the decision, and I think over time that became more and more the scenario, that you got a decision and your task was to find the evidence to support that decision, rather than find the evidence which demonstrated what the most sensible way forward would be.' (EW-CS-CJ2: Former Senior Home Office Civil Servant)

Technical feasibility

A final component of the policy stream relates to the technical feasibility of policy change. The reclassification of cannabis was not a proposal to subvert the classification system or attempt anything radical. Rather, it was a simplistic, but symbolic, move within the already-established framework. For some, including a former chair of the ACMD, the Misuse of Drugs Act had become outdated and was not accurately representing its intended purpose of scheduling drugs according to harm:

> 'The Misuse of Drugs Act is no longer fit for purpose. I mean that's bloody clear. A lot of the drugs are in the wrong places. … It just shows there is no relationship between harms and their position in the Act. The Act is wrong, it is flawed. And if it is flawed, it is unjust.

> It determines penalties and the penalties are incorrect.' (EW-A-AC-H1: Former Chair of the ACMD)

However, the Misuse of Drugs Act operates as an important framing device for politicians when considering policy change. Given the dominant perspective that behavioural change is achieved through law and order and punishment, the 'politico-logic' is that increased problems surrounding cannabis should be accompanied by an upgrading of its classification. As such, the 2009 reclassification did not challenge any legislative orthodoxies, but instead reproduced the already dominant philosophies and discourses surrounding cannabis, and by doing so it fulfilled the criterion of being technically feasible.

Moreover, the policy predicament that Garland (2001) articulated appears to be particularly salient in the case of cannabis. On the one hand, there is a view that firm action needs to be taken to counter the reported negative consequences of consumption; but on the other hand, there is a benign acceptance of its consumption in society and a belief that being too tough would be counterproductive, as this would create significant administrative burdens on control agencies. The policy alternative of reclassification to Class B fitted both these needs. It did little to change existing practices, which have arguably allowed for the de facto depenalization of low-level cannabis offences (see Sentencing Council, 2011; Shiner, 2015); but the change signalled that the government was somehow taking action and responding to public and media fears. In this sense, the political value of reclassification was not in its evidence-based problem-solving capacity, but its symbolic value.

Finding the 'golden angling' in the Netherlands

In the Netherlands, changes to the criteria relating to coffeeshops in 2012–13 represented a long struggle between competing agendas and alternatives, resulting in a form of compromise and a "middle of the road"[11] stalemate. This section examines the various factors that shaped how policy alternatives were narrowed down and selected from the primeval soup.

Political feasibility

The particular values of political parties in power are of extreme relevance. All three parties in the Rutte I coalition were aligned on the policy preference to respond to cannabis issues through a strengthening of law enforcement (see Table 4 in the Appendix). More will be said about this political constellation in Chapter 6, but here it is worth highlighting the values and role of one key player, Ivo Opstelten of the VVD, who held the position of Minister of Security and Justice in the Rutte I and Rutte II governments.

A common view of Opstelten was that he was a respected, charismatic and "successful crime fighter"[12] who was more on the conservative than liberal side of the VVD. Indeed, it was postulated that he perfected a "very visible yet selective approach"[13] while mayor in Rotterdam, where he had to compete with Pim Fortuyn's populist party, the LPF, on issues of law and order. Set in the context of increasingly hostile public and political views on crime and disorder, cannabis and coffeeshops provided an "easy target"[14] to symbolically demonstrate the VVD's, and Opstelten's, abilities in this sphere.

> 'Opstelten is a minister who always says in those words, we are going to get them and a very aggressive style of speech, especially on crime nowadays. It's we're going to get them, punishment has to be harsher, harder, crime cannot pay off, that kind of rhetoric. It's the same with drugs, especially cannabis.' (NL-A-NGO3: Independent Research Organization)

This can also be seen in the official rhetoric of 'strengthening and broadening the fight against organized crime' and employing a 'vigorous approach' to dealing with nuisance (House of Representatives of the States General, 2011a: 2, author's translation).

The role of the international sphere was also extremely pertinent, not just in the sense of "west wind" policy influence, with more punitive countries such as the United Kingdom and the United States "dominating the debate",[15] but also in the sense of sustained international tensions created by Dutch drugs policy, which were "cultivated" by Dutch politicians and contributed to an "internalization of criticism".[16] "I think they [Rutte I] wanted to end this pressure, they didn't want to be the odd one out any more, they didn't want to explain. And that's why they said let's not sell to foreigners any more."[17] Such international pressures have created significant barriers to alternative, liberalizing reforms, thereby contributing to plausible solutions being sought in measures – such as the residency criterion – which, from an international point of view, attempt to reduce the problem rather than simply tolerate it.

Yet despite an apparent shift to a tougher criminal justice-oriented perspective on cannabis, there is still political space to consider more liberalizing approaches. Whereas such perspectives were found to be largely maligned in both major political parties in England & Wales, there are still deep-rooted attachments in the Netherlands to the benefits of a market separation policy, which are supported by many political parties. Harm reduction and health-oriented goals remain at the stated core of cannabis policy, with coffeeshops seen as a way of achieving such goals. While most interviewees recognized that there has been a broad shift away from such ideas being ruling discourses on crime, deviancy and control, there was some variation in opinion as to the degree to which such perspectives have diminished. For some, notions such as resocialization are still favoured by a "large minority",[18] but for others, concepts such as *gedogen* have been transformed. "I would say that tolerance as an ideal, as a humanitarian ideal, has disappeared, but tolerance as a pragmatic strategy is alive and kicking. We still solve problems that way."[19]

In this sense, traditional liberal beliefs have undergone a 'recoding' (Garland, 2001) to become embedded within narratives of pragmatism. Such beliefs are entrenched in most institutions and agencies that deal with cannabis, predominantly in the health field, but they can also be seen across public prosecution, the Ministry of Justice and Security, the police and many municipality governments. Unlike in England & Wales, where arguing *for* liberal reforms is seen as putting one's head 'above the parapet', it was suggested in the Netherlands that advocating for the complete removal of the coffeeshop system would elicit the same view. "I imagine if someone would stand up and say let's close down all the coffeeshops, that would be putting his head above the field here … this is not an option, there would be a lot of opposition."[20]

As such, the primeval soup of policy in the Netherlands is not as limited as in England & Wales. There are a host of political parties, largely existing on the Left of the political spectrum, that advocate a more liberalized and/or pragmatic approach to cannabis (notably, D'66; GroenLinks – the Green Party; the Socialist Party (SP)]; and the PvdA). Given that the PvdA made up part of the Rutte II cabinet, it is worth noting that their political values had an influence on the political feasibility of policy measures within this coalition (see Table 4 in the Appendix). Thus, analysis of the changes in policy under Rutte II should take account of the political values of the parties involved and the extent to which these allowed certain policy proposals to take precedence over others. The juxtaposition between a shift towards a tougher approach to crime and drugs and a strong counter-perspective reaffirming the need for a market separation policy lends itself to policy compromise and finding a "middle of the road"[21] solution for all parties.

Research and expertise

Given the long-standing fragmented and polarized positions on cannabis policy across varying coalition governments in the Netherlands, the results and recommendations of pragmatic problem-solving committees have played a vital role in finding and legitimizing a middle ground in coalition policy. Problematizations of cannabis came to a head in the late 2000s, leading the Balkenende IV government to seek to create a 'new, integrated policy document on drugs' (Advisory Committee on Drugs Policy, 2009: Appendix I). This involved the use of research and expertise to inform the debate. An evaluation of drugs policy was commissioned prior to the establishment of an expert committee (chaired by van de Donk) to make recommendations for cannabis policy reform (see Advisory Committee on Drugs Policy, 2009; van Laar and van Ooyen-Houben, 2009). The challenge for the van de Donk Committee, despite it operating in the political realm, was to try and find a common, shared position, or "golden angling",[22] between two broad factions representing health and criminal justice perspectives.

There was an extremely pragmatic, compromise-based approach written into the committee's objectives, and consensus was found through the use of a policy matrix to open up multiple solutions to the problem (see Advisory Committee on Drugs Policy, 2009: 42). For the van de Donk Committee, the most rational policy option was to move from a system of open, one-sided regulation to a system involving a closed coffeeshop type, which would serve the local market. The need to restrict foreign visitors was also imagined in a more 'radical' measure, to turn coffeeshops into private clubs (Advisory Committee on Drugs Policy, 2009: 46). This would require local users to have club memberships, which could be restricted to a particular region. These ideas were adopted by the Rutte I coalition with the residency and closed club coffeeshop criteria.

These lines of thought allowed for the finding of common ground in the committee, with a shared recognition that to solve the "burden of our own policy", the only way is through "damage control",[23] with coffeeshops returning to their original purpose. "If you want to keep the coffeeshops alive, then we have to reduce them to what they were originally meant to be. Local facilities for Dutch people, and the framework of public health."[24] Thus, the committee framed solutions to problems via a fundamental acceptance of coffeeshops. As already mentioned, the option to completely ban coffeeshops was not conceivable, as this would threaten what is, in the dominant view, the beneficial separation of markets.

But in addition to more central direction on policy options, there was recognition of a need for 'tailor-made approaches' (Advisory Committee on Drugs Policy, 2009: 49). Similar to the original intentions of the Baan and Hulsman committees, the van de Donk Committee favoured local experimentation to develop and test pragmatic solutions.

Overall, it is evident that the van de Donk Committee was very influential in producing recommendations that were used in the creation of new coffeeshop criteria under Rutte I. The proposal to limit foreign visitors was seen as a prerequisite for any further changes, and this came to fruition in the shape of the residency criterion. Moreover, the closed club criterion came out of this report as a way to control the size of coffeeshops and, in turn, the domestic cultivation of cannabis in order to maintain supply.

The van de Donk Committee was tasked with looking at the future direction of Dutch drugs policy, but a major point of consideration related to drugs legislation and the system of classification used to control illegal substances. The committee recommended a new committee to look at the Opium Act list system and consider whether moves should be made to introduce a single list of illicit substances. A committee was established, led by Professor Henk Garretsen. The Garretsen Committee made a recommendation to categorise cannabis according to high and low potency so that stronger forms would be in Schedule I (hard drugs) of the Opium Act, (Expert Committee on the List System of the Opium Act, 2011). This would put all offences related to cannabis on the same level as those relating to hard drugs such as cocaine, heroin and ecstasy.

Thus, a number of potential policy options were presented by these two commissions. The search for policy alternatives had a broad remit in the Netherlands, and as such the list of policy proposals for serious consideration were wide, but these were narrowed down through a rational and logical process involving varied, and somewhat polarized, perspectives.

Research and expertise had a very pragmatic "content-driven"[25] problem-solving capacity. The formation of committees prior to the enactment of new policy measures is a clear example of this, with most of the measures introduced under Rutte I (with the exception of the school distance criterion) based on proposals made by these committees. In contrast to England & Wales, where evidence had to fit with preferred policy options – for example, expertise and advice from the ACMD was drawn on as a statutory obligation prior to policy change but then swiftly rejected – in the Netherlands, research played an important part in discussions and development of policy. This is evident in the evaluation of the residency and closed club measures, which was an important shaper of the coffeeshop policy (see Research and Documentation Centre, 2013).

Not only does research serve as a pragmatic tool to solve policy problems, but it also provides coalition governments legitimacy in following a particular direction or proposal. Expert committees are seen as a way to find solutions that represent a wide variety of interests. This was apparent in the views of those working in the commissions as well as politicians.

> 'Because this topic is so controversial … they follow more the content of these reports … in these two cases, the policy is to a quite a large extent content driven and not politically driven. But perhaps that is just because that is so controversial and they couldn't come to a solution themselves, and that was the reason to form a committee.' (NL-A-AC-H2: Academic Expert in Health and Member of Garretsen Committee)

> 'Because a coalition system really needs to have a basis, someone will always have to move their position to get a decision. That means they should have reason to change, which they cannot get from their

> manifesto, because they are changing from this. So there is some necessity for facts or expert judgement or something like that to support the moving of the political position.' (NL-P4: CDA Politician, Utrecht)

However, the relationship between research, expertise and policy is not purely evidence driven. There were some accounts of using research to fit political agendas, similar to the findings for England & Wales. As one committee member noted, the debate is "very ideologically driven, so it is very difficult to see the research outcome in a neutral way. People use it for their own point of view".[26] The challenge to expertise from the growth of populism and the toughening of perspectives on cannabis has driven short-term political point-scoring and choosing a "standpoint" over "facts".[27] Such trends, especially in the context of the popularity of Geert Wilders' PVV party since the late 2000s, have called into question the use of research and expertise in guiding decisions, with one politician noting that "the PVV don't believe in research".[28]

The prioritization of a "fact-free politics"[29] over one based on scientific evidence and expert advice can be seen with the planned introduction of the school distance criterion despite there being no evidence to support the policy measure and no clear and logical rationale for its effectiveness. "There was one research project in Rotterdam, they applied such a distance criterion already, 250 metres not 350 metres, and the research showed that it did not have any effect on the youngsters, not any."[30] This measure was favoured by the Christian Democrats and Minister Opstelten, but their support was based on the measure's potential to reinforce a moral and ideological position that attempted to symbolically de-normalize cannabis and coffeeshops, rather than it offering a more effective way to reduce and prevent youth consumption.

Nevertheless, despite the use of research findings and expert advice in this way, they continue to perform an important function within Dutch politics. While populist forces may drive policy to a degree, research and expertise also serves as a correcting force for measures which "are not successful in practice",[31] as was the case with the evaluation of the closed club and residency criteria.

Technical feasibility

Alongside political feasibility and the use of research and expertise, technical feasibility plays a fundamental role in the selection of policy options in the Netherlands. Dutch drugs policy is positioned awkwardly between regulation and prohibition, one of the main reasons being that international conventions and regulations limit the extent to which cannabis can be liberalized. As with much of the debate surrounding cannabis and drugs policy, the scope for policy development is not clear: some believe that, particularly with growing liberalization internationally, there is room within existing frameworks to experiment with policies to regulate the back door problem; others believe that the conventions are set in stone and that little variability is possible beyond the already strained *gedoogbeleid*.

Following the latter view, the Rutte I and Rutte II governments clearly stated that experiments which would bring into question the allegiance of the Netherlands to the spirit of the international conventions were not feasible: 'The core of our policy is that any kind of cultivation of cannabis is illegal and remains prohibited. Experiments such as the municipality of Utrecht represent conflict with applicable legislation and international obligations' (House of Representatives of the States General, 2011a: 5, author's translation). This implies the impossibility of full regulation and justifies the view that stricter policy is the only logical solution in the context of the Netherlands.

Moreover, tensions between national and local levels reveal different views on technical feasibility. This is illustrated by the attempts to introduce policies to restrict foreign visitors to coffeeshops. When local municipalities attempted to introduce such measures, they were faced with lawsuits by coffeeshop owners who argued that the policy unfairly discriminated against other Europeans and unfairly targeted coffeeshop businesses in selected areas. Rather than municipalities adding measures to their own rules and regulations, which lacked technical feasibility, the Dutch government had to introduce new national policy in the form of the national residency criterion for coffeeshops. That worked, despite the continued challenges from coffeeshops, because the rules had to comply with international and European regulations, the *Grondwet* (Dutch Constitution) and the Opium Act.

Thus, technical feasibility has played a crucial role in development of new policy measures, as it limited the possibilities for change within existing approaches. Legal regulation of the back door was not seen as an option, but neither was the complete prohibition of cannabis or the closing down of coffeeshops. In a political context that favoured a punitive shift in relation to cannabis policy, issues of technical feasibility served to advance tougher measures on tackling drug-related crime.

The primeval soup in global perspective

The policy changes in England & Wales and the Netherlands discussed here illustrate the ways in which responses to identified policy problems take substantive form in the policy stream, being shaped by political feasibility, the use (or not) of research and expertise, and technical feasibility. These components can be located in cannabis policy processes in other contexts too, and this section briefly explores two other settings – Australia and Spain – to further elucidate their influence. Given the nature of cannabis policy making in each of these countries, where states and regions have significant powers to legislate, issues of technical feasibility in particular prime our attention to the dynamics between national and subnational levels (which forms the substantive focus of Chapter 7).

Australia

Australia is a federal parliamentary constitutional monarchy comprised of six states and two territories. In the control of non-medical illegal drug use, Commonwealth (federal) authorities are predominantly responsible for border control as well as drug trafficking and manufacture. At this level, possession and cultivation offences are also legally prohibited, but approaches to these offences are principally matters of the state and territorial authorities, which hold considerable legislative powers (Hughes, 2020).

Overall, the past few decades have witnessed considerable policy movement at the subnational level, with the broad trajectory in respect of cannabis consumption and cultivation for personal use displaying growing institutionalization of decriminalization and depenalization approaches (Ritter et al, 2011; Shanahan et al, 2017; Hughes, 2020). Indicatively, at the time of writing, all states have some form of diversionary approach for cannabis use and possession offences (Hughes et al, 2019; Hughes, 2020).

Nevertheless, this trajectory has by no means been a smooth one, with the rhetoric surrounding cannabis changing from 'harmless substance' to 'potentially harmful substance', and a series of policy 'contractions' along the way (Ritter and Sotade, 2017; Hughes, 2020). Here, we briefly explore the policy stream in relation to two recent, contrasting cannabis policy movements: the 2011 changes to earlier depenalization reforms in Western Australia; and the 2018 decriminalization reforms in the Australian Capital Territory (ACT).

In many respects, the 2011 policy changes in Western Australia resemble developments in England & Wales across a very similar time frame. In 2004, the Cannabis Infringement Notice (CIN) – a scheme involving civil penalties for various acts related to adult possession and cultivation – was introduced by a Labor-led government (Lenton, 2004; Lenton and Allsop, 2010). Then, in 2011, a government led by the Liberal Party and the National Party replaced the CIN with the Cannabis Intervention Requirement (CIR) – a policy instrument that requires adults to complete a Cannabis Intervention Session (CIS) or face criminal prosecution – and recriminalized all cultivation activities (Drug and Alcohol Office, 2011). While the 2011 changes were not all that radical, as diversionary measures were retained for possession cases, they did represent a significant tightening of the rules and an increased risk of criminalization.

In respect of the policy stream, there are several notable aspects of this policy contraction. First was the lack of supporting evidence for policy change. On the contrary, research had demonstrated the benefits of the 2004 reforms in terms of changes in cannabis markets, public health goals and cost-effectiveness (Drug and Alcohol Office, 2007; Fetherston and Lenton, 2007; Hughes, 2020).

Second was political feasibility, which was more pertinent as the 2004 reforms were an important issue in election campaigns, especially for the two major parties – the Labor Party and the Liberal Party – becoming an avenue through which party positions could be clearly distinguished. When it was clear that the Labor Party was both willing and in a political position to legislate on cannabis, the Liberal Party took an opposing stance, despite having introduced the cautioning scheme that preceded these reforms.

Revising the 2004 changes along the lines of a 'get tough' approach was clearly politically beneficial, particularly given sustained criticism levelled by media outlets and the police that the CIN was soft – and, despite evidence to the contrary – and had sent the wrong message, which had led to increases in use (ABC News, 2007; Australian Associated Press, 2007, 2011; Lenton and Allsop, 2010). Thus, similar to the situation in England & Wales, for a party that had embraced a wider law and order positioning, the CIR and CIS policy had political feasibility, as it allowed political actors to assert that more punitive action was being taken against an identified problem while, at the same time, was not so sweeping as to be unpalatable to voters, retaining a core, adaptive-style diversionary approach.

In contrast to the changes in Western Australia, the passing of the Drugs of Dependence (Personal Cannabis Use) Amendment Bill 2018 in the ACT was indicative of greater liberalization, with adult possession and cultivation for personal use becoming decriminalized.[32]

The origin of this Bill was a private members bill, introduced by the Labor Party backbencher Michael Pettersson, which was subsequently referred to the Standing Committee on Health, Ageing and Community Services. Based on the inquiry and recommendations of this Committee, which involved 36 written submissions and four public hearings, a series of revisions were made to the Bill and it was then passed into law by the ACT Government.

For the Bill's proponents, this change was a 'logical next step' to earlier diversionary schemes, arguing that prohibitive approaches had failed to eradicate drug use while also placing considerable burdens on criminal justice agencies. Moreover, it was contended that through this Bill, the government would continue to show 'a commitment to evidence-based and practice-informed responses to drug use that minimize harm in our community', with the measures creating 'opportunities to better reach people who are already using the drug and connect them with the services or supports they need' (Legislative Assembly for the Australian Capital Territory, 2019).

While at first glance the reforms appear to be aligned with a strong evidence base, submissions to the Committee inquiry suggested that stakeholders, particularly from the police and medical associations, were not convinced of the Bill's necessity, with claims that the existing Simple Cannabis Offence Notice scheme was effective in reducing use and diverting users away from the criminal justice system and into education and health services (Standing Committee on Health, Ageing and Community Services, 2019).

These were legitimate points, particularly since the provisions under the Bill did little to radically alter the black market. Despite initial indications that a fully regulated legal market was the preferred policy solution (Legislative Assembly for the Australian Capital Territory, 2018b), the form that the policy change assumed was very much influenced by issues of technical feasibility and political feasibility. In the first case, considerable hurdles were presented by federal laws that prohibit the selling of cannabis and place limitations on the amounts an individual may possess without facing federal enforcement (Australian Associated Press, 2019;Evans and Hayne, 2019; Keyzer, 2020). But, as ACT lawmakers explained, keeping possession and cultivation offences within the Drugs of Dependence Act 1989 but with the exception that they do not apply to those aged 18 and over was 'designed to resolve potential incompatibilities with Commonwealth laws' (Legislative Assembly for the Australian Capital Territory, 2019).

Sensitivity about clashes with federal authorities was matched by political sensitivity regarding law enforcement. In this sense, the need to distinguish between 'innocent' users and 'bad' black market actors in cultivation and supply can be detected. For example, the recommendation of the Standing Committee on Health, Ageing and Community Services to allow for indoor and artificial growing was rejected on the basis that 'the Government supports police being able to make a clear distinction between cultivation for personal use and cultivation for large-scale or commercial purposes by criminal operators' (Legislative Assembly for the Australian Capital Territory, 2019). Similar policing-related reasons were given for rejecting shared cultivation, such as that under a CSC model. Thus, regardless of whether such measures would support harm reduction – a key rationale underpinning the reforms – the placation of concerns emanating from law enforcement agencies made the reforms more politically feasible.

Spain

Similar in respects to Australia, Spain is a comparatively decentralized country, constituted of 17 autonomous communities. While at the national level, Spanish drug policy has historically had, and continues to have, a tendency towards repressive drugs policy (Gamella and Jimenez Rodrigo, 2004; Pares and Bouso, 2015; Quintas and Arana, 2017), the freedoms granted to individuals and autonomous communities under the Spanish Constitution have also allowed for alternative approaches to cannabis to flourish.

Most prominent in this regard is the emergence of CSCs – groups of users which, as a collective, cultivate and distribute cannabis among members. The first CSC was formed in 2001 and numbers have since grown significantly, with 800–1,000 estimated to be currently in operation (Arana and Pares, 2020). The existence of CSCs as non-profit closed-circuit organizations has been made possible by the configuration of laws and judgements by the Supreme Court of Spain. In short, while possession and consumption in public, along with commercialization of cannabis activities, are punishable offences, the use and possession of cannabis intended for private use are not. Moreover, owing to the law on non-profit organizations and a Supreme Court ruling that shared consumption is lawful, individual users are able to form associations to cultivate and consume cannabis (Gamella and Jimenez Rodrigo, 2004; Pares and Bouso, 2015; Belackova et al, 2016; Decorte et al, 2017; Marks, 2019; Pares et al, 2019).

With CSCs originating as a grassroots innovation and not from policy intervention by authorities, government responses to their existence at national and subnational levels have contrasted considerably, reflecting core differences in conceptualizations of CSCs as either a user-based community solution to the harms of black market interaction or criminal organizations which are a threat to public health. As such, a range of policy proposals exist in the primeval soup, with the broad patterns suggestive of regulatory approaches being more strongly advocated in regions and municipalities while prohibitive approaches are more favoured at national level (Arana and Pares, 2020).

Most of the recent policy developments concerning CSCs sprouted initially at regional or municipal levels, facilitated by autonomous communities and municipal governments possessing legislative abilities in respect of public health, social welfare and public safety (Arana and Pares, 2020). Policy discussions at this level have, overall, been oriented around how best to align and regulate the activities of CSCs in accordance with particular public policy goals.

To take an example, in the Basque Country – one of three autonomous communities to have made good progress advancing CSC policy reforms – formal policy discussions to regulate CSCs have been ongoing since at least 2012, when the ruling government formed a commission in the Basque Parliament. Indicative of political feasibility as well as the role of research and expertise in this process, Pares and Bouso (2015) note that the commission drew on approximately 30 specialists and the final report, published in 2014, had the support of all but one political party. The main recommendations of the commission were to provide legal security through introducing rules, programmes and protocols for CSCs based on principles of harm reduction and the human rights of people who use drugs (Pares and Bouso, 2015; Arana and Pares, 2020). The influence of the commission was felt in the passing of the Law on Addictions 2016 – while not expressly concerning CSCs, its provisions do allow for CSCs to fall under legal regulation if they meet a set of conditions (registration, non-profit status, adults-only).

Nevertheless, a key component of cannabis policy processes in Spain relates to technical feasibility; provincial and municipal regulations need to be in accordance with national statutes and directives, and so while attempts have been made to introduce new laws and by-laws at subnational level, these have been met in equal measure by challenges by the national government in the courts, largely on the grounds that such regional legislation impedes on the Spanish government's authority (Arana and Pares, 2020). In an exception, the Constitutional Court in the Basque Country found that the regional government can legitimately legislate on CSCs under the Law on Addictions, though this has also narrowed the scope of CSCs by tying their existence to public health aims (Arana, 2019; Arana and Pares, 2020). In other areas, however, most of the initial judgements made by the Constitutional Court and Supreme Court have been in the national government's favour, though subsequent appeals and challenges to prosecutions have often been won by regional authorities and cannabis activists.

Thus, the outcome of these processes has led to a rather complex situation in which a considerable grey area continues to exist, affording limited legal protections to CSCs while simultaneously recognizing the rights of individual and communal users. This speaks to the tensions and difficulties, particularly in terms of political feasibility and technical feasibility, that exist in the policy stream between national and subnational levels in this context. This theme is picked up and explored further in Chapter 7.

Summary

In this chapter, we have explored how identified problems become coupled with tangible policy proposals. One thing that has become apparent is that such processes do not always follow a linear pattern; a given problem does not necessarily, in and of itself, predetermine the approach that will be taken. Rather, a multitude of ideas about cannabis policy are in existence at any given time, and those which emerge from the primeval soup of policy are shaped by a number of factors, including political feasibility and technical feasibility.

Most obviously, a policy proposal needs to be aligned with the sorts of expressive and instrumental dispositions that exist among those in positions of political decision-making. Across the cases considered here, there are clear indications that dispositions which favour reactive and repressive approaches are heavily prevalent in (national) political landscapes. In part, such beliefs are enmeshed with the sociocultural context in which deeply held beliefs emerge, but instrumental political goals which tend to favour punitive populism have also been exacerbated by social, economic and political changes over the past 40 years or so. Nevertheless, these cannot be said to be the sole feature of late modern societies; there are plenty of indications that alternative positions exist, and indeed in many contexts across the globe, these are outcompeting those which favour approaches based on prohibitive frameworks. This is certainly the case at a subnational level, which is explored further in Chapter 7.

Additionally, the influence of research and expertise has also been variable; in England & Wales, expert advice was a second thought to a predetermined policy action, while in the Netherlands there was a more thorough attempt to engage and listen to experts. Nevertheless, a broad conclusion to draw is that while most political decisions are claimed to be based on expertise, the apolitical use of research does not exist, with actors often using the research that fits with their political agendas.

A final aspect discussed here was the technical feasibility of changes in cannabis policy. The binding national and international laws, legal judgements and regulations play a crucial role in shaping the contours of possibility, or at least what is thought to be possible. In many cases, changing policy *within* existing prohibitive frameworks is perceived to be far more technically viable. At the same time, especially where the recorded number of cannabis users is relatively high, the actual content of reforms purporting to be 'tougher' often retain mechanisms which allow for policy adaptation. Moreover, the often complex nature of the basic laws, rights and precedents often leaves a grey zone which can be exploited by those who possess the will to do so.

This speaks to a core theme underlying the above discussion – the importance of political will. Whether or not preferred policy alternatives actually manifest is tied to currents in the political stream which provide the mechanisms and impetus for windows of opportunity to open or be forced open. It is to this idea that we turn next.

6

The Political Environment and Windows of Opportunity

Introduction

The final component of Kingdon's multiple streams model is the political stream. Already, several themes have been discussed which have touched on innately political aspects, such as electoral insecurity and the needs of political actors to appear tough on cannabis. In this chapter, we delve further into the national-level political environment through an examination of three main components: changes in administration, the national mood and organized political forces. The first of these relates to the political colours and constellations that comprise a ruling government and how these change over time. The national mood refers to public opinion and, arguably more important, how perceptions and artificial constructions of this are used as a tool of politicking. Finally, organized political forces refers to the alignment of actors and organizations around a given policy position and their efforts to shape the outcome of policy-making processes. As with preceding chapters, an empirically based discussion of these aspects in England & Wales and the Netherlands is first presented, before complementing and contrasting these contexts with two further cases: the legalization of cannabis in Uruguay in 2013 and the unsuccessful attempt to legally regulate non-medical cannabis in New Zealand in 2020.

England & Wales: an inevitable policy reversal?

The 2009 reclassification of cannabis in England & Wales usefully illuminates the role of changes in administration, the national mood, and organized political forces in policy change, and how these aspects are conditioned in an adversarial political environment which is dominated by two large parties. Indeed, it is argued that the competition both between and within political parties that such structured relations foster has, under contemporary conditions, made cannabis policy making particularly vulnerable to penetration by populist forces and knee-jerk reactions.

Changes in administration

Owing to the nature of the UK Parliament, which tends to favour one party forming a government, individual ruling politicians, and particularly the prime minister, have the capacity to take on a more influential role in decision-making processes than could be expected in other forms of democratic governance. Even within the same party, a key element of political manoeuvring is the need to distinguish oneself from predecessors, and this is further compounded by the relatively short terms of office which politicians serve. Indeed, changes in senior political offices during the 2000s opened key windows of opportunity for decisions surrounding cannabis classification to occur.

The Labour Party came into power in 1997, after 18 years in opposition, with the self-projected image that they had made a break from Old Labour on issues of law and order. There was intensive focus on the link between illegal drugs and crime, and especially with Class A substances such as heroin and cocaine. The reclassification of cannabis to Class C was driven forward by Home Secretary David Blunkett. An insider noted, "almost one of the first things he said was 'I want to reclassify cannabis from B to C', or 'I'm going to' more likely was his phrase".[1] This policy shift became acceptable under the leadership of Tony Blair because of initial favourable media pressure for reform, the "embarrassment"[2] that would be entailed with not reclassifying and the rationale that this would allow police forces to redirect resources away from what was, at the time, considered a relatively benign substance and towards tackling Class A substances. In addition, Labour had secured a landslide majority in the 2001 general election, thus giving room for more controversial policies to take shape, and other events of political significance started to occur at around the same time, such as the hugely controversial war in Iraq.

It is significant to note, however, that the 2004 reclassification was done without the full support of New Labour, with one former senior Home Office civil servant noting the perennial political fear of appearing "soft" and "the caricature that people have got of New Labour on law and order".[3] Without the full support of those in power, and given prevailing political and moral tendencies inherent in drugs policy (see Chapter 4), the reclassification to Class C was never based on secure foundations. Thus, when opposing actors occupied key positions, the classification of cannabis became a "hostage to fortune".[4]

When Charles Clarke became home secretary, the possibility of reversing the 2004 decision was openly voiced, with Labour MP Ed Balls stating on election night in May 2005 that the government had to learn from its 'mistakes' on 'cannabis … Iraq' (Sare, 2009). Amid the wider political pressures, Clarke requested that the ACMD review the cannabis classification in March 2005. According to some participants, Clarke's decision to follow the ACMD's advice not to reclassify was a close one, and given Clarke's feelings about the earlier downwards reclassification, it seems clear that he was in favour of the reclassification to Class B. The ACMD chair at the time said: "When I handed in the report in 2005, we declined to reclassify, [and] he said this wasn't the report that [he] wanted, but he said that [we] made the case so strongly and so clearly that [he would] have to accept it."[5]

Clarke's decision was seen as being partially fuelled by his own characteristics, in the sense of respecting the "advice of civil servants, the role that civil servants play, and the role that advisors play".[6] Nevertheless, with more politically urgent issues, such as the war in Iraq and immigration policy, it was possible for Clarke to defer a decision to reverse the reclassification, using the recommendations from the ACMD to add scientific legitimacy to this decision.

After Clarke was replaced as home secretary by John Reid in 2006, the classification issue did not surface again until there were further changes to the cabinet in 2007, following Tony Blair's resignation and succession by Gordon Brown. The tension and disagreements between Blair and Brown were a focal point of New Labour's rule during the mid-2000s, and when Brown eventually succeeded Blair, this created the sense that there was a dearth in political legitimacy given that Brown was not democratically elected as prime minister. Many interviewees suggested that with Brown facing strong media criticism and pressures to hold a general election, the change in power had opened a space in which he had to show that he was a strong and capable leader.

Gordon Brown became prime minister on 27 June 2007, and the following month he made the announcement that cannabis classification was to be revisited. The immediate focus on cannabis classification could be seen as a way of "making a break from the past". Alongside Brown's own "Presbyterian conscience", the concentration on this issue became a way in which he could distinguish himself from Blair and "put a stamp, a rebranding on what his version of New Labour was like".[7]

Thus, establishing political legitimacy through the reclassification of cannabis was important for Gordon Brown, and this shaped the relationship between Brown and Home Secretary Jacqui Smith. Importantly, Smith was characterized as being a weak home secretary who simply followed the wishes of Gordon Brown and was more prone to media influence than her predecessors had been:

> 'I thought Jacqui Smith was a deficient Home Secretary … she was unable to project complex arguments or even to understand them I think.' (EW-CS-CJ: Former Senior Home Office Civil Servant)

> 'the one home secretary whom I found particularly unhelpful was Jacqui Smith. ... She wasn't really interested in the evidence, she was wanting to do the bidding of the Prime Minister.' (EW-A-AC-H2: Former Chair of the ACMD)

Indeed, such depictions were later substantiated, both by Gordon Brown, who stated, 'I may say that probably I used my position to persuade members of the government who were not as keen on that policy as I was' (Leveson Inquiry, 2012: 72), and by Jacqui Smith, who, after leaving public office, broadcast a radio programme entitled *Stoned Again* (2012) where she suggested that the reclassification may have been a mistake.

In attempting to explain why Brown was able to exert so much influence in the cannabis debate, it was suggested that by the time these events were unfolding the government was 'old', and as such it became more prone to orders from the top. As one interviewee said, "when governments get old ... they become less functional. Ministers become of a lower quality and more compliant to direction from the very top."[8] Whereas Tony Blair seemingly gave home secretaries room to manoeuvre, Brown was reportedly much stricter. This again alludes to the powers to govern in a majoritarian political system that tends to lead to single-party government. With a majority in government, Prime Minister Brown was able to advance his moral preferences and play a fundamental role in the shaping of policy, with little political opposition. That is not to say that there should have been an expectation of resistance at this moment in time, given the favourable context in which these developments were occurring. This was a "quick win"[9] policy for an old government in decline and in need of popular support after critical changes in administration.

The national mood

Sensing a critical national mood in relation to cannabis, in light of the perceived failures of the 2004 reclassification and the growing recognition of problems attributed to cannabis, the government viewed reclassification back to Class B as a simple decision which prima facie attempted to satisfy an increasingly critical public and media. Indeed, even *The Independent* newspaper – which had started a campaign to decriminalize cannabis in 1997 – wrote an editorial admitting it had got it wrong (Owen, 2007). The lack of influential critique of the proposed reclassification to Class B reduced the political damage (or increased the political feasibility) of such a move.

Significantly though, the issue of cannabis classification became a way for the New Labour administration under Brown to attract voter confidence in a key demographic, that of middle England.[10]

> 'It probably served the broader purpose of trying to connect with middle England or that base that Tony Blair had in his pocket, just by virtue of who he was and how he looked and came over. … If [Brown] could pursue a policy on drugs that was somehow in tune with that *Daily Mail* middle England constituency, then clearly it did, for him anyway, it had a broader purpose.' (EW-A3: Academic and Former BBC Home Affairs Correspondent)

In this way, the reclassification of cannabis was largely viewed as a political manoeuvre to gain support after Brown came to power. In particular, it chimed with the feelings of conservative voters and the Right-wing media, which had been critical of Brown and the 2004 reclassification. In this sense, the national mood was not one of general consensus towards cannabis, but reflected the fears and concerns of specific 'noisy' segments of the population. The Right-leaning tabloid media was seen as a key driver of this noise, which in turn produced unstable and "frail"[11] policy processes. "There is still a hangover within government, that view remains, [that] if the *Daily Mail* takes a particularly strong line on an issue, then this is something we have got to take very seriously in terms of policy."[12] The hugely complicated, and sometimes contradictory, evidence base on cannabis and drugs policy opened a space for criticism from the main political opposition, and within this context, the media had a greater role in influencing which issues to respond to, and in asserting the ways these *should* be responded to.[13]

A controversial narrative to have emerged from several of the elite interviews was the suggestion that Brown made a deal with Paul Dacre, the editor of the *Daily Mail* at the time, that if certain policies were pursued, the paper would be softer in its reporting of Brown.

> 'When Gordon Brown took over from Blair, Brown is reputedly done a deal with the *Daily Mail* that the *Mail* would support him.' (EW-A-AC-H1: Former Chair of the ACMD)

> 'It was too neat, and the speed at which the *Daily Mail* responded with its editorial saying what a brave man.' (EW-A2: Academic Expert in Criminology and Former Home Office Researcher)

These claims are virtually impossible to verify or falsify without an unlikely confession from either party. Indeed the idea that the *Daily Mail* had influence over the cannabis reclassification was denied by Brown in the Leveson Inquiry (see Leveson Inquiry, 2012: 71–2).

Whether this is true or false is not the point of interest here; rather, it is that the reclassification had political ramifications as it was supported by the Right-wing media[14] and, in that sense, was beneficial in establishing

Brown's credentials among a demographic which was valuable but highly contested. Within this demographic, appealing to the moral entrepreneurs of concerned mothers who were "so angry at the down classification that they had to really push"[15] was a central concern for New Labour, to appease their fears about cannabis. Interviewees cynical of the justification for the policy change suggested that the reclassification was not targeted at cannabis users per se, as they are likely to be largely marginalized from the political process, but was more important as a symbolic gesture for concerned parents and the Right-wing media.

> 'The politician will do his press release, do his TV, and maybe a bit of parliament, and then very self-consciously hoping for favour of courage in certain media outlets which is read by the parents of the people taking the substances, and the young people themselves aren't part of that conversation.' (EW-CS-CJ: Former Senior Home Office Civil Servant)

Importantly, the reclassification appealed to those who were more likely to vote, rather than politically disinterested youth. Moreover, that the changes to legislation and police guidelines made *no* difference to the treatment of young offenders adds further weight to the perceived importance of policy symbolism over substance. Thus, for all the policy talk emphasizing the need to protect young individuals from the effects of cannabis, it seems that the change in legislation was designed as a reassuring mechanism for parents' ontological insecurities regarding cannabis.

Organized political forces

Thus far, it has been argued that the role of the media was extremely significant in putting the issue of cannabis classification on the policy agenda, but it was the combination of a variety of individuals and groups, who formed a loose set of policy entrepreneurs, along with the lack of influential critique that allowed the reclassification to Class B to occur without major contestation. "The sorts of stories that were being told by the conservative advocates fitted with the ways that politicians wanted to use the power that they have, to shore up their own political and ideological positions."[16] This set of actors was inter alia comprised of the Conservative Party, mothers' groups (such as those headed by Mary Brett and Debra Bell), doctors and psychiatrists, and the ACPO. The ACPO came to support the reclassification, but it is important to note that this is a relatively disparate organization consisting of a 'broad church' of views towards the policing of cannabis, and the general perception of the organization was that the effect of the reclassification was negligible.[17] Located within the 'institutional rationalities'

(Townley, 2008) of law enforcement, the reclassification did not challenge or serve as a detriment to existing practices, but only increased their legitimacy as owners of the problem.

The combination of all these political factors – changes in administration and the need to appear tough on drugs; the personal characteristics and views of those in power; and the support for (or lack of influential critique of) reclassification from a wide range of influential individuals and agencies who campaigned to put (or retain) the issue on the policy agenda – contributed to the decision to reclassify. Thus, the reclassification of cannabis to Class B fitted with a set of dominant moral preferences and was politically beneficial for Brown and his colleagues. In this way, this policy movement could be considered as a knee-jerk reaction from the government against the perceived mistake of downgrading to Class C. The government were antagonized by a "rapacious"[18] media and an adversarial opposition, which tormented Labour's capability to be tough on law and order. The process was not about searching for the most rational, evidence-based solution to a set of concerns; rather, it was intended to send a message, to a key demographic, that the government was strong in the face of perceived adversity.

The Netherlands: an uncomfortable middle ground

In the Netherlands, with the elevation of policy problems and possible solutions cemented following the conclusion and report of the expert committee chaired by van de Donk, a window of opportunity was opened for the Rutte I government to introduce a stricter set of measures, which would have heavily reduced the overall number of coffeeshops and limited their use to residents of the Netherlands. However, with a further change in the political colours of government, the window remained open, and the proposed and trialled measures were revised under a new coalition agreement. This removed the measures that were seen as being a "step too far"[19] (the school distance and closed club criteria) and gave greater flexibility to local municipalities in how and when to implement the residency criterion as a national rule. These incremental movements reflect both the structural characteristics of the political environment in the Netherlands and how changes in administration, the national mood and activities of organized political forces all served to shape the policy process.

Changes in administration

A key aspect in accounting for the 2012–13 changes to coffeeshop policy in the Netherlands was the decisive changes in government that shifted the political constellation from a balanced centrist coalition between two religious parties (the CDA and the CU) and the PvdA, under Balkenende

IV, to a Right-leaning cabinet made up of the CDA and the VVD with parliamentary support by the PVV, under Rutte I, then back to the centre with a balance between the VVD and the PvdA, under Rutte II.

Set within the context of increased voter volatility and mobility since depillarization, the penetration of populist-driven law and order policy agendas and a disdain for the *gedogen* policy, these shifts heighted the political need for parties to have a strong "profile".[20] For some parties, this increasingly meant basing policy on popular appeal rather than on rational problem-solving.

> 'We feel more and more pressure as politicians, we have to get very clear and tough. … You have to do your best to be a more distinctive politician because we also have to look at the polls, we also have to look at the voters, we also have to look at the media … to distinguish yourself you sometimes have to be focusing on a distinctive policy than really the best policy.' (NL-P2: VVD Politician, Utrecht)

Indeed, the rising popularity of Geert Wilders' PVV, the third-largest party in the 2010 election (see Aarts and van der Kolk, 2011), was crucial in creating competition, particularly with the centre/centre-Right-leaning CDA and VVD, for voters on crime and disorder issues (see also van Kessel, 2011).

> 'Even a minister of the Christian Democrats who was very in the middle, he was getting signals from his party that he had to be stiff on crime to get the wind out of the sails of Mr Wilders. So when it became clear that crime was going down tremendously, we had to work for a year to get our minister to say it out loud. He said it is not politically convenient for me to say it.' (BL-CS-AC-CJ: Senior Civil Servant in Ministry of Justice and Security and Member of van de Donk Committee)

Thus, the importance of being *seen* to be responding, over and above the actual quality of policy responses, put pressure on each party and government to make their mark while in power. With cannabis policy deeply politicized, there was pressure on politicians to respond quickly, clearly and authoritatively, and this allowed a reactionary politics to foster. Indeed, the measures introduced in Rutte I signalled that the government was taking some action against recognised problems. This was particularly the case with regards to the school distance criterion, but can also be seen more broadly, as the tighter measures offered little in the way of effectively addressing the back-door problem, other than tough rhetoric emphasizing a 'vigorous approach' and 'strengthening and broadening the fight' against criminality (House of Representatives of the States General, 2011a: 2, author's translation).

Importantly, it was the combination of political parties within the Rutte I coalition, and their dispositional values, that helped shape the choice of responses and reject alternatives. The distinctive shift to further repression was made possible because of the "unique cabinet", composed of "completely Right-wing, or centre-Right-wing" parties.[21]

However, while political parties may take extreme initial positions, especially during election campaigns, in many ways the Dutch political system follows a process which necessarily results in a more balanced approach. This is due to the very nature of having to form a coalition, structured by a political system of proportional representation. There are loyalties and preferences attached to working with particular coalition partners, but compromise and agreement are required, between at least two parties, on how they are to govern the country. Taking an initially more extreme position becomes politically useful in negotiations, as less political ground is lost than if you were to start bargaining at the centre.

> 'One thing, that is campaigning, and secondly, that is also negotiating. I was quite fierce in the media about, for instance, the *wietpas*, then you get a sort of pressure always that the others are getting fiercer, and in the end I don't have to move this much but I only have to move this much because I already took a very radical position in the beginning.' (NL-P2: VVD Politician, Utrecht)

Where compromise cannot be readily found, a process of "wheeling and dealing"[22] "backstage"[23] is required, or it may be that the issue is so contested that it creates a stalemate and is left to one side until a future coalition can find some form of agreement on how to proceed. The result of these negotiating processes is that policy change tends to be relatively slow and incremental, with parties retreating from extreme initial positions in order to find a balance.

Relatedly, there is an acceptance that new coalitions cannot completely undo the decisions made before it, especially given that parties often transition across ruling coalitions, providing some continuity.[24] This is clearly seen in the way cannabis policy unfolded, with initial movements under Balkenende IV to revise drugs policy carried on and introduced under Rutte I, and then revised under Rutte II, with the more contested elements softened down. Thus, policy making consisted of small steps within existing boundaries, which were then counteracted by further changes in government. In this way, policies aimed to "please the Right with tough talk"[25] but satisfy liberal actors with more pragmatic and flexible measures.

The second change in administration, from Rutte I to Rutte II, is of key importance in this regard. The VVD's new coalition partner, the PvdA, had a completely different perspective from its previous coalition partners, the CDA and the PVV, on how to respond to cannabis. The change in administration brought more balance between the polarized Right and Left, and, as a result, there was a shift from repression in Rutte I to "water treading"[26] in Rutte II. It was noted that without the "threat" of the extreme Right-wing PVV in government, coffeeshop policy could be less strict and more flexible than what had originally been intended. "The Right-wing extremists [the PVV] are smaller, the threat is less I think on that side of politics, and they [the VVD] made a deal to govern. … Part of the deal was, I think, more liberal, more tolerant approach of the coffeeshop policy."[27] This created an interesting situation for Minister of Justice Ivo Opstelten, who while being forced to be more flexible and compromise with his PvdA counterparts, also maintained a political desire to "save face" and keep up his own political image as a "hardliner".[28] Nevertheless, the politics of coalitions, coupled with timely and decisive changes in administration, provided a powerful mechanism by which more extreme or contested policy measures were rejected or revised.

The national mood

The national mood in the Netherlands at the time was as polarized as the political parties. Greater media coverage of policy problems arguably increased public and political support for tougher measures against cannabis. However, once the new measures were introduced, there was a severe backlash from a liberal community who felt their rights were under threat. While it is broadly recognized that the Dutch media is not as febrile as the tabloid press in the United Kingdom,[29] the media still plays an important role in shaping debates and informing political opinions, increasingly influencing a more reactive and immediate type of politics.

As in England & Wales, interviewees noted that concerns and fears were primarily driven from the conservative middle class, in response to perceived threats from outsiders.[30] But, despite the punitive framing of cannabis policy, the issue of cannabis divides people sharply. While overall views on responses to crime have hardened, there is still strong support for liberal policies regarding cannabis. "Most people in the Netherlands are still in favour of the use of soft drugs, 70 per cent or so, maybe 80. … The same people voting for Wilders, PVV, are in favour of soft drugs."[31] Interviewees suggested that media perspectives on cannabis policy were fairly balanced on the whole, but liberal values really came to the surface as a dominant counter-narrative when it became apparent coffeeshops were under threat, with the public "really waking up"[32] and media critiques of the *wietpas* further fuelling a desire to regulate the back door. "From the media it has become clear that this *wietpas* has been strongly criticized and has negative side effects in those cities which had these tourists."[33]

Thus, the national mood propelled concerns into the political sphere, but also served to counter what was seen as an overly repressive set of measures, helping influence the revision of the measures introduced by Rutte I. While not leading to a full policy reversal, which is rather uncharacteristic in policy making in the Netherlands, the national mood was a key contributory factor in accounting for how and why policy took the direction it did.

Organized political forces

In understanding both the introduction and "mellowing out"[34] of national coffeeshop policy measures, the role of local municipalities is a vital component. In many ways, cannabis policy is grounded in the needs and experiences of the local level. However, local mayors faced technical difficulties when trying, within an *international* context, to carve policy solutions to the influx of foreign visitors in affected southern municipalities. An effect of this was to bring together a loose coalition of local mayors that lobbied the national government to intervene. The call of these mayors, from varying political backgrounds, for support to tackle a salient problem was in line with the political desires and needs of the Right-wing political parties who took power in Rutte I.

> 'Mayors, liberal mayors, Left-wing mayors, who said, "we can't handle it anymore, we just close it down" ... this gave a lot of discussion in ... centre-Left, Left-wing parties, because their own mayors close down. It was not just these awful Right-wing extremists who are using the fear of crime ... they are just mayors of flesh and blood who are doing it.' (NL-A-AC-CJ: Academic Expert in Criminology and Member of van de Donk Committee)

While mayoral and municipal pressure was initially a factor in advocating for more repressive measures, once the new measures began to be trialled, a rather different picture emerged, one centred on resistance to their national implementation. A structural mechanism granting the local level considerable political voice can be found in the powers of governance relating to cannabis policy. Primarily, issues concerning coffeeshops relate to public order and health issues, which fall under the governance of the local mayors, alderpersons and councils. As noted in Chapter 3, these actors and structures are influential in the Netherlands. However, the picture is complicated by the differences in political orientations found at a local level. These are much more varied than one would find at national level, with divergence not only between national and local levels but also within the same party.

Interviewees noted that broadly speaking, rural areas were characterized more by conservative political coalitions, whereas cities were more likely to have liberal coalitions and mayors that generally supported the existing coffeeshop system. This is pertinent given that municipalities with coffeeshops had over four times more inhabitants than municipalities without. In other words, coffeeshops are associated with urban density, with 53 per cent of the total number of coffeeshops being in municipalities with over 200,000 inhabitants in 2011 (Bieleman et al, 2012). Significantly, of the 11 largest municipalities, 9 were governed by 'progressive' parties (most often the PvdA) at the end of the 2000s (Wouters et al, 2010). This is especially important given the political dynamics of the VVD being in a national coalition with the PvdA in the Rutte II government.

Aside from coffeeshops, the *grote vier* (big four) of Amsterdam, Rotterdam, The Hague and Utrecht occupy a "special position"[35] in the political realm, as they experience the bulk of problems found in urban environments. In these larger municipalities, mayors often have a "political history" and "still have a lot of influence, so they don't take anything for granted and they are a force, they can speak against the minister".[36] This grants these municipalities and actors more political relevance in directing and influencing policy change at the national level. Among the big four, Amsterdam has an even more privileged position, especially concerning coffeeshop policy. Amsterdam had more coffeeshops than any other city in the Netherlands in 2011, with over a third of the total (222 out of 651) (see Bieleman et al, 2012). The measures proposed under Rutte I would have had a devastating effect on the number of coffeeshops in Amsterdam, and its economic interests would have been threatened by a ban on tourists visiting one of its more liberal attractions.

Moreover, the proposals to introduce a nationwide policy requiring these large municipalities to apply new rules, even where they were not experiencing cannabis-related nuisance problems, created significant tensions and resistance. In reaction to the new measures, the big four offered "strong opposition"[37] and rallied against implementation.[38] The power of the big four in rejecting policy proposals raised serious questions about government legitimacy, and the government had to compromise with these municipalities, and others, in order to proceed.

Liberal values that remain strongly entrenched in local governance are also complemented by a sense of pragmatism held by some actors involved in drugs policy at national level. Indicatively, policy actors in the Public Prosecutor's Office noted their resistance to the proposed reclassification of cannabis with a THC content of over 15 per cent as a hard drug, due to the lack of resources required for adequate enforcement. There was a suggestion that their work involved "policy prevention" rather than developing new policy.

> 'We often say inside here that we are busy doing the prevention of new measures, policy prevention, instead of developing or formulating

> new policies, because there are so many new ideas and a lot of them don't make much sense, so we try to stop them instead of further development.' (NL-PP4: Policy Worker, Public Prosecutor's Office)

Moreover, given that drugs policy is driven by a health-oriented harm reduction perspective, there were clear divides in relation to cannabis policy between the Ministry of Health, Welfare and Sport and the Ministry of Justice and Security. This can be seen, for example, in terms of discussions with stakeholders.

> 'The ministry that is responsible for security and justice does not talk with anyone having a coffeeshop or producing cannabis, because for them they are all criminals and they say it like this. … They have their closed circuit, we try to be open-minded and talk with everybody.' (NL-CS-AC-H1: Senior Civil Servant in Ministry of Health, Welfare and Sport and Member of Garretsen Committee)

The placing of responsibility for cannabis policy within the Ministry of Health, Welfare and Sport provided a valuable political voice, which appeared more grounded in reliable research data and evidence and less prone to emotional and expressive displays of power than was the case with stakeholders in the Ministry of Justice and Security. While the health ministry may have had limited power to prevent the criminal justice measures, it served as a further disgruntled voice against the coffeeshop measures introduced by the Rutte I government. This was especially the case for the *wietpas*.

> 'We said it is going to be a big problem because markets are going to be diffused, a lot of people do not want to be in a database. … We said if you are going to do it like this, nobody will come. And they [the Ministry of Justice and Security] said oh no these people are way too stoned, they are not going to care. Really, that was the answer. … And, oh, what a coincidence, when the pass was introduced, we saw a dramatic decrease in people going to coffeeshops, because they had to be in a database.' (NL-CS-AC-H1: Senior Civil Servant in Ministry of Health, Welfare and Sport and Member of Garretsen Committee)

The *wietpas* generated a fear that the government was overextending its powers in relation to the civil liberties of its citizens, as it would essentially create a list of those taking part in what was technically an illegal activity (see House of Representatives of the States General, 2011c: 1–2). Thus, the *wietpas* served as a suitable target around which policy communities opposed to the government initiatives could coalesce, with resistance coming "from users, coffeeshop owners, politicians, the local, everyone".[39]

Thus, organized political forces lying dormant reacted strongly to the planned introduction of a set of measures which were largely seen as counterproductive and ineffective. The measures threatened a set of practices that existed largely without serious nuisance and youth problems. Across a range of national and local institutions and agencies, liberal orientations towards cannabis policy retained significant influence. This was made possible through structural and contingent relations of governance, which granted a wide range of actors and organizations a political voice and allowed for more rational, pragmatic and evidence-based views to surface.

The political environment in global perspective

In England & Wales and the Netherlands, a common theme in the political environments at the time of the policy changes discussed here was the existence of a punitive public climate in which political parties sought to exhibit their law and order credentials when responding to identified problems. Yet differences in political environments also played a crucial role in shaping the windows of opportunity that were available for decision makers. In other democratic contexts too, changes in administration, the national mood and organized political forces are foundational for generating opportunities for policy change. Here, our discussion turns to consider two cases that further illuminate the dynamics and relationships between political opportunity, public opinion and policy advocacy, and the differentiated outcomes that can emerge. The first case is the case of Uruguay, which, in 2013, became the first country to adopt a national legal framework for regulating cannabis; the second is New Zealand, where there was an unsuccessful attempt to legalize non-medical cannabis via a public referendum in 2020.

Uruguay

In England & Wales and the Netherlands, political actors' sensitivities towards the national mood on cannabis policy and how this may have affected poll ratings was a crucial factor in shaping developments in the political stream. Yet the legalization of cannabis in Uruguay in 2013 is an interesting case to consider precisely because it occurred in the context of public disapproval of the reforms.[40]

This is not to suggest that support for liberalization of cannabis policy did not exist or was without precedent in Uruguay. For example, even under military dictatorship, a law was introduced in 1974 which de jure decriminalized cannabis possession for personal use, and when the country returned to democracy in 1985, a pro-legalization movement emerged (Walsh and Ramsey, 2016). These efforts historically centred around the wide discretion afforded to judges in applying the existing law, which led to the criminalization of users (Queirolo, 2020).

The issue was brought into the political spotlight during the 2000s in the context of growing rates of use among youth populations, and it was elevated by pro-cannabis grassroots organizations from around 2010 (Kilmer et al, 2013). In addition to pointing out the harms caused by criminalization, reform advocates argued that there was a blurring of the cannabis market with that of 'pasta base', a paste similar in effect to crack cocaine. Owing to the stringent penalties for cultivation and the nature of the illegal market, it was asserted that young people were purchasing cannabis from individuals who were simultaneously involved in cross-national trafficking networks supplying pasta base. In response, akin to the model in the Netherlands, reform advocates pushed for separation of the markets for cannabis and other, hard drugs (Walsh and Ramsey, 2016).

Moreover, international currents at the time helped shape the legitimacy of political discourse surrounding liberalization of cannabis policy. These currents included developments towards legalization in Washington and Colorado in the United States and the influential Global Commission on Drug Policy's 2011 report, which was supported by a number of former and active high-profile Latin American political actors (Global Commission on Drug Policy, 2011; Walsh and Ramsey, 2016).

Interestingly, despite Uruguay experiencing crime victimization rates lower than the average for Latin America, not having suffered the sorts of drug trafficking-related violence witnessed in places such as Mexico, levels of insecurity were relatively high (Walsh and Ramsey, 2016). In this sense, the articulation of problems of international drug trafficking and violence, which were driven by both domestic and international policy networks, complemented and played off the anxieties concerning public safety in Uruguayan society. Spurred on by these parallel organized political forces, such developments undoubtedly provided a fertile ground for the policy solution of legalization to emerge. Crucially, however, the advancement of the legalization bill largely resulted from a change in administration that saw the rise of the Broad Front political party with the remarkably humble yet charismatic José Mujica as the country's president.

Thus, the perceived existence of problems, particularly surrounding pasta base and public safety, served as a key rationale for reform efforts. In short, cannabis legalization was advanced by the president and his inner circle as a solution to problems of public insecurity, with the proposal included as part of the Strategy for Life and Coexistence (Walsh and Ramsey, 2016; see also Kilmer et al, 2013; Queirolo, 2020). Following the establishment of the Commission on Addiction, which formulated a proposal for legal regulation, almost all political parties agreed to one single bill for passage in 2011. Then, in 2012 Mujica's government submitted a bill, which passed in 2013 by a narrow margin (Kilmer et al, 2013). Yet, as mentioned earlier, an extremely interesting facet of the policy-making process, alongside its drawn-out introduction in Uruguay, was the lack of public support, with public opinion surveys conducted in 2013 and 2014 suggesting that over 60 per cent of respondents were against the legalization reforms (Kilmer et al, 2013; Cruz et al, 2017, 2018). Thus, the radical change in direction was heavily driven by the president and legislature in a top-down manner (Cruz et al, 2016), and as Queirolo (2020: 116) suggests, 'neither activists, nor public opinion, nor a party's mandate towards its electorate played a decisive role in introducing the topic into the public agenda'.

New Zealand

In stark contrast to Uruguay, the outcome of efforts to legalize non-medical cannabis in New Zealand – culminating in the proposed Cannabis Legalisation and Control Bill 2020 – was determined entirely by the public via a referendum.

This policy proposal originated in the context of comparatively high and sustained self-reported cannabis use, especially among young people, and historical over-representation of Māori populations as subjects of law enforcement. At the same time, the enforcement of criminal laws had been 'substantially eased' over the past decade (Fischer and Bullen, 2020: 1; see also Wilkins and Sweetsur, 2012), and a series of political debates on liberalizing cannabis policy reform had taken place since the 1990s (Abel and Casswell, 1998).

Nevertheless, it wasn't until the coalition agreement between the Labour Party and the New Zealand First party, supported by the Green Party, following the 2017 election that the first concrete proposal for substantive legal reform surfaced. This was indicative of a key change in administration that aligned political actors and groups around agendas of social justice and public health, and had the means to advance these goals in relation to cannabis policy in a domestic and global context that also favoured liberalizing reform. As part of the coalition agreement, concrete proposals to legalize the non-medical cannabis market were developed in the form of the Cannabis Legalization and Control Bill, which represented a fairly balanced approach between public health and public safety concerns. A decision was made to hold a public referendum on whether to enact the Bill, and this took place on 17 October 2020.

The use of public referenda represents a powerful way for the ruling government to assert legitimacy over a contentious policy reform, even if, as was the case in the United Kingdom's referendum on leaving the EU, the margin of victory is so narrow as to question the existence of a unified public will or national mood. In contexts where referenda are frequently part of the political process (such as in Switzerland or in US states), such proposals are often binding; in other words, notwithstanding later possible legal challenges, the result determines the subsequent enacting or repealing of a legal bill. However, the referendum concerning cannabis legalization in New Zealand was non-binding, suggesting that, regardless of the result, the government maintained ultimate power over the final decision. Yet, even in such a case, once a policy decision is put to a public referendum, it becomes very difficult for governments to *not* follow the outcome of the vote, lest it risk undermining the trust of the electorate.

The holding of a public referendum also fundamentally affects the dynamics of policy processes. For the sake of public comprehensibility, the fine-grained complexities of policy negotiation are put aside in favour of offering a selection between a finite range of choices – usually, either for or against the proposal. Also, the role of lobbying, often done behind closed doors, becomes heightened or at least more overt, with coalitions forming to publicly advocate for their respective positions.

Thus, use of a public referendum relinquishes the power of political actors and pivots the decision-making process almost entirely towards the national mood and the ability of organized political forces to influence public opinion. Of course, the corollary of this, for those in political office who are supportive of policy reform, is a substantial political gamble, given the potential for the public to reject the policy proposal. In the United States, public referenda on cannabis policy have generally worked in favour of reform advocates (Fischer and Hall, 2021), but in the case of New Zealand, the national referendum resulted in 50.7 per cent voting *against* the legalization proposal.

In some ways, the result of the referendum was unexpected. The Bill itself represented a rational and evidence-based reform, it was supported by leading academics, and pro-reform advocates had the advantage of greater spending on campaigning, particularly via digital platforms which have been a highly effective – if not controversial – means of campaigning in recent years. Yet, in reflecting on the reasons why the legalization bill was rejected, commentators suggest a series of factors. Rychert and Wilkins (2021) point to the ineffectiveness of pro-legalization campaigners and the lack of elite support for reform. Telling in this latter regard was the reluctance of the widely popular Prime Minister Jacinda Ardern to disclose her voting preference.

However, the referendum took place in the broader context of a set of parallel developments, including, inter alia: declining rates of arrest for cannabis over the past few decades; the decision to regulate medical cannabis months before the referendum; and the public policy goal of a 'smoke-free' New Zealand (Wilkins and Sweetsur, 2012; Pacula, 2021; Wilkins and Rychert, 2021). These factors may have served to undermine the need for legal regulation of non-medical cannabis.

Added to this, various concerns were voiced about the logistical components of regulatory mechanisms that could potentially lead to increased use and negative health outcomes. Yet for Rychert and Wilkins (2021: 3), the campaign environment itself 'encouraged persuasion and selective use of evidence rather than rational discussion of all the evidence and gaps'. Similarly, it was claimed that 'for many opponents legalization remains an issue [of] morality' (Fischer and Hall, 2021: 1), with voting patterns following 'established conservative-liberal, urban-rural and age divides' (Rychert and Wilkins, 2021: 1).

Nevertheless, while this paints a picture of an uninformed public driven by non-rational moral values, other commentators have instead argued that the public were informed but were simply 'unconvinced by the public health arguments supporting [legalization]' (Smyth and Christie, 2021: 1). Indeed, it is possible that such views could were shaped by prior negative experiences of New Zealand's novel psychoactive substances legalization experiment (Rychert et al, 2018; Rychert and Wilkins, 2020; Pacula, 2021). In this regard, it is pertinent that the strongest opposition came from lower socio-economic areas and rural areas, which suffer greatest health harms from alcohol and tobacco and were briefly targeted for sales of novel psychoactive substances (Pacula, 2021).

In sum, while a change of administration brought a ruling coalition of political parties that were aligned around a preferred policy solution and set of related problems, the decision to hold a public referendum and the lingering political anxieties around enacting controversial policy reforms exemplify the fragilities of the policy making process.

Summary

It is possible to see how changes in administration, the national mood, and organized political forces serve to facilitate or hinder the preferred representations and policy proposals concerning cannabis. Clearly, key changes in administration present ideal windows of opportunity for policy change, as actors and parties seek to distinguish themselves from their predecessors and have the means to advance problems and policies aligned with their dispositional tendencies.

However, even if there is alignment among decision makers, this is not to suppose that change necessarily occurs. The failed attempt at legalization in New Zealand alerts us to the importance of the mechanisms by which policy/legislation is formalized, which in this case, deferred the final decision to a public referendum.

Relatedly, this speaks to the influence of the national mood and organized political forces. In the cases considered, cannabis became an important political signifier which was intimately connected – either tangibly or symbolically – to other problems; in other words, seldom are changes to cannabis policy solely about cannabis. Rather, the cannabis issue is often cannon fodder for political motivations concerning other agendas, whether that be law and order, public health or human rights.

The cases of England & Wales, the Netherlands and also in some respects New Zealand demonstrated how public debates and representations of cannabis policy have become highly polarized, with a simplified artificial bifurcation emerging between those who are seen to support prohibition and those who are seen to oppose it. This heightens political sensitivities and anxieties over perceptions of the national mood and the ramifications, for parties' political image and standing, of landing on the wrong side of public opinion. Certainly, this is further driven by interest groups, who utilize their available resources to influence the direction of public sentiment and the views of policy makers. With contemporary conditions of policy making in this sphere often extremely politicized and subject to fierce scrutiny, there are arguably greater political risks for actors and parties seeking to reform policies and laws that have been embedded for decades. Nevertheless, the case of Uruguay (and also Canada) illuminates how the national mood, and artificial constructions of it via public opinion surveys, do not in themselves necessarily determine the direction of policy, with ruling political actors driving forward policy reforms despite noticeably negative public sentiment in these contexts.

Overriding and conditioning all of these aspects are the broader institutional elements of political systems, which structure possibilities and constraints in the political stream. Key aspects in this regard are the differences between adversarial and proportional representational systems as well as the policy-making norms that these systems foster, with the former arguably more vulnerable to penetration by a more polarizing and populist style of politics. Such institutional and normative components are further examined in Chapter 7, where we turn to consider cannabis policy making at the subnational level.

7

Beyond the National: Policy Negotiation, Resistance and Subversion

Introduction

Through examination of the problem stream (Chapter 4), the policy stream (Chapter 5) and the political stream (Chapter 6), we have been piecing together how movements in cannabis policy come into fruition. Thus far, the discussion has largely focused on the national level of decision making, and for good reason: changes in cannabis policy often relate to legislation determined by a national sovereign entity. However, it would be a mistake to assume that decision-making beneath the national level is irrelevant or that it simply mirrors national policy. Rather, spheres of governance beyond the national can be pivotal in the generation and unfolding of policy (see Stenson and Edwards, 2004; Edwards and Hughes, 2005; Devroe et al, 2017).

Accordingly, this chapter aims to identify different mechanisms and relations of decision-making that facilitate or hinder the negotiation, resistance and subversion of cannabis policy at the subnational level. First, the empirical focus on England & Wales and the Netherlands is continued, comparing and contrasting the representation of problems at the national level and looking at the unfolding of nationally introduced policy changes in two contexts: Cardiff/Wales and Utrecht. From there, taking a broader lens, the role and nature of the subnational in two further countries – the United States and Japan – are considered, to exemplify contrasting settings for manifestations of cannabis policy.

A muted dragon? Reclassification in Wales

As alluded to in Chapter 1, owing to the legal provisions afforded under devolution settlements in the United Kingdom since 1998, the notion of a clear and singular subnational level in England & Wales has become a somewhat awkward and clunky proposition. In respect of the Welsh context, the Welsh Government and affiliated Wales-level agencies are now important players with lawmaking and decision-making abilities directly affecting substance use policy (see Brewster and Jones, 2019; Jones, 2020; Evans et al, 2021). In addition, as is the case across the United Kingdom, local authorities represent a key level at which policy is determined and implemented. For the sake of clarity and to contrast with the national jurisdiction of England & Wales, here we focus jointly on Wales – as a partially devolved legislature – and Cardiff – as a site of local governance – in respect of the 2009 reclassification of cannabis to Class B.

Overall, there were points of crossover in the way cannabis was constructed as a policy problem at the national level, particularly in recognition of the abundance of commercial cultivation and health problems attributed to the consumption of cannabis. Nevertheless, owing to the political environment of Wales, which tends to foster more welfare-oriented policies and faces less populist punitive-driven demands, as well as the abilities of actors to resist and rework policy decisions in ways which fit their working agendas, there was also evidence of divergence at a subnational level.

Problem representation

Historically, one of the most distinguishing aspects of drugs policy in Wales is that all substances (both legal and illegal) that can potentially cause dependence and harm are placed within the same strategy. This has been the case since before the establishment of the Welsh Government and well before England had even produced a harm reduction strategy on alcohol (Welsh Office, 1996; National Assembly for Wales, 2000; Cabinet Office Strategy Unit, 2004). This is due not least to an overt recognition of the high levels of harm emanating from alcohol (Welsh Government, 2008: 12) as well as shared factors which contribute to, and are consequences of, different forms substance use (National Assembly for Wales, 2000; Welsh Government, 2008). Moreover, in several regards, drugs policy discourse in this setting at the end of the 2000s demonstrated a more rational and pragmatic approach than was found in England. The framing of issues regarding substance misuse was seen to be more "sympathetic"[1] towards the individual user: "We are more likely to use the softer language of, these could be people you know, these could be people like you, and if they fall into difficulty we ought to be able to help them because you might be in difficulty one day."[2]

A significant contributory factor for the development of this 'Welsh approach' relates to the technical feasibility to formally shape certain policies and laws in Wales. Interviewees noted that even prior to the establishment of the Welsh Assembly Government in 1999, the Welsh Office had freedoms to shape policies around health that it did not have for criminal justice, and a health-led framework became further solidified following devolution of powers in this area.[3]

Thus, by the late 2000s, the Welsh Government's lack of ability to shape criminal justice matters had led to a sharpening of those areas in which policy movement was attainable. This was further shaped by a belief that law enforcement efforts had 'made less impact in this area', with the government's admission that illegal drugs are 'easy to access and the prices have continued to drop' (Welsh Government, 2008: 48). Moreover, there was a belief that enforcement should prioritize 'those who supply drugs to children and young people' (Welsh Government, 2008: 52). Consequentially, there was an implicit framing of the law enforcement lens away from applying punitive responses to users (qua simple possession offences), thereby contributing to an aim of 'not stigmatising substance misusers' (Welsh Government, 2008: 21). Through the dominant health-led narrative, there was a preference for a harm reduction approach that minimizes the impact of law enforcement on individual users.

This provided an important conditioning environment in which local authorities in Wales conceptualised problems, especially in the capital of Cardiff. At this level, the policy talk further evidenced the centrality of the provision of treatment and harm reduction services in responding to substance misuse. A range of participants from police officers to health officials noted that this predominantly referred to alcohol and injecting drug users, which were seen as "the bigger concern", with cannabis "stuck there in the middle"[4] between criminal justice and public health priorities.

However, despite cannabis being seen as less harmful than other drugs, a common concern among interviewees was that cannabis is widely available, especially for young people. In respect of mental health, there were mixed views about the extent to which its use causes health and social problems. On one hand, interviewees across health and criminal justice and from non-governmental organizations noted that the consumption of cannabis did appear to present problems for young people. However, in relation to increased reports of mental health and social problems, a contrasting perspective suggested that the increases in recorded problems was not due to an actual change in behaviours, but rather to reporting, recognition and perception that cannabis was causing mental health and other social problems.

> 'I think the competent skills of the mental health workforce have improved to enable them to make the association more often. … Because we weren't asking the question, you don't know the extent to which it proliferated before.' (EW-CS-H1: Substance Misuse Policy Worker, Cardiff and Welsh Government)

> 'Often it is a convenient cause that a parent or relative or whoever can pinpoint and say it is the drugs, whereas there might be a whole

raft of things going on and perhaps the drug use isn't helping but it's certainly not the root cause.' (EW-NGO3: Third Sector Substance Misuse Worker, Cardiff)

From a law enforcement perspective, despite consumption being prevalent, the issue of cannabis cultivation was seen as more problematic. A key concern surrounded the connections between larger operations and organized crime groups, with problems related to these practices including property damage, human trafficking and other serious forms of criminality. "It's certainly connected to organized crime. … Houses have been rented and houses have been ripped apart, electricity has been stolen, people are getting injured … you have got people from the Far East, Vietnam, who have been associated with growing cannabis in houses."[5]

Thus, in some ways the construction of cannabis as a problem at the subnational level corresponds with the national problematization of cannabis prior to the 2009 reclassification. However, in the Welsh context, the more "sympathetic"[6] approach to substance misuse and the greater focus on alcohol and Class A drugs meant that low-level possession was not considered the most pressing problem. Where cannabis was concerned, the focus was on supply and cultivation, which was connected to organized crime, and the health perspective in which policy actors sought to reduce harm to young individuals.

Policy negotiation

Overall, there does not appear to have been a Welsh voice in the reclassification process. There was little attempt to formally carve alternative criminal justice responses to cannabis. While the framing of substance misuse in Wales was based on a more rational and pragmatic understanding of the problems that affect individuals and communities, it was still locked into broader dominant frameworks of how illegal drugs should be controlled and responded to. In this sense, there was a lack of debate, or even acknowledgement, of alternative ways in which illegal substances could be managed – such a debate could have led to the Welsh Government's harm reduction aims being more readily achieved. Rhetoric such as "making sure that services are equipped to meet the health needs of substance users is our top priority" and "developing policies and strategies we know work"[7] were based within a broader prevailing paradigm that affects the types of evidence sought out and used.

Policy making in Wales involves a fairly narrow set of policy makers. One criticism levelled at the Welsh system was that there "isn't enough grit in the oyster",[8] signifying a lack of critical debate with a "pooling of stupidity and prejudice".[9] As such, it was suggested that dominant philosophies and discourses were accepted and re-performed, with a range of stakeholders – from politicians, civil servants, experts (in the form of the Advisory Panel on Substance Misuse) to practitioners – seemingly not engaging in the debate.

> 'It's like the debate doesn't happen at all, so I get very straightforward advice within the parameters of the way that policy is currently configured … people like that [the Advisory Panel on Substance Misuse] who are not in the government machine but are there to advise it, even there they don't raise it as an issue at all. They simply talk within the tram lines.' (EW-P1, Senior Political Figure)

> 'I don't see any pressure on the Welsh Government to lobby the Westminster Government in opposition to any of the decisions around classification, and I don't see there currently being any appetite for them to do that either … it's just not on the radar at all.' (EW-CS-H1: Substance Misuse Policy Worker, Cardiff and Welsh Government)

This lack of engagement is partially connected to political sensitivities and anxieties about potential threats to the legitimacy of the devolution project, which is conditioned by the relationship between Welsh Government and Whitehall. As one senior political figure noted, the Welsh Government had to be "tentative" in the "fights to fight":

> 'we have a series of difficult discussions that go on between ourselves and Westminster government. Would we choose to add this one [substance misuse] to the list? I think probably not, because the other things that are on the list are, you could argue in some ways are more pressing … you always worry that if you introduce another argument into that, you will lose ground on some more important ones.' (EW-P1: Senior Political Figure)

At the time of the 2009 reclassification, the transferral and use of powers from London to Cardiff was still in its early stages, and so there was a lack of willingness to engage critically in a highly contested area which could compromise the granting of powers and laws in other areas. A further political aspect worth considering in the context of the 2009 reclassification was the relationship between the specific governing parties of the Welsh Government and the UK government. Both governments were led by Labour parties, and if the Welsh Government had challenged the policy measure, this would have resulted in political problems for both governments, creating suspicion of infighting. "When there was a Labour government at both ends, it was trying to find ways of explaining difference that [would] minimize what was sometimes genuine differences of view. … If the Tories are in charge, who cares?"[10]

Thus, the Welsh Government was largely a passive observer in the 2009 reclassification, with little interest in rocking the boat. At the local level of Cardiff, there was also a distinct lack of official challenge to the reclassification of cannabis. However, there was evidence that cannabis policy was being reworked in more unofficial ways at the local level. On the part of law enforcement, this was driven by a perception that "the fight in respect of cannabis is lost".[11] In turn, this led to an informal pragmatic adaptation of the way resources were directed and managed. This was made possible by the large amount of discretion given to police constables in dealing with possession offences. For most interviewees representing the police, the reclassification back to Class B "[didn't] make a great deal of difference"[12] to how the police approached cannabis offences; the approach was influenced much more by factors such as time and resources.

> 'The arrests that are generated as a result of drug possession generally will create paperwork and obstructions at key points in time when you have got a limited number of officers … that can be a real factor in the minds of middle managers and sergeants who will give that clear direction.' (EW-POL-CS1: South Wales Police and Welsh Government)

Rather than enforcing a stringent approach, it was seen as more beneficial to deal with circumstances flexibly and in combination with actors and agencies supporting a harm reduction agenda. Feeding into this, interviewees from the police often saw themselves as protective agents, in the sense that there was recognition of the potentially harmful effects of criminalization combined with a paternalistic rhetoric.

> 'In many areas drugs policy can be murky. Clear messages will always come out of the Home Office, stamp all over these people, and the reality is, how would you like your kids to be dealt with? And that's how we try to police.' (EW-POL-CS1: South Wales Police and Welsh Government)

> 'Cannabis warnings … there were loads and loads of them issued and then that was seen as maybe not the best way of tackling the problem because you're criminalizing somebody for having a little bit of cannabis on them, and that stays with them their whole life.' (EW-POL-CS2: South Wales Police, Welsh Government and ACPO Cymru).

Nevertheless, in the policing of cannabis at local level, more influential than the reclassification of the drug was the removal of the centralized police targets, which had skewed police performance. Following this, local performance targets regarding illegal drugs related only to recorded instances of drug trafficking (South Wales Police, 2011). As such, the incentive for officers to record cannabis possession offences disappeared, and priority was placed on improving 'community satisfaction' and 'value for money' (South Wales Police, 2011:1-8). As a result, attention shifted to large-scale cannabis cultivation and crimes such as burglary.[13] This demonstrates divergence between the political pressures found in the national policy realm and the pragmatic strategies of managing issues at a subnational level.

Additionally, responses to cannabis from other agencies reflected the perspective that cannabis poses far less risks and harms to the individual and society than other substances, particularly alcohol and opiates. The perceived relative risks of cannabis as well as pressure on resources led to prioritization of responses to the more problematic substances. Cannabis users usually do not require, or do not present themselves, for clinical treatment or services, and they do not pose the same risks as the alcohol-fuelled night-time economy. As such, policy selection and management at the local level were more about education and prevention.

> 'We are struggling in order to cope with managing the substances that put a much greater degree of pressure on public services ... we're not going out proactively trying to identify more people to come into services because of their cannabis use when our resources are already stretched as a result of the other substances.' (EW-CS-H1: Substance Misuse Policy Worker, Cardiff and Welsh Government)

The reality is that there exists a paradox in the policing and management of cannabis and cannabis-related issues; to follow a strategy of proactive law enforcement and treatment with cannabis users would create a huge burden across the criminal justice system and treatment agencies. Such an approach was largely seen as ineffective and wasteful. Among interviewees, a dominant view of the 2009 reclassification at the local level was that existing practices were not affected significantly. Placed within the context of a health-dominated substance misuse field in Wales, the talk and decisions corroborated the notion that police officers act as 'street-level bureaucrats', as they bend and rework official policy and guidelines to fit the circumstances they are in (Lipsky, 2010).

Thus, at local level, problem disposition and resource management are important components in understanding the overall significance of the reclassification. It is suggested that national cannabis policy decisions have been channelled in a way which accords with the political and technical feasibilities of policy in Wales and at a local level. However, what is less clear from these empirical findings is whether subnational polities in England deflected punitive approaches to cannabis in a similar fashion, even with the lack of a 'buffering' mechanism similar to that in the Welsh context.

Nevertheless, since the 2009 reclassification, there have been increasing signs that directions in cannabis policy are driven less by national law and more by the multitude of other factors shaping decision-making at a local level. Alongside the removal of centralized performance indicators, neutralizing the perverse incentive to actively pursue cannabis possession cases, a reduction in the financial resources of police forces due to a prolonged period of austerity has been important in decisions about which offences to prioritize. This is particularly pertinent given that the political noise surrounding cannabis quietened significantly following the reclassification, with the emergence of other drug scares, such as the county lines phenomenon, higher on police and political agendas (Spicer, 2021). Another equally significant development was the introduction of directly elected PCCs, who wield considerable power in determining budgets and priorities. As a result, a significant number of forces appear to be adapting to current circumstances by deprioritizing or diverting cannabis offences. Also, there have been reports of a limited, but noteworthy, number of senior police officials exploring the role of grassroots CSCs in more controlled cultivation practices (Gayle, 2015; Transform Drug Policy Foundation, 2022). Nevertheless, in other cases, particularly with regards to the Metropolitan Police Service, it is evident that cannabis offences remain a key tool through which to police 'suspect communities', with stop-and-search for cannabis offences continuing to drive significant racial disparities (Shiner et al, 2018) (see Chapter 3). Such developments point to the importance of other mechanisms shaping policy processes across England & Wales, and the overall patterns appear to indicate the return of localization in responses to cannabis.

'Policy prevention': challenging policy in Utrecht

Contrasting with England & Wales, cannabis policy at subnational level in the Netherlands is vibrant and overtly politically contested. To clarify how and why this is the case, we consider the case of Utrecht, the fourth-biggest municipality in the Netherlands. This illuminates how the "force field"[14] of the local level was significant in raising problems, setting agendas and reworking policy introduced under the Rutte I and Rutte II governments.

Policy representation

Overall, findings from the subnational level in the Netherlands are suggestive of both convergence and divergence with the national level in respect of how cannabis and coffeeshops were conceptualized as policy problems.

There were similar increases in awareness, number of incidents and types of responses to illegal activities operating around the back door of coffeeshops in Utrecht. Whereas in former years the issue of cannabis cultivation was not perceived to be a serious issue by senior police officers and received relatively little police attention, there was a shift in attention and resources, aided by national prioritization. Moreover, data collection and analysis originating from within the local police force started to shift the internal culture to acknowledge the negative aspects of the cannabis trade. For example, it was noted that there were serious problems such as a death threat to the mayor, violence, arms trading and gang wars.[15]

More mundanely, one of the most commonly reported concerns around coffeeshops in Utrecht related to parking. At the time of the research, the city's coffeeshops were mainly located in the inner-city area, which is characterized by narrow streets. The constant flow of customers using bicycle lanes for parking created points of nuisance for local residents.[16] Interviewees suggested that this more visible problem was of greater concern to the police than organized crime, since it impacted the daily lived experiences of residents. As one politician suggested:

> 'It is not that it is about the health issue, it is not about the huge black [market] of criminality behind it, because people actually say, do we care if people shoot each other whilst they are both criminals trading with each other? No, I am more irritated by the fact that there is dog poo on the street or I can't park my car. … As a representative of Utrecht … I am more focusing on these inconvenience problems.' (NL-P2: VVD Politician, Utrecht)

The parking problem was not the only visible issue; public nuisance and degradation to the area were also concerns. While most clearly articulated by a CDA politician, such views were noted by most interviewees. There was also a perception that coffeeshops and the public consumption of cannabis serve as a bad example for young people,[17] and this presented itself in a 'not in my backyard' syndrome in relation to the opening or moving of coffeeshops.[18]

Despite these problems being raised, the coffeeshops in Utrecht were not seen to be overly problematic, especially in comparison to the problems in the southern municipalities with regards to drug-related tourists. "The drug problem in this city was a homelessness hard drug problem, and the coffeeshops, well they just functioned, there was not much public nuisance of the coffeeshops, not comparable to what you have in Maastricht near the border or in other cities."[19]

Conversely, coffeeshops were valued as useful social outlets. This was noted particularly by representatives from the police and prosecution service, who argued that the visibility of coffeeshops is a positive when it comes to managing problems.

> 'I think it is a good system … as the police, you can manage what is going on about that building, the people that come. Most of the time we don't have complaints about the people around the coffeeshops … we also know that we never get rid of it, because you know it's here and it always has been.' (NL-POL4: Utrecht Police)

With acceptance of the inevitability of cannabis consumption, the coffeeshops were seen as providing a useful and relatively unproblematic outlet where the sale of cannabis is more controllable and manageable than sale via non-tolerated sources, thus affirming the market separation philosophy.

At the time of the Rutte I and Rutte II governments, there were points of overlap with the national level in the construction of problems, particularly in respect of the back-door. Overall, however, the issues felt at a local level were not overly problematic. Rather, coffeeshops were largely valued as social institutions. Any minor nuisance problems could be dealt with through existing tools, and cultivation problems were seen as being due solely to state failure to regulate the back door. As such, the national changes to the *gedoogbeleid* were seen as counterproductive, contributing to existing problems and creating new ones.

> 'We don't have any problems with tourists in coffeeshops, so we don't see the idea of installing permits or something, and 350 metres, we don't have any problems yet and we don't see the advantage of that, only that we have to close down a lot of coffeeshops.' (NL-P5: D'66 Alderperson, Utrecht)

A somewhat ironic policy problem highlighted by this interviewee was that there were "too few coffeeshops"[20] in the municipality. Further, in relation to the school distance criterion, the main objections were centred around the fact that this would lead to most coffeeshops being closed down and the lack of sound evidence that it would be effective in reducing cannabis use among young people.[21]

The "big problem"[22] was not with coffeeshops and nuisance, but production and supply of cannabis to coffeeshops. In this respect, the main issue with the planned introduction of the closed club criterion and the actual introduction of the residency criterion was that Utrecht was not experiencing problems related to drug tourists – it was estimated that only approximately 10 per cent of coffeeshop visitors were from other countries. As a policy advisor to the mayor noted, "we cause a problem by introducing [the residency criterion] and by enforcing it".[23] Consequently, there were fears in local government that the introduction of this measure would "start up dealing in the streets again"[24] due to the necessity of checks and recording of user information.

Policy negotiation

The measures introduced in 2012 under the Rutte I government were met with significant resistance by ruling political parties in Utrecht, with the dominant perception being that they were unnecessary and would actually create problems. As a result, while the residency criterion appeared in the national guidelines, there was no intention to enforce it. This is evidenced both in interviewees' comments and in the subtle way in which it was codified into the local coffeeshop policy published in July 2013.

> 'The Residents Criterion, which is part of the national tolerance criteria (AHOJ-G), will be listed in the Utrecht enforcement strategy on hotel and catering, indicating that enforcement will be undertaken as [it is] objectively determined that the visit of non-residents at the Utrecht coffeeshops leads to trouble.' (City of Utrecht, 2013, author's translation)

> 'We think it is necessary if people who can't show they live in our country are causing problems, but they don't at this moment, so we don't implement it now, and we will implement it as soon as that is the case. … As long as we don't have that problem, there is no duty to implement it.' (NL-PA3: Policy Advisor to the Mayor, Utrecht)

Thus, while the residency criterion became formally recognized in local policy, there were no intentions to enforce it as long as foreign consumers were not considered a problem. Interestingly, though, despite the questioning of the school distance criterion, municipal coffeeshop policy partially included this into its guidelines: a distance of 250 metres applies in the inner city, while 350 metres applies in residential areas outside the inner city – the distance criterion is not applied in the outskirts of the city (City of Utrecht, 2013). This could be the result of the growing prominence of the 'broken windows' perspective and negative stigma that has come to circulate around coffeeshops, both of which signal a need to protect families and children from the perceived threat of cannabis.

At the subnational level, alongside dissatisfaction with measures initiated at national level, the ability to create policy solutions to problems that are experienced locally was viewed as being important. An example was the establishment of drive-in coffeeshops at the periphery of the city.[25] In addition, one of the most important developments to have emerged from the local level at this time was the proposal to introduce a CSC-style model of regulating cultivation (see Wouters and Korf, 2011).

Under the prosecutor's guidelines, individuals may grow up to five plants without being prosecuted, but under a club model, the idea was that operating as a collective, 200 individuals would be able to grow up to 1,000 plants, which would then be shared among club members. The plans, originating from the alderperson for health, carved a clear rationale for the experiment, drawing on research and evidence (City of Utrecht Municipal Executive, 2011). Moreover, it was argued that these plans were possible within existing national and international frameworks, on the basis of scientific and medical purposes as well as benefiting public health,[26] thereby contesting national policy talk that such experimentations are not technically feasible. Interestingly, following the conclusion of the fieldwork for this research, while the national government has made advances in establishing cultivation experiments, Utrecht and the other big cities subsequently declined to participate, citing concerns over restrictions that would be imposed (see Advisory Committee Experiment Closed Cannabis Chain, 2018; Kreulen, 2019; Korf, 2020).

Thus, there is a considerable degree of manoeuvre available to local municipalities in the translation of national policy and the creation of new policy. At national level, regulation of cultivation was not considered an option, because it did not fit with the particular values and ideologies of those in the Rutte I government; yet at subnational level, alternative discourses provided the rationale to drive forward policy measures relating to cultivation.

Nevertheless, it is pertinent to note that municipal politics have similar dynamics to national-level politics in terms of the need for processes of coalition-building and governance. For example, the proposal in Utrecht to start a cultivation experiment was not universally agreed on in the city council, with parties such as the CDA heavily against the plan.[27] Moreover, it was suggested that increasing pressure on the local council to counter nuisance problems is slowly shifting attitudes towards being tougher against coffeeshops that transgress the rules. In some cases, this has been successful in the sense of granting extra resources to police troublesome streets and areas.

However, a further point is relevant here: even though there may be pressures exhibited at a local electoral level, there is a demarcation between locally elected politicians who form the municipal council and the executive body consisting of the mayor and alderpersons. Thus, while the remit of the council is to decide the municipality's broad policies and oversee their implementation, the administration of policy falls to individuals who are not directly elected.[28] This is particularly complex regarding cannabis policy, which at a local level is considered both a health issue and a public order issue, thus falling under the remit of an alderperson and the mayor. Such structures of governance may provide some counterbalance to negative feelings towards cannabis and coffeeshops, as the mayor and alderperson are insulated from local electoral opinion. Moreover, as described in Chapter 3, the mayor has a special duty to engage in 'tripartite consultations' with the chiefs of police and the prosecution service, who negotiate on and determine priorities and allocate resources according to mayoral, national and police/prosecution needs. In terms of accountability, the responsibility of alderpersons and the mayor is first to the local council, rather than the national government, and this provides a structural mechanism whereby support is fostered for local policy development and resistance against unfavourable national measures.

> 'They [national government] can't control local governments . ... I am responsible for health issues in my home town, and there is nobody who can say if I have to do this or that. That is my way how I can go forward if I still have the majority in the city council who is supporting me.' (NL-P5: D'66 Alderperson, Utrecht)

This has a very important role in the development of policy, with most drugs policy initiatives starting at the local level before being translated into national policy. This is facilitated by the ability to trial and experiment, as enshrined under the Opium Act 1976. With regards to the cultivation experiment, it was the fact that this was justified as a health project, which hypothetically removed it from the remit of 'justice and security', that allowed the plan to move forward. Such manoeuvrings at the subnational level are allowed because it is recognized that the local level has to deal in practical terms with surfacing problems, while these become abstracted at the national level of policy making.[29]

The specific direction of local policy responses was driven by a municipal coalition comprised of Left-wing parties. It was noted that the "spirit of the people"[30] supports a "real"[31] and "full"[32] Left-wing political representation within the local council. While there has been a degree of voter movement, as experienced throughout the Netherlands, support for liberal parties has been largely consistent. During 2010–14, the municipal coalition was comprised of GroenLinks, D'66 and the PvdA. When it comes to cannabis policy, all these parties supported measures that would regulate the back door – none more so than D'66, which saw this as a key measure and took issue with the direction of policy that was initiated by Rutte I. Moreover, there were historical trends in Utrecht for support of liberal drugs programmes – for example, the introduction of heroin prescriptions, another measure that went against the national grain of drugs policy at the time (see Central Committee on the Treatment of Heroin Addicts, 2002). Since the 2010 election, the council remained heavily Left leaning, with D'66 and GroenLinks winning a combined 22 seats out of 45 in both the 2014 and 2018 elections and being part of both ruling coalitions. This helps to explain the continued support for the cultivation experiment.

Thus, while cannabis policy may have been, and continues to be, contested within the city council, it has been predominantly controlled by Left-leaning coalitions. In addition, even Right-leaning politicians accepted the inevitability of cannabis consumption and the use of coffeeshops locally, and this prevented consideration of any radical changes, such as complete closure. "We understand the market is going to be there anyway … you cannot say Utrecht is a drugs-free zone, because if you are going to the streets somewhere, you cannot control it."[33] As such, political negotiations from the perspective of Right-leaning parties within the city council were more fixed on dealing with the undesirable social effects that are associated with coffeeshops. This was particularly the case when a set of Left-leaning parties, all broadly agreed on the issue of coffeeshops, had control of the local council and had representatives in the positions of alderpersons and mayor.

Looking outward, from the local to the national, it is conceivable that the specific combination of parties in control of the municipal council at the time of the Rutte I government was the key factor in the challenge to the 'full' Right-wing government. The national measures rubbed uneasily against the political preferences of the municipal council, who wanted to move in a different direction with cannabis policy. Moreover, the Utrecht coalition's advancement of alternative policy agendas (notably the cultivation experiment) might not have been agreed on had there been different parties represented in the ruling coalition. This highlights the finite windows of opportunity for moments of resistance or advocacy of alternative policies.

In an important way, resistance against the new national measures transcended the issue of cannabis to represent broader disdain with the politics of national government within a particular political climate. The proposals for cannabis cultivation were seen by some as a symbolic attempt to confront the national approach, with Utrecht serving as the "spokesperson"[34] of resistance.

> 'It is really symbolic to say locally, we are going against the national trend and we believe we as Utrecht can be the front runner and can do things which are on the edge of what is legally allowed to start moving this way.' (NL-P4: CDA politician, Utrecht)

> 'Everything that government [Rutte I] did was reflected here in the opposite way in Utrecht because it is the fourth-biggest city and it has a full Left government, and at that time it was seen as a sort of, the opposition against the national government.' (NL-P2: VVD Politician, Utrecht)

Thus, the complex features of subnational governance not only shape policy debates at national level but also, due to relations of governance that grant significant power to municipalities, allow for resistance and policy alternatives to flourish at subnational level. The position of Utrecht as a member of the big four elevated its powerful status, which, coupled with a firm political coalition of Left-wing parties and the liberal "spirit of the people", gave it significant room for manoeuvre in both the non-enforcement of the residency criterion and attempts to move in a different direction with cannabis policy.

The role of the subnational in policy negotiation in global perspective

In the chapter so far, a common theme of cannabis policy processes at subnational level in England & Wales and the Netherlands was the ability of actors and organizations to rework policy in ways that accorded with their preferred dispositions and goals. Nevertheless, the means by which this was achieved and the level of success varied greatly, owing to key differences in the mechanisms and relations of policy making, both between national and subnational authorities and within a particular subnational sphere. To further elucidate the ways such components intimately influence manifestations of cannabis policy, we now turn to consider two contrasting cases of the United States and Japan.

United States

The United States is a federal republic comprised of 50 states, a federal district and 5 major territories. The existence of these subnational entities, and the powers to govern which are endowed under the Constitution of the United States, produces an interesting set of dynamics between national and subnational levels.

Since the Marijuana Tax Act 1937 and under the Controlled Substances Act 1970, activities relating to cannabis are prohibited at a federal level. On a national level, the United States has been at the forefront of both domestic and international attempts to eradicate cannabis and its use through populist–punitive rhetoric, legislation and interventions. The country has come to be seen as the lead protagonist in a war on drugs since the 1970s (Andreas and Nadelmann, 2006; Bewley-Taylor and Jelsma, 2012).

Nevertheless, this masks a much more diverse picture of how cannabis policy has unfolded at subnational level. Even following Nixon's infamous 'public enemy number one' speech and his subsequent call to arms in 1971, a number of states and cities chose, by the end of the 1970s, to pursue a policy of decriminalization (Single et al, 2000; Eastwood, 2020). In more recent times, while the federal stance has, in substantive terms, changed little, cannabis policy reform at subnational level has advanced considerably. At the time of writing, 37 states, the District of Columbia and 3 territories have passed legislation permitting medical cannabis, and 18 states, the District of Columbia and 2 territories have passed legislation which regulates the sale, possession and use of non-medical cannabis (Booker et al, 2021).

The problems such policy movements are intended to resolve are multifaceted, being contingent on different geohistorical contexts (see Edwards and Hughes, 2005). In Washington state, for example, proponents of the 2012 initiative to legalize non-medical cannabis focused on several issues: the legitimization of widespread medical cannabis use, which had resulted from the loose patchwork of regulations of the preceding two decades; the reduction of policing, judicial and social costs, which disproportionately affected ethnic minorities; and the championing of individual and civil rights (Cambron et al, 2017; Mosher and Akins, 2020; Obradovic, 2021). In other states, arguments for legalization have centred around, inter alia, improvements to public safety and/or expected tax revenues (Leon and Weitzer, 2014).

What makes these representations of the cannabis problem relevant at subnational level are the mechanisms that can facilitate policy change. In this regard, the Tenth Amendment of the US Constitution and its 'anti-commandeering doctrine' grants considerable sovereignty to individual states. Moreover, within the constitutions of almost all states, there are provisions allowing for direct voting on proposals or legislative reforms. Depending on the state, such referenda may be initiated by an individual citizen or group which has gathered the requisite amount of support, or they may originate from the state legislature (Mikos, 2009; Cambron et al, 2017). These provisions have facilitated considerable movement in cannabis policy at the state level. It is also worth noting variation *within* states. Depending on a state's constitution and the nature of legislation, counties and cities in some states can, for example, implement ordinances banning cannabis businesses (see Mosher and Akins, 2020).

As mentioned in Chapter 6 in relation to New Zealand's 2020 referendum, such direct forms of democratic decision-making enable greater political participation, and similar to processes at a national level, the roles of the national mood and organized political forces become pivotal. In this latter regard, especially given the remarkable success of states radically shifting course after decades of prohibition, the overwhelming disparities in campaign spending are not insignificant. For example, supporters of Washington State's Initiative 502 raised US$6.2 million while opposition groups raised just US$16,000, and the disparity in Mississippi's 2020 ballot on Initiative 65 was US$7.6 million to US$315,000 in favour of reform advocates (Leon and Weitzer, 2014; Mosher and Akins, 2020; Ballotpedia,

2021). Of course, spending is not the only decisive factor, as demonstrated by cases such as California's 2010 Proposition 19, which was not passed despite a difference in spending by almost 10:1 in favour of the supporters. Thus, along with the actual content of proposals and their palatability to voters, successful campaigns have also been underpinned by a scheme of cooperation including, inter alia, political figures, newspapers, business leaders, medical groups, civil rights organizations and cannabis advocacy groups (Leon and Weitzer, 2014).

Returning to dynamics between national and subnational levels, while the federal government cannot force a state to criminalize an act under state law (Garvey and Yeh, 2014), it is important to remember that federal law supersedes state law, and federal government can pre-empt state law if it so wishes. Nevertheless, with a growing number of states passing legislation in direct conflict with federal statutes, the collective efforts of states appears to be weakening the position of federal government. In other words, as more states legalize cannabis, it becomes more difficult for the federal government to reverse direct democratic decisions. Moreover, enforcement of laws in relation to small-scale offences (such as possession and cultivation for personal consumption) are, in the first instance, the remit of state organs, and federal authorities do not possess the resources necessary for consistent and effective law enforcement, even if they so desired. Accordingly, Schwartz (2013) suggests that the anti-commandeering doctrine versus pre-emption dynamic in contemporary cannabis policy has created a crisis of federalism.

In response to the state-level reforms, policy memoranda were issued by the Department of Justice under successive Obama administrations. In 2013, the most significant of these, the Cole Memorandum, essentially gave safe passage to the implementation of state laws without interference by federal authorities so long as they did not 'threaten' a set of eight federal priorities (Department of Justice, 2013; Pardo, 2014; Cambron et al, 2017). This memorandum was rescinded by the Trump administration (Office of the Attorney General, 2018), but minimum federal intervention was de facto continued, possibly owing to the severity of an 'opioid crisis' (Mead, 2019). At the time of writing, with a further change of administration to President Biden, there are signals that there may be a return to the previous Obama-era guidance (Radler, 2021). Additionally, a number of legislative bills have been submitted but there remain difficulties in getting these passed in the Senate (see, for example, the Marijuana Opportunity, Reinvestment and Expungement Act).

Nevertheless, developments in cannabis policy in the United States demonstrate the powerful role of government authorities and democratic processes at subnational level, not just in negotiating existing policy but also in driving forward local and national reforms. Complementing the earlier discussion of England & Wales and the Netherlands, this draws further attention to the dangers of assuming policy linearity and the structural mechanisms of the political environment by which divergence and policy change can emerge.

Japan

In contrast to the United States, but similar in some respects to England & Wales, Japan is a unitary state whose central organs of policy and legislative decision-making concerning policy related to cannabis command considerable control in comparison to subnational government authorities.

Strikingly, since Japan first introduced the Cannabis Control Act 1948, a result of the pressures exerted under the American occupation, the Act has remained largely untouched (Nagayoshi, 2019). Under this original law, alongside acts relating to cultivation, trafficking and supply, the possession of cannabis was made a criminal offence. A key contrast with legislation concerning other prohibited substances, however, is that the actual use of the substance was left out of the legislation. Even so, the Japanese government and its main organs – including the Ministry of Health, Labour and Welfare, the Ministry of Justice and the National Police Agency – have traditionally held a zero-tolerance stance on cannabis, with little to suggest that the official approach is anything other than active enforcement of criminal laws (Vaughn et al, 1995). Moreover, while self-reported cannabis use and recorded arrests have been very low since the Act came into effect, there is extreme sensitivity about even modest increases (Brewster, 2018a).

In recent years, as arrests for cannabis offences have increased, especially among younger people (National Police Agency, 2021), and with the shifting positions of supranational organizations, particularly in respect of medical cannabis, cannabis legislation in Japan has been drawn into the political spotlight. Since January 2021, there have been concrete signs of change in motion, with the Ministry of Health, Labour and Welfare forming an expert committee to consider revising the Cannabis Control Act. At the time of writing, two main proposals have surfaced: regulation of some medical forms of cannabis and criminalization of cannabis use (Ministry of Health, Labour and Welfare, 2021; The Mainichi, 2021).

That this policy process is primarily located in a national bureaucratic committee is not surprising; indeed, it is reflective of how most policy has been created in Japan from at least the post-war period. Notwithstanding some considerable shifts in the sociopolitical environment of Japan since the 1990s, which generated greater instability and somewhat eroded the previously high trust in elites, national bureaucrats still wield considerable resources in shaping the nature and content of policy reforms – even more, it has been argued, than democratically elected lawmakers (Tsurutani, 1998; Nakamura, 2002; Inatsugu, 2011).

Thus, once concrete proposals concerning cannabis law reform move up the bureaucratic ladder and are decided, these will almost certainly be passed into law by the Liberal Democratic Party, which has dominated the political landscape since its formation in 1955. At the time of writing, this is expected to happen sometime in 2022 (ATA-Net, 2021).

So where does this leave the subnational sphere in cannabis policy making in Japan? First, it is important to note that there has been, and still is, very little indication of a willingness to challenge the status quo. Since the 1950s, subnational authorities – largely in the form of prefectural and municipal governments, along with criminal justice, health and education bodies – have been key stakeholders in the provision of anti-drug policy efforts, particularly in respect of education and prevention (Vaughn et al, 1995). Indeed, one of the key elements of the Japanese government's success in maintaining a prohibitive regime has been the ability to enrol actors and agencies beyond central bodies into a scheme of cooperation. Thus, the normative positions on cannabis have historically been diffused and shared between national and local authorities, with the goal of eradication through criminal justice-based approaches remaining dominant. As such, Japanese prefectures and municipalities are willing participants in the prohibitive regime and continue to actively participate in anti-drug campaigns, the messaging of which has remained largely untouched for around four decades.

However, it is not simply a case of normative alignment between central and subnational authorities leading to low resistance or subversion. Rather than simply label everything under the umbrella of 'Japanese collectivism', we need to understand the mechanisms and relations of power that contribute to patterns of alignment (Brewster, 2020). Important in this regard is that prefectural and municipal authorities lack the resources necessary to do anything, even if they wanted to. Once the amendment to the Cannabis Control Act becomes national law, a directive will be given to subnational governing bodies, and they must obey this. In this sense, the relationship with central government concerning this policy area is largely top-down, with subnational authorities lacking the constitutional–legal resources required for variation.

This is further compounded by the organizational culture pervasive in bureaucratic organizations in Japan, in which strong hierarchical-based relations and frequent job transfers have a strong grip over individuals and their future career prospects (Inatsugu, 2011). In combination with a lack of organizational and financial resources at subnational level, such relations promote 'institutional isomorphism' rather than innovation (Edwards, 2016).

Thus, in many ways, the case of Japan reflects similar circumstances to those of England & Wales, but the space for adaptation, resistance and subversion at the subnational level is arguably more restricted, owing to the sorts of contingent relations that shape the interactions of policy actors.

Summary

This chapter has considered the nature of cannabis policy decision-making at a subnational level of governance, and it has illuminated the considerable potential for variation. A central point on the generation of variation concerns the 'constitutional-legal' resources available to policy actors at this level (Edwards and Hughes, 2012; Edwards, 2016). Contexts such as England & Wales and Japan exemplify environments where key decision-making in cannabis policy operates in a top-down manner, with subnational actors not possessing the requisite legal powers to challenge national legal statutes. In contrast, the discussion of the political systems of the Netherlands and the United States showed that where subnational authorities do possess sufficient constitutional-legal resources, the scope for negotiation, resistance and/or subversion of national policy, and the ability to introduce alternative bottom-up policies, is much larger.

Yet, crucially, even where subnational governors occupy a more submissive status in an asymmetrical relation with national governors, such a structured relation does not automatically result in a flat translation of national policy into the subnational sphere. Key differences in respect of the dispositional tendences of actors, organizational cultures and political relations between subnational and national levels have facilitated policy adaptation – in the case of England & Wales – or policy concordance – in the case of Japan.

Likewise, considerable differences exist between the Netherlands and the United States. In addition to those factors noted above, the availability of constitutional-legal resources also shapes or enhances other dynamics in cannabis policy. In the Netherlands, decision-making power is concentrated in the ruling municipal council, which in turn elevates the importance of political representation. The location of the majority of coffeeshops in municipalities represented by parties holding liberal and progressive positions provides a strong counter voice to any repressive policies emerging at the national level. This is further bolstered by the presence of non-elected decision makers, who are shielded from electoral pressures and anxieties. It is in this respect, to borrow a Dutch phrase, that 'the soup is never eaten as hot as it is served'. In contrast, the direct forms of democracy that are possible and often used in local cannabis policy reform in the United States mimic dynamics found at a national level, with public opinion and campaign support central components shaping decision-making.

Notwithstanding such differences, in the United States such mechanisms also have the potential to mellow out or even serve as the foundation to reform more punitive policies found at a national level. However, in either context we should be cautious in assuming this is always the case, for it is equally plausible that such relations of governance can facilitate shifts towards more punitive or illiberal policies.

What this chapter has alerted us to is how different contingent social relations, as well as the favoured dispositions and available resources of policy actors, can lead to very different outcomes in cannabis policy. Having explored different aspects of policy change across and within different contexts, we turn next to connect together these components and consider what this means for understanding and explaining convergence and divergence in cannabis policy.

8

Cultures of Cannabis Control

Introduction

What are the overall patterns in cannabis policy-making processes, and how can we understand and explain converging and diverging tendencies across different contexts? A key assumption underpinning assertions of a punitive turn in crime control is that late modern globalizing conditions are *necessarily* accompanied by convergence in issues and representations which are particularly favourable to non-adaptive policy processes.

Certainly, aspects such as technological advances, ease of cross-national movement, rapid knowledge transfer and political insecurity and instability have all contributed to similar shifts in the nature of cannabis-related acts, as well as in the environments in which policy is determined, across a number of contexts. However, what is clear from preceding chapters is that while there are degrees of similarity, there is also considerable variation both cross-nationally and between national and subnational levels of governance.

Through synthesizing the findings of previous chapters, this chapter first discusses policy processes in cannabis control in England & Wales and the Netherlands and then turns to consider what shapes such trends through examining the role of political institutions and relations of power. In each section, broader reflections from the other international cases that have been examined are also considered. In this way, the comparison identifies ways in which policy making is facilitated, resisted or reworked at national and subnational levels, and illuminates the contingently messy configurations of cannabis policy making which give rise to variegated cultures of control.

Policy processes in cannabis control

In the late 2000s, cannabis had taken on a number of shared problematizations across both England & Wales and the Netherlands, particularly in respect of public disorder, organized crime and mental health. In considering why these particular representations prevailed in these contexts, and how they came to be connected to more restrictive policy responses, we have to understand that problem recognition is not simply a reflection of an objective state of affairs, but involves coupling to moral and normative judgements in a vacuum of power struggles. The definition of a problem serves to diagnose and respond to behaviours in a way that accords with belief systems or which justifies further power and control of definition-givers (Freidson, 1970). This pertains not only to political imperatives, but also to the expressive beliefs of actors and 'bureau-rationalities' of organizational settings (Edwards and Hughes, 2012). In both countries, the dominant framing of cannabis problems was advanced by a series of loosely connected policy entrepreneurs who lobbied political actors to take action. Some of these individuals and organizations were more firmly aligned in the traditional political sense (for example, concerned constituents and lobby groups), while others coalesced around a common desire for change in pursuit of their own normative and organizational interests (for example, law enforcement, health professionals, municipal councils and media outlets).

In both England & Wales and the Netherlands, concerns with nuisance, public disorder, cultivation and organized crime were propelled onto political agendas, particularly by law enforcement agencies who were spending more time tackling these issues and were reporting a growing problem. Recognition of the existence of large-scale commercial *domestic* cultivation with links to organized networks came to represent an altogether different problem from that which preceded it; no longer did production exist only beyond the borders of these nation states – it had become deeply embedded within them.

This became coupled with fears surrounding the growing demand for cannabis, which was seen to be fuelling the increase of cultivation practices as well as leading to public disorder by users. In the Netherlands, the erosion of state borders following the creation of the Schengen Agreement and the EU facilitated the movement of vast numbers of individuals from neighbouring countries seeking a more "friendly climate"[1] for buying cannabis, in coffeeshops, than in their more hostile native countries. This led the authorities of those municipalities lying on the borders of Belgium and Germany to feel that they were suffering more from cannabis-related nuisance, and local mayors requested intervention from the national government. In England & Wales, especially given the heightened fears over antisocial behaviour in the early 2000s (see Hughes, 2007; Squires, 2008), the 2004 reclassification was perceived as a relaxation of the laws that led to a disrespect of police authority and an increase in public consumption.

As such, in both countries a strong narrative to emerge was that law enforcement agencies and local authorities were not adequately equipped to tackle the issues that had arisen in part from existing policy responses. For example, in England & Wales, the 2004 reclassification was projected as causing a loss of police authority to deal with increasing numbers of law-breaking cannabis users and as encouraging criminal entrepreneurs to cultivate cannabis in large-scale operations; in the Netherlands, not resolving the back door problem was seen as encouraging criminal entrepreneurs to take advantage of increased market demand.

As concerns over cannabis-related public disorder and criminality grew from the early 2000s on, this fused with a further (resurfaced) problem: the transformation of the perception of cannabis as a relatively harmless substance to one of a drug that is extremely dangerous for mental health, particularly in relation to young people. Psychiatric studies provided evidence of a link to schizophrenia, and these worries were amplified by health institutions being confronted by more people entering treatment and a connection to high-potency cannabis commonly found in domestic cultivation practices.

These commonalities are not surprising under globalized conditions, particularly in settings such as the EU. Research and knowledge networks facilitate a global exchange of ideas, techniques of data generation and monitoring are expedited through computerization, and communication has been made easier through the establishment of international bodies and agencies such as Interpol, the UNODC and the European Monitoring Centre for Drugs and Drug Addiction. The direction of travel is not balanced, however, with several Dutch interviewees (police and academics) suggesting that there had been a degree of "west wind"[2] knowledge transfer in crime control from the United Kingdom and the United States. Such patterns have been empirically observed elsewhere in the area of policing, with 'policy learning' between England & Wales and the Netherlands (Jones, 1995; Jones et al, 2009).

Arguably at the heart of constructing, cementing and further accentuating problem construction was the role of the media in criticizing the respective governments while also providing a voice to anti-cannabis groups who shared powerful and emotional experiences. In England & Wales, the national tabloid press – particularly those of a Right-leaning persuasion – held considerable influence in shaping political agendas and debates. While it can be suggested that the Dutch media are far less dramatic than the British, similar pressures are being faced to produce dramatic, newsworthy stories at a time marked by declining print press circulation and increased competition from digital outlets. This has a discernible impact on how problems are represented, as local concerns become extrapolated to become 'everyone's problem' (Garland, 2001: 86). In this sense, coffeeshop-related nuisance and the relationship to criminal organizations became generalized to cover all coffeeshops in all municipalities, and the perception of damaging harm came to be present in every cannabis consumer.

The issues surrounding criminal justice, public disorder and health became all the more alarming in the public domain due to the fact that cannabis was the most widely used illegal drug. The threat was constructed as not only lying in the margins of society with undeserving social undesirables, but also permeating social strata in a perceptively widespread manner. Moreover, in several ways, this also drew on and cemented historical racialized narratives about the role of 'outsiders' in illegal drug markets. The effect of the emergence and projection of these problematizations contributed to a "negative societal feeling"[3] in both countries, which grew from the early 2000s.

Yet, while some problems may have an objective reality to them and were supported by research evidence – millions of people were crossing the border to buy cannabis in the Netherlands; domestic cultivation had increased; cannabis does have the potential to seriously affect the brains of young people – this did not necessitate a determined course of action. Rather, why the problems took root and resulted in more restrictive measures is connected to the nature of the policy-making environment and how they coalesced with the expressive value systems of national political actors in power in these contexts. This reaffirms the notion that evidence is often used by political actors in ways which fit with their dispositional tendencies and policy agendas (Stevens, 2007; Lenton and Allsop, 2010).

In both jurisdictions, patterns of political representation over the past few decades suggest a shift towards the political Right, which has granted a more influential space for moral authoritarian arguments to gain traction in responses to cannabis. Such shifts in both jurisdictions are vital to understanding why particular narratives came to dominate the debate. The notion that cannabis use is a threat to the moral order and must be firmly responded to through criminal justice measures is, of course, by no means new in cannabis policy, having been a constant feature since the earliest formations of national and international control frameworks (see Chapter 2). Nevertheless, a reinvigorated and reconstituted understanding of cannabis-related acts as immoral was facilitated through the social, legal and medical harms that had been attributed to it during the 2000s.

Problems were constructed in a way that promoted criminal justice institutions as a logical device through which to re-establish social order. In this vein, the problem was not one resulting from prohibitive conditions, but one which could be resolved by them. This was legitimated by a self-justifying circular argument often made by political actors: the illegality of cannabis is premised on notions of harm, and notions of harm are confirmed by virtue of its illegality. As more objective assessments have aptly demonstrated, however, the connection between drug harms and legal status is a fallacy (Nutt et al, 2007; Nutt et al, 2010). Nonetheless, it serves to disguise the more subtle and embedded moral judgements which underpin modes of control.

Moral imperatives, then, were heavily enmeshed in processes of defining cannabis use as a form of medical deviance. As Conrad and Schneider

(1992: 1) note, 'deviant behaviors that were once defined as immoral, sinful, or criminal have been given medical meanings … in many cases medical treatments have become a new form of punishment and social control'. However, it is not just that the renewed focus on links between cannabis and mental health was accompanied with increased activities to diagnose and treat; research evidence of these connections was used by political actors in a way that complemented and reaffirmed the legal separation of cannabis from other substances.

Medical concerns that have emerged about cannabis over the past two decades have mainly focused on schizophrenia, but there has been growing emphasis at the political level on the link between young people, cannabis and deviancy, which reflects a degree of biological determinism. This centres problematic behaviour around the psychopharmacological effects of cannabis, with reduced attention paid to wider social structures and developments that may also contribute to problematic behaviour. In this sense, political actors employ 'criminologies of the other' to frame social abnormalities as a cause of cannabis use (Garland 1996, 2001): the danger of the foreign substance in the pure body which triggers the onset of socially deviant behaviours and deteriorates the moral order.

However, it is not necessarily the case that political actors are fundamentally committed to notions of drug taking as immoral and to repressive measures as the solution – indeed, most politicians in England & Wales have privately recognized the ineffectiveness of prohibitive approaches (UK Drug Policy Commission, 2012) – but that the performance of such public positions are largely believed to be the only tenable ones for politicians who are competing over key contested voting populations in an environment favouring law and order approaches.

In both England & Wales and the Netherlands, political volatility and ambivalence concerning issues of crime, security and disorder have generated heightened pressure to assume a punitive stance on cannabis policy through non-adaptive strategies of control. In this sense, the triggering of a sense of crisis by vocal policy communities not only resonated with the sorts of expressive beliefs about drug taking dominantly held by those in political office but was also met with 'punitive display' in order to demonstrate to key segments of the electorate the capabilities of governors in protecting these citizens from a series of threats which cannabis was seen to pose.

Such dynamics become particularly heightened with changes in administration, which often provide key windows of opportunity for policy change to occur (Kingdon, 1995). In England & Wales, New Labour reacted to the perceived mistake of their own earlier decision to reclassify cannabis to Class C. When Gordon Brown came to power, he had a political desire to demarcate himself from Tony Blair, which, in addition to his religious and moral values, appealed to the critical voters from conservative middle England who had been so vocal in objecting to the downgrading of cannabis.

Similarly, in the Netherlands, the VVD and the CDA appear to have taken a more repressive stance concerning cannabis and criminality in a context where 'grey' responses, such as the tolerance policy, are increasingly unpopular. The success of the extreme political Right, particularly Geert Wilders' PVV, in the areas of crime control and immigration has generated greater volatility and competition for voters in an increasingly politicized environment with political parties keen to demonstrate their law and order credentials. While the issue of coffeeshop policy has not been a central theme in this overall development, cannabis became an important symbolic issue in which battles for political legitimacy were to be won (or lost).

Alongside convergence in terms of political feasibility and the desirability of selecting more repressive measures to project a sense of authority in dealing with perceived problems, another point of similarity in the selection of more repressive policy measures can be found in the technical feasibility of policy proposals.

Since the Netherlands departed from the global and European norm in the 1970s, the pressure to come back in line with surrounding countries has been a constant presence in policy debates. Again, this is particularly relevant given the geography of the Netherlands and the impact of relatively easy cross-border movements. The 2012–13 changes to cannabis policy attest to such pressures by trying to close the market off from non-Dutch residents, which in turn would relieve accusations that the coffeeshops supply cannabis to neighbouring countries. Moreover, European and domestic legislation was cited as a reason behind the introduction of *national* measures (the residency and closed club criteria) while also rationalizing the blocking of more liberalizing options. In England & Wales too the consideration of policy alternatives took place within the existing parameters of the Misuse of Drugs Act. When asked to review the classification issue, the ACMD was tasked only with looking at what class cannabis should be in, and so alternatives which went beyond the model of prohibition were automatically filtered out.

These descriptions show how the problem and policy streams became coupled with the political stream and took policy in a specific direction; a direction which, in both jurisdictions, facilitated the need and desire for governments to project an image of paternalistic protector from a reconstructed threat.

However, while the political environments in England & Wales and the Netherlands may have garnered support for moral authoritarian positions on cannabis, this should not be taken to suggest that rival positions do not exist or that they do not also feature in policy processes. A major point of divergence in policy-making processes between these two countries was the degree of influential counter-voices in conceptualizing and responding to policy problems. While it would be unfair to suggest that there was little or no reaction from opponents of the 2009 reclassification in England & Wales,[4] the impact of such protests was largely in vain and did not impact in any meaningful way on the policy-making process. However, in the Netherlands a sustained resistance against the planned measures from various sectors of society ultimately contributed to a revisiting of the issue and the relaxing of the initial rules. Later, we explore what made it possible for policy actors in the Netherlands to more meaningfully challenge national policy than those in England & Wales; for now, it suffices to identify other ways that issues of cannabis were problematized and what sort of values underpinned this. In particular, two tendencies broadly falling under the disposition of social justice can be identified as important in the Dutch case: liberal pragmatism and social liberalism.

First, it is important to stress that liberal pragmatism and social liberalism are not unique to the Netherlands; there is also evidence of such positions in cannabis policy processes in England & Wales. For example, the Wootton Report and momentum for reform in the late 1960s was very much driven by ideals of social liberalism (Seddon, 2020). Moreover, the 2004 reclassification from Class B to Class C demonstrated the triumph of liberally pragmatic values over competing dispositions (Monaghan, 2011). Nevertheless, such episodes have been relatively few, and certainly what followed in cannabis policy in England & Wales is indicative of the lack of resources and influence that actors holding such dispositions have had to advance their goals.

In contrast, liberal pragmatism has been a prominent feature not just of cannabis policy but across a range of contentious policy spheres in the Netherlands, connected to its social, cultural and political history (see Chapter 3). With coffeeshops in existence for four decades prior to the proposed policy changes and with overall patterns of consumption comparable to other Western countries during this period (MacCoun and Reuter, 1997, 2001; Room et al, 2008; European Monitoring Centre for Drugs and Drug Addiction, 2014), there remains continued support for the role of coffeeshops, which are seen to fulfil their intended purpose of separating soft and hard drug markets. This market separation philosophy is underpinned by a liberal pragmatic disposition; in other words, it is accepted that people, especially younger people, may experiment with illegal drugs and it is therefore preferable to provide suitable conditions in which they are able to purchase and use cannabis without being exposed to the dangers of other, more dangerous, illegal drugs. Thus, although cannabis may have taken on new and renewed negative meanings, it is still demarcated from other illegal drugs. Second, while the political environment may have become more volatile and favourable to 'sovereign state' strategies of control, antiauthoritarian strands of social liberalism retain a strong influence in many parts of the country. In this sense, policy measures that were perceived as an overreach of central government's power in relation to the civil liberties of citizens became deeply contested.

These values continue to underpin widespread support for the coffeeshop system, most strongly emanating from national political parties such as D'66, the PvdA and GroenLinks, the larger urban municipal councils, civil servants in the Ministry of Health, Welfare and Sport, scientific experts and, of course, coffeeshop owners and users. Even actors within criminal justice organizations, stretching from the Ministry of Justice and Security to the Public Prosecutor's Office and police agencies, continue to recognize the benefits of the market separation policy. In this latter respect, even though such organizations have often been at the forefront of advocating for stricter measures, this appears to be born out of frustration over the lack of a conclusive solution to the weaknesses in existing policy, which has generated problems of crime and disorder rather than a fervent desire to eradicate coffeeshops entirely. It is this breadth of influential policy actors with liberally pragmatic and socially liberal values that provided a strong counter-voice against policies which threatened the separation of markets philosophy.

Looking beyond the cases of England & Wales and the Netherlands, concerns of public disorder, criminality and mental health are by no means unique, with changes in the use, supply and production of cannabis intimately connected to developments in technology, communication, mobility and broader sociocultural transformations which have been felt to similar degrees in many advanced countries. These have both challenged and exerted strains on pre-existing modes of control and generated opportunities for innovation within an unregulated illegal drug market (Decorte and Potter, 2015).

Yet, even where there are similarities in recognized problems – such as the dangers posed by organized crime in the black market or connections between youth cannabis use and mental health – it has become clear that there exists a range of alternative values which have underpinned movements away from punitive modes of cannabis control.

In contexts where there have been movements towards depenalization, decriminalization or legal regulation over the past decade, 'successful' discourses have been aligned around a social justice disposition; in other words, prohibitive approaches, contrary to their intentions, have failed to protect the health and safety of individuals and have encroached on fundamental rights. Thus, whether it be attempts to regulate CSCs in the autonomous regions of Spain, the decriminalization of possession and cultivation in the ACT or legalization in Canada, notions of social justice have underpinned policy reforms.

Given recent social movements, such as the internationally influential Black Lives Matter, it is clear that a dispositional tendency towards social justice in matters of public safety and public health has also coalesced in other issues. As we saw particularly with the cases of Jamaica, New Zealand and parts of the United States, growing attention has been paid to the discriminatory effects of prohibitive cannabis control measures on Indigenous peoples and ethnic minorities.

Moreover, in contexts where cannabis use has remained relatively high, this sense of failure is not constructed only in terms of the harms or injustice to individuals, but also as one of economic wastefulness. In other words, prohibitive approaches are seen as having been enormously costly, and there has been little indication that they result in the desired outcome of reducing use (see, for example, Legislative Assembly for the Australian Capital Territory, 2018a). Certainly, it is difficult to detach the growing political credibility of views from a broader 'sustainable development' agenda, which has become prominent following the 2008 global economic crisis.

Related to but also somewhat distinct from notions of fiscal waste, a further disposition that has been an important driving force in some recent cannabis policy reforms is that of economic liberalism. This is hardly a new position to take in the sphere of drugs control, not least given that most of the world's colonial powers in the late 19th century and early 20th century were at the forefront of economic gain in international drug markets. Yet the reason why this has become influential in policy reform advocacy in recent years is arguably because it sidesteps questions of morality which have dogged cannabis policy debates, instead highlighting the benefits that legal regulation brings to tax revenues. It is perhaps this aspect which, again in the broader context of economic instability over the past decade, has made the economic rationale for policy reform influential across the political spectrum. This has manifested most strongly in the United States, arguably the most fervent advocate of free market capitalism, but it has also become a prominent line of argument in many other contexts too.

Thus, while particular problematizations of cannabis, the political environments they thrive in, and the non-adaptive policy responses that they drive may be a prominent feature of cannabis policy in late modern societies, they are by no means determined, nor do they prevent the flourishing of alternatives in policy processes.

Political institutions and relations of power

Building on this, we now seek to explain why some crime control strategies are more 'successful' than others, and the ways in which these manifest in policy processes. In particular, we consider the nature of political institutions and the relations of governing they give rise to which enable or frustrate policy actors in advancing their policy agendas. Here, we examine two spheres through which power traverses and is negotiated and performed: the national level of governance and the subnational level of governance.

National governing relations

Clearly, the sorts of values and motivations of political parties and policy actors is shaped by the particular social and cultural context in which they exist. As noted already, similar shocks in the social, economic and political environments in both England & Wales and the Netherlands generated electoral anxiety, political volatility and voter mobility. Such shifts have arguably generated a favourable space for the flourishing of non-adaptive strategies of crime control. However, their manifestation in the policy realm is also further shaped by political structures.

In brief, under the Dutch system of proportional representation, multiple political parties are necessarily involved in government administrations. This system ensures that those in government hold different positions on policy issues and, as such, necessitates a need to generate agreement in order to form a governing coalition. Thus, even if a 'politics of consensus' has deteriorated in spirit in the Netherlands (see Chapter 3), it continues to be reproduced through the structured actions of political actors who have to compromise in order to govern. In contrast, the adversarial style of politics of England & Wales has been dominated by two major parties with, ordinarily, one party forming the government and the other forming the opposition. This system lends itself to a style of governing whereby the ruling party is ordinarily able to push through its preferred policies without having to negotiate with the opposition, and it grants a greater level of policy influence to senior political actors such as the prime minister.

These dynamics are important when considering the dispositions towards cannabis policy. In the Netherlands is a long history of political parties supporting a range of policy positions. While there has been increased politicization around issues of law and order, this has not marginalized liberal perspectives on cannabis, but rather has led to greater polarization between those supporting more liberalization and those supporting repression. Indeed, spells of voter dissatisfaction towards the traditional centrist parties have provided a space for smaller parties on both sides of the political spectrum – from the Right-wing populist PVV to the social liberal D'66 – to make gains and participate in governments.

In the Westminster political system, the historical dominance of criminal justice dispositions and the vulnerability to accusations of being soft on crime have produced competition for who can claim to be the party of law and order. This political competition between two main parties that have never taken contraposing positions to prohibitive cannabis control frameworks severely weakens the potential for alternative positions to penetrate the debate. Accordingly, political debates concerning cannabis and illegal drug policy are narrow, with both the Conservative Party and the Labour Party sharing broadly similar positions. Indicatively, the legislation relating to the

2009 reclassification – the Misuse of Drugs Act (Amendment) Order – passed through the House of Commons with 76.3 per cent of the House supporting the motion, and only six MPs from the Conservative and Labour parties rebelled (see House of Commons, 2008b).

In comparison to the Netherlands, where the power to govern is diffused among several parties and parties that hold a range of positions on cannabis have greater scope to enter government, the adversarial style of politics in England & Wales accentuates the pressure on the two main parties. Under these conditions, so long as the ruling government commands the confidence of its own party, the need of the core executive to give consideration to the desires of other political parties is limited. Nevertheless, this generates greater susceptibility to the influence of media-driven concerns, knee-jerk reactions and policy reversals. Expertise is more likely to be utilized where it is seen to progress ideological and political goals, but it can also be readily discarded (Stevens, 2007; Lenton and Allsop, 2010). This was very clearly the case with the 2009 reclassification, where the decision to reclassify had seemingly been determined prior to seeking advice, as is statutorily required, from the ACMD.

Similar political behaviour can also be found in the Netherlands, with incident-driven events focusing policy concerns and short sound bites entering the political lexicon. However, the shift does not appear to be as extreme, or to have unfolded in the same ways, as in England & Wales. In the Netherlands, the political environment has changed significantly since the post-war peak of consociational democracy, with greater movement of parties in and out of government (see Chapter 3), and while it is often the case that there is continuity of parties across coalitions, it is also possible that in a subsequent coalition an incoming party will hold a contrasting position to an incumbent. So, although alignments around criminal justice-oriented dispositions may be found at particular moments, these do not automatically dominate the political landscape in other ruling administrations as has largely been the case in England & Wales. Indicatively, while Rutte I (2010–12) represented a Right-leaning cabinet made up of the VVD and the CDA, supported by the PVV, Rutte II (2012–17) brought back political balance between the VVD and the PvdA. The subsequent cabinet, Rutte III (2017–21), was represented by three Right-leaning parties – the VVD, the CDA and CU – while also including the socially liberal D'66.

Arising from these dynamics is a broad understanding that to completely reverse policy is counterproductive, ensuring a more incremental style of policy making rather than the quick policy reversals that often occur in England & Wales. However, it is important to remember that this need to find a working consensus, often across polarized parties, has also produced problems of governing. Polarization on policy issues – with cannabis being a prime example – has made it incredibly difficult to find agreement. It is this which has contributed to stagnation in national policy development and reform, with discussions surrounding problems of nuisance and organized crime continuing since the early 1990s.

Yet at the same time, consensus-building provides a more important role for expert advice, which can provide the glue to governing and act as a buffer against populist-driven pressures. Where decisions are difficult to make, commissions provide legitimacy in decision-making through pragmatic advice that enables parties to move from their original starting points. This role of expertise in the Netherlands, with most of the key recommendations of the Dutch commissions adopted, provides a striking point of difference to the role of expertise in the 2009 reclassification in England & Wales.

Consequently, processes of consensus-building in the Netherlands require careful negotiation and time, often stretching over different coalitions. Over the four years from the announcement of plans to revise *gedoogbeleid* in 2009 to the actual introduction of national measures in 2013, three coalition governments and five political parties were in power. Contrast that with the 18 months it took the Labour Party to expeditiously reverse its own decision on cannabis classification in England & Wales.

Moreover, the recommendations of Baan and Hulsman from the late 1960s that Dutch drugs policy should allow for local experiments are still followed. The trialling of some coffeeshop measures, as opposed to mandatory national implementation, facilitated debate over the advantages, disadvantages and effects of the measures, providing a space for competing dispositions on the problem to surface and for contested elements to be addressed. It this component which has since allowed for advances in regulation of the back door through cannabis cultivation trials, again using an expert commission (Advisory Committee Experiment Closed Cannabis Chain, 2018).

It is clear from this discussion that contextual differences in democratic institutions play a central role in shaping the power of political actors to govern in cannabis policy and the opportunities for non-political actors, such as the media and expert advisors, to influence the direction of policy (Brewster, 2017).

Further to this, it is also necessary to consider power relations in respect of responsible government departments and auxiliary organizations who are involved in the oversight and development of policy, and the sorts of opportunities this provides these actors to advance their goals.

In both England & Wales and the Netherlands, owing to the illegal status of acts relating to cannabis, responsibilities for governing cannabis-related problems are *necessarily* tied to government departments and statutory organizations relating to criminal justice. In England & Wales, the Home Office has a firm and leading position in drugs policy, with, inter alia, police forces – represented through the National Police Chiefs' Council (formerly the ACPO) – being key players in policy debates. Of course, considering the way in which the UK government blindsided the ACPO in the 2004 downward reclassification decision, their support cannot be said to be a precondition for policy change. Nevertheless, the ACPO's broad welcoming of the 2009 reclassification – which would see increased powers available for policing cannabis offences – coalesced with the government's push for reform.

This is not to ignore other departments that are involved in drug policy, but it is clear that policy is driven through a criminal justice lens in a notoriously stringent state department which holds most of the power. The implication of this is that cannabis policy (and wider drugs policy) is constrained within a narrow tunnel vision dominated by actors and organizations which tend to hold law and order dispositions, with little space for alternative dispositions to meaningfully impact policy processes.

Developments in the Netherlands indicate that the Ministry of Justice and Security has become an important voice in directing cannabis policy. In relation to the 2012–13 changes, for example, Minister Opstelten was a domineering force who was at the forefront of debates and pushed forward policy movements. Moreover, similar to England & Wales, policing organizations, such as the Taskforce on Organized Cannabis Cultivation, played an important role in legitimating criminal justice policy concerns.

Nevertheless, while criminal justice involvement may reflect a necessary relation of governing regimes in which cannabis is prohibited under legal statutes, in the Netherlands there is much greater diffusion of power and responsibility owing to the existence of historically shaped contingent relations which provide greater opportunities for actors advocating rival dispositions to challenge, resist and subvert punitive tendencies. Principally, this refers to the responsibilization of the Ministry of Health, Welfare and Sport in cannabis policy. This is also reflected in the way the *gedoogbeleid* empowers the Public Prosecutor's Office while removing police interference in coffeeshop issues in the first instance. In these departments, policy actors command a powerful voice in raising objections to policies. This was seen in the case of the resident criterion, with those in the Ministry of Health, Welfare and Sport strongly arguing that this would destroy the separation of markets and be counterproductive to public health goals. In this way, coffeeshop policy is afforded some protection from a pure criminal justice lens by the nature of organizational relations and responsibilities, which empower a range of policy actors – who hold rival dispositions – within policy-making processes (Brewster, 2017).

Nevertheless, we must be careful about making blanket assertions about the relationship between systems of democratic governance and organizational relations to policy processes. If we turn to consider the above findings in the context of developments from other democratic settings from across the world, a more complicated picture emerges. For example, a system of proportional representation does not in itself facilitate a form of governing by consensus across different parties. In Uruguay, while the legislative branch of government is based on proportional representation, the core executive is appointed by a directly elected president. This places far greater power in the hands of the country's leader, which became evident in the instrumental role of President Mujica and his inner circle in the 2013 legalization reforms (Cruz et al, 2016; Queirolo, 2020). Additionally, legalization reform was achieved in Canada, a country whose governance is historically based on a Westminster system and dominated by two large parties. The experiences of both these countries demonstrate the potential for governments to push through liberal policy change even in the face of political and public opposition (Fischer et al, 2020). Finally, we ought to be careful in assuming that where drug policy is positioned as the primary remit of a health or welfare-based government department, this will serve as a counterforce to punitive shifts. For example, in Japan the primary responsibility for drug policy lies in the Ministry of Health, Labour and Welfare, but this ministry has been among the leading advocates of a strict zero-tolerance approach (Vaughn et al, 1995).

What this suggests, then, is that we can only understand the role of structural political institutions and organizational relations in the sociocultural and historical context in which they exist and according to the sorts of dispositions which have prevailed within such settings.

Subnational governing relations

The above line of argument, that differences in structurally and culturally shaped political institutions and organizational relations are central in accounting for the existence of variegated cultures of control, is further bolstered when comparing how policy responses have developed within the subnational sphere.

In the subnational case sites that were empirically examined in England & Wales and the Netherlands, social democratic values remained fairly consistent over time. Such values influenced how cannabis policy (and substance misuse policy) has evolved, with both sites seeking an approach that reduces stigma and harm to marginalized groups while also improving health outcomes. However, differences in the constitutional-legal resources of governing actors in the two jurisdictions generated differentiated abilities to resist, rework and subvert policy (Brewster, 2017).

Subnational governance in the United Kingdom has been described as 'hypercentralized' in comparison to European norms (Loughlin, 2001; House of Commons, 2009), with a history of distrust between central and local governments (Chandler, 2001). Although local authorities have degrees of autonomy in respect of cannabis policy, especially when considering the devolved powers of health in Welsh responses to substance misuse and the operational independence of the police, this is largely a *distribution* of responsibility rather than *power* to govern. In the Welsh setting, policy can be differentiated from the broader UK drugs strategy, but decisions still take place within the parameters of a broader prohibitive structure imposed by the UK government, with little official movement beyond this possible. Moreover, findings suggest there is little desire to rock the boat in this area, given the desires to establish broader political legitimacy. In this context, cannabis policy falls prey to the same fears and political pressures that exist in the wider UK context, with Welsh politicians unable and unwilling to look beyond prescribed policy alternatives (see Brewster and Jones, 2019).

However, in the Netherlands, structural empowerment grants significant powers to municipal councils and mayors in determining local cannabis policy. In this context, local political representation is more relevant, not only in the translation of policy from national to local spheres but also in the role of the local in challenging national policy formation. This is not to suggest that local representation *necessarily* causes resistance to national policy measures, but rather that powers located in particular geohistorical contexts present opportunities to rework policy in unique ways (Edwards and Hughes, 2005).

The relationship between subnational authorities and central government during the period of policy change that was examined is of central importance in this regard. In the Netherlands, most of the largest municipalities, which contain the vast majority of the coffeeshops, were led by PvdA mayors and municipal councils. This, combined with the fact that the PvdA became a national coalition partner, created political pressure for Minister for Justice and Security Ivo Opstelten, from the VVD, to be more flexible with the new arrangements. For example, the school distance criterion, which did not originate from any tangible municipal concern, but was based more on symbolism and ideology, was rescinded following pressure from municipalities arguing that it would lead to the closure of most coffeeshops – an effect which would be unwelcome in most urbanized municipalities, where the role of coffeeshops is valued.

Here, it is relevant that larger municipalities have more influence than others; so while policy responses are contingently related to political representation at the local level, the ability to rework policy is also related to the size and geopolitical power of municipal authorities. The local case site in question, Utrecht, is a major city – one of the big four – and also has dominant Left-wing political representation. It is these facets that granted Utrecht more influence in shaping the debates on the new coffeeshop measures and which continue to serve as a springboard for propelling concerns and alternative responses into the political sphere, such as with regulated cultivation.

The prominent role of some mayors in the larger cities, who often have political experience at the national level, places more bargaining power in their hands. This is further bolstered by the detachment of important key players at the local level from electoral anxieties and pressures. For example, executive power rests with the College of Mayor and Alderpersons, which consists of appointed individuals who are separate from the directly elected municipal council.

While the analysis of England & Wales indicated that the framing of substance misuse in Wales may be a factor in facilitating the diversion of police resources away from individual cannabis users and subverting overly punitive policy responses, it is not clear whether such patterns exist in other subnational spheres. The waters become muddied in England & Wales given the apparent lack of governance capabilities in this area, whereas in the Netherlands there can be greater certainty that political representation at the subnational level is an important mechanism. When triggered (in this case by counterproductive national policy), the authority and power granted to the municipal level can react and rework national policy in a more meaningful way than is possible in England & Wales (Brewster, 2017).

Reflecting on these differences between England & Wales and the Netherlands, it might be tempting to assert that liberal, adaptive-style policy reform is more likely where subnational contexts have increased powers. However, is this always the case?

Considering the other cases examined in this book, despite tougher stances adopted by national authorities, there are certainly solid indications that where there is freedom to experiment at a subnational level, this has been instrumental in contributing to depenalization, decriminalization and legal regulation reforms. For example, in Spain, proposals to regulate CSCs originated in the governments of autonomous regions rather than at the national level (Arana and Pares, 2020). Similarly, it was the ACT Government, rather than the national government, that took forward cannabis policy reform in Australia (Hughes, 2020). And within the United States, the ability of individual states to change policy by popular democratic vote has clearly been vital (Pardo, 2014; Mosher and Akins, 2020; Obradovic, 2021). In contrast, and somewhat similar to England & Wales, the lack of constitutional-legal, organizational and financial resources in Japan has been extremely effective in preventing alternative problematizations and policy proposals to emerge in prefectural governments.

Nevertheless, the 'policy retraction' in Western Australia is a reminder that subnational movement towards liberalizing policies doesn't necessarily happen (Hughes, 2020), and just because contemporary currents may be moving towards such policy frameworks, the possibility of more punitive policies being introduced in the future is not ruled out. This suggests that national–subnational relations are contingent in policy reform. In other words, where subnational authorities possess the requisite resources to govern, this elevates the role they may play but does not guarantee a particular policy direction. This reaffirms the importance of considering the configuration of these relations in respect of other contingent relations and conditions.

While the discussion here draws attention to core differences in the abilities of actors at subnational level, it is important to consider another aspect of policy – 'structured ambivalence' (Garland, 2001) – which results in more adaptive, pragmatic responses in policy on the ground (Shiner, 2015; Brewster, 2018b). In both England & Wales and the Netherlands, national policy talk of key politicians, Opstelten and Brown, surrounding the policy changes was deeply expressive, assertive, and protective. Examples include Brown's suggestion that skunk was 'lethal' (BBC News, 2008) and Opstelten's sustained sound bites on the need to 'attack' and 'combat' criminality. However, the actual policy decisions had very little impact on the problematized populations. In England & Wales, the reclassification made *no* change to how young people were policed – as it further cemented a system of out-of-court disposals for dealing with adult cannabis users – and the notion of reclassifying for 'policing priorities' was a bit of a misnomer given police forces already had operational discretion in how resources could be directed. In the Netherlands, the three coffeeshop measures were reduced to one, the school distance criterion. This was then given flexibility in its application at the local level: while the school distance criterion aimed to add 100 metres to most existing practices, coffeeshops were already largely abiding by the well-ingrained criterion not to allow admission to those under 18 years (see de Bruin et al, 2008). Moreover, while there were significant policy concerns over large-scale cultivation, the actual measures did little to effectively address these problems. Although the idea behind closing off supply from non-Dutch residents had a rational basis in reducing coffeeshop-related nuisance, it ignored the national police's own estimations that 48–97 per cent of cannabis is exported (van der Giessen et al, 2014).

Responses to cannabis in contexts where use is relatively high are necessarily conditioned by a realization that to be overly repressive would create serious administrative burdens, and as a result there is a pragmatic adjustment by control agencies working within available parameters. Thus, the construction of cannabis as a danger sits alongside the implicit acceptance of cannabis use in contemporary society, reflecting, in Garland's (2001) terms, a policy predicament in how to respond.

The sheer volume of cannabis users presents a set of administrative burdens in the application of repressive legislation. It is wholly unforeseeable that every one of the estimated 2.6 million past-year users in England & Wales could be caught, processed and given a custodial sentence given that the current prison population of almost 79,000 is at 97.8 per cent of useable operational capacity (Office for National Statistics, 2020; Ministry of Justice, 2021). Similarly, the prospect of the Dutch relinquishing the coffeeshop system in favour of enforced criminalization would create a whole host of additional burdens, not only on the courts and prison system but also with police forces having to tackle increased dealing and possession offences.

Contemporary responses to cannabis within prohibitive regimes have to take account of this predicament, and in some ways the policy decisions represent an adaptation to the situation by either managing risks and threats or through minimal changes to practice. There appears to be an implicit acceptance of the inability of law enforcement agencies to eradicate the problem, but this occurs within a broader symbolic stamp that the national government is acting on the problem, thus evidencing a simultaneous degree of denial and acting out (Garland, 2001). Such a relation of 'hypocrisy' allows different spheres to orient themselves to different audiences and mandates; politicians can talk tough, and practitioners can pragmatically adjust (Brunsson, 1993; Brewster, 2018b).

The overall picture suggests patterns of convergent divergence (Levi-Faur and Jordana, 2005) in that subnational spheres of governance demonstrate degrees of divergence from the more punitive responses initiated at a national level. In some regards, this is a necessary component of policy making in any society; the national level exists in an abstract reality, removed from the everyday realities of policy problems, and is required to formulate broad responses across diverse settings. The local level, meanwhile, is firmly rooted in concrete situations and encounters a set of issues in relation to how to actually implement measures and react to situations that arise.

Summary

Overall, developments in cannabis policy in England & Wales and the Netherlands exhibit several common features suggestive of convergence under late modern conditions. Primarily, the political environment in which decisions are made has become more politicized, more volatile and more ambivalent. In turn, this has generated a space in which moral authoritarian dispositions, and non-adaptive strategies of control, are dominant in the attempts of political actors to respond to cannabis problems. Nevertheless, it is evident that such a political environment does not *necessitate* such problem constructions and response types, and neither does it result in homogeneous policy processes, with a series of relations and conditions existing at national and subnational levels which have been found to support, resist and rework policy in uneven ways. The result of these dynamics, in the case of England & Wales and the Netherlands, has been that the latter has been able to mitigate punitive forces in a more meaningful way than the former. Moreover, looking at other cases from across the globe, similar social phenomena are being constructed as problems in a variety of different ways with an increasing number of jurisdictions advancing adaptive alternatives to punitive control frameworks. Often, the sorts of problematizations and policy proposals that underpin such movements are not new; but they have found suitable windows of opportunity to gain traction in their respective political environments.

In making sense of the contemporary landscape of cannabis policy, it is the dispositions of policy actors, the abilities they have to advance their agendas, and how these components are structurally and culturally shaped within particular social and historical contexts which are key to understanding the flourishing of variegated cultures of control.

9

Conclusions and Future Directions

Introduction

The contemporary control of cannabis reflects a myriad of rapidly changing policy responses. If it was even possible to speak of a broad convergence and consensus around the use of prohibitive regimes throughout the 20th century, developments in the 21st century certainly bring such an assertion into question. In some contexts, prohibitive frameworks have been renewed and strengthened, while in a growing number of others, these have been diluted by depenalization or decriminalization reforms or else entirely replaced by legal regulation.

In order to better understand why this is the case, grasping the processes by which such responses have manifested is clearly vital. As such, the aim of this book was to explore inter- and intra-national policy convergence and divergence in cannabis control, and how similarities and differences in policy-making processes may be best understood and explained.

Principally, this was based on an empirical study of two advanced liberal democracies in Western Europe – England & Wales and the Netherlands – whose recent policy changes, prima facie, appeared to show similarities in the employment of non-adaptive strategies of control. This was further supported by drawing on a range of contrasting cases from around the world, which, overall, have exhibited what could be broadly thought of as adaptive-style reforms.

In this final chapter, we consider the main arguments set forth in the book in the context of their implications for cultures of control, cannabis policy making and criminology, before finishing with a reflection on the methodological approach that underpinned the empirical research and a consideration of future directions in comparative criminology.

Cultures of control, cannabis policy making and criminology

David Garland's *The Culture of Control* was heavily criticized for underplaying the influence of different national and local political institutions and cultures, and for failing to recognize the fundamental messiness, unpredictability and contestation involved in the policy-making process (Matthews, 2002; Young, 2002; Edwards and Hughes, 2005; Tonry, 2009). These critiques are relevant not just to this work, but arguably more so to those who have overly concentrated on the punitive turn, with a dominant assumption of these 'criminologies of catastrophe' that globalizing late modern conditions are necessarily accompanied by convergence around ever more restrictive and punitive policy responses (O'Malley, 2000). The problem then, as Garland himself recognizes, was the lack of consideration paid towards the 'non-punitive modes of managing crime that these deep transformations make possible' (2004: 170). As such, the challenge put forth was to examine how different societies have 'adapted and reacted to the new risks, insecurities and opportunities inherent in the social organization of everyday life under late modern conditions' (Garland, 2004: 179–80).

In both England & Wales and the Netherlands, changes to cannabis policy around the late 2000s and early 2010s prima facie indicated a toughening stance, and there are several points which do appear to indicate convergence in control cultures. Cannabis has undergone a series of transformations that have been similarly problematized in terms of criminal justice, public disorder, health and morality. Moreover, how such societies have attempted to understand such risks also indicates convergence; more professionalized and skilled law enforcement bodies, an ever-present need to diagnose social problems as medical issues and the renewal of quasi-religious moral arguments have all shaped what counts as a problem and provide ready-made solutions for its remedy.

How problems have been constructed is also connected to the political environment of policy making at the national level, with both jurisdictions in this study exhibiting a highly politicized policy arena in which there are pressures for politicians to be seen to be taking clear, authoritative decisions. For similar, but differently experienced, reasons, appealing to populist law and order demands has become a prominent aspect in both countries, and this has shaped the taking up and placing of particular representations of cannabis on the policy agenda. In this respect, the Netherlands has arguably shifted more than England & Wales towards a more conflictual and ambivalent set of control strategies.

In both settings, it was not the case that policy advocates of alternatives to restrictive measures were absent from policy debates; nor can it be asserted that they have not played a significant role in the past. For example, in

England & Wales the Runciman Report gained significant traction and was used to partially justify the 2004 reclassification (see Monaghan, 2011), while in the Netherlands a significant coalition of actors coalesced to challenge the more restrictive measures passed under the Rutte I coalition government. Nevertheless, the stories that were listened to and re-performed accorded with a set of dominant political values at the time and fitted within existing technical parameters, making a more repressive direction in policy attractive. In these ways, under late modern conditions, the sorts of windows of opportunity for particular narratives and evidence to be used by a willing set of political actors appears to be favourable to law and order politics and policies that impose greater restrictions and enhance the role of law enforcement.

However, the danger of assuming 'flat' convergence in cannabis policy misses the fine-grained complexities of the motivations, pressures, negotiations and power manoeuvres involved in agenda setting, policy development and it's unfolding across different geopolitical spaces. An in-depth examination of the policy process helped illuminate such dynamics. As the findings of this research suggest, the residues of modern political institutions, practices and cultures evident in each national and subnational setting bear importance for how particular responses are able to be facilitated, resisted or subverted by policy actors. To reiterate these for clarity, this predominantly refers to the qualities of political systems that structure relations between political actors and the sorts of political culture this gives rise to, which provide a more inclusive/exclusive and incremental/reactive policy environment; the sociohistorical values concerning cannabis, which produce varying degrees of policy support and opposition; the (dis)empowerment of the local and political representation at this level; the ownership of the problem by policy stakeholders; the role of, and windows for, expertise, the mass media and public sentiment to shape policy debates; and, relatedly, the 'structured ambivalence' (Garland, 2001) that exists between policy at national and subnational levels.

Such factors help explain how adaptive and non-adaptive strategies take the particular shape they do across and within different levels of governance. As such, control culture is not a uniformly experienced phenomenon, but is constantly performed and reproduced, diversifying and mutating across varying structure–agency relations.

As this research has demonstrated, such 'empirical particulars' are necessary for producing a more nuanced account of the way in which different national and subnational policy spheres react to many of the same fundamental structural shifts associated with late modernity. The development of punitive responses is not objectively determined, but rather the result of particular interests and situated decisions within broader structural constraints. However, the illumination of divergence from such responses and the identification of conditions that support alternative modalities of control open up possibilities for progressive change.

This is precisely what has been happening in recent years in many contexts across the globe, with the overall direction being towards liberalizing reforms. Indeed, similar to how globalized conditions may have contributed to points of convergence around non-adaptive strategies, they may also facilitate divergence from them. In this respect, the sharing of information has never been quicker or easier, and momentum for alternatives to prohibitive frameworks continues to grow as the number of countries and locales that adopt such policies increases. It is possible to see how the events happening in one context can and do have implications in another. For example, policy makers in the ACT very clearly stated the reforms of the Americas in support for their own policy changes (Legislative Assembly for the Australian Capital Territory, 2018a), and researchers and policy advocates are often well connected to others across the globe.

These developments have also generated growing diversification in the international community over policy approaches where once there may have been a relatively stable consensus. In turn, and while dragging behind individual countries, we have witnessed several important changes at the international level, such as the rescheduling of cannabis in international conventions and revisions to language in communiques, favouring non-penal measures for individual use (WHO, 2017; Collins, 2018; Sischy and Blaustein, 2018; CND, 2020).

One may be tempted then, as van Swaaningen (2013) has pointed to in relation to the decreasing use of imprisonment in the Netherlands, to assert that such developments indicate a reversing of the punitive turn. Yet, while windows of opportunity appear to be increasingly opening for alternatives to prohibitive frameworks, it is extremely difficult to predict when a policy window will open and how long for. Moreover, in some contexts, policy windows may remain non-existent for many years to come, either due to the political sensitivities and anxieties over cannabis and illegal drugs and/or because other issues are dominating policy agendas. For example, in the UK policy landscape, issues such as Brexit and COVID-19 have dominated political discussions in recent years, so there has been little room for proposals like decriminalization or legal regulation of cannabis to make their way onto policy agendas, while in Japan, there remains very little political or public appetite for policy liberalization in respect of non-medical use.

This is precisely why the research findings presented here are important. It no longer suffices to paint broad-brush pictures of overall movements – whether that be convergence around punitivism or convergence around alternatives to punitivism; rather, we need to possess knowledge about concrete contexts, the dispositions and resources of policy actors and their relations of power which generate such policy windows and manifestations of control (Edwards, 2016).

Such an endeavour of 'reducing illusions' of cannabis policy making is important not just because it brings us to a closer understanding of the social world, but also because it is intrinsically connected to the normative role of criminological research. In other words, it is necessary for criminology, as a social science, to 'acknowledge its often hidden or repressed premise – that its evaluations of practices imply a conception of human flourishing' (Sayer, 2011: 245). In turn, thinking about flourishing or well-being requires us to think about 'ill-being', and in this sense a guiding universal principle ought to be the reduction of unnecessary harm and suffering (Bhaskar, 1986).

In the context of this research, this raises questions about the sort of policy-making processes that are preferrable and what the role of criminological expertise ought to be in these processes. This is not unique to the area of cannabis policy, but reflects core issues about what processes are best for contemporary liberal democracies.

There is an underlying assumption that the 'dystopic' visions attributed to works such as *The Culture of Control* represent an undesirable set of conditions (Zedner, 2002), not least in respect of the relationship between criminological expertise and political decision-making. Certainly, the existence of an ambivalent duality between the loss of rationality in political decision-making and particular bounded rationalities based on economic reasoning and risk management presents a set of challenges for the criminological academy and critical studies of crime control. In many cases, it has been challenged on knowledge production and legitimacy by the rise of populist punitivism and silenced by a managerialist 'what works' agenda (Hillyard et al, 2004; Casey, 2008; Hope, 2009; Sherman, 2009;Tilley, 2009). The implication is that under such conditions, processes of policy making risk contributing to unnecessary harm.

As this research has found, the area of cannabis control is by no means immune to such forces, and in many cases exemplifies the dangers of irrational, fear-driven swings in public sentiment driving policy change. Thus, independent expertise and evidence is vital for making decisions on cannabis; this brings us closer to understanding the objective state of affairs and the effects of different policies on identified problems. One clear example of this can be seen with studies which have effectively deconstructed the myth that illegal drugs are inherently more harmful than legal drugs (see Nutt et al, 2007; van Amsterdam et al, 2009). Other research has demonstrated the utility of harm assessment frameworks, which have been applied to the usual foci of individual and social harms but also have encompassed policy frameworks themselves as a potential aggravator or mitigator of harm (see Greenfield and Paoli, 2012, 2013; Paoli et al, 2013). Here, there is clear scope to combine such analytical models with deliberative methods such as the 'policy Delphi' panel, which has been effectively in other criminological research (Edwards et al, 2013a, 2013b), in order to generate shared understandings of the scale and severity of harms as well as generating consensus among expert participants on how substance policy *ought* to be governed.

However, is it realistic or even desirable for decision-making to take place behind closed doors, guided only by expert advice? In our contemporary times, given the lack of direct participation and popular legitimacy as well as a sense of distrust towards experts and elites, this appears problematic. More so, expertise and evidence by itself cannot necessarily answer the question of what *ought* to be done. Ultimately, decisions in cannabis policy are not neutral; as we have seen, evidence may conclusively point to the same problem, but the acting on it, and the nature of that response, entails moral reasoning. This is what makes debates around cannabis and illegal drug policy so difficult; such moral positionings are deeply contested and are also inseparable from broader questions about what rights, freedoms and responsibilities individuals and governments should have.

In a democratic society, the ability to translate moral preferences into tangible policy responses is legitimized by the confidence of the public. It is in this regard that a central challenge is how to protect policy-making processes from irrational forces of penal populism that may undermine and harm the political institutions we entrust our security and freedom to. As has been argued, configurations of political institutions – such as the consensus-driven governance of the Netherlands – may serve to do this, but this does not address, and may only aggravate, the sense of disconnect between politics and the public.

In David Garland's keynote speech at the 12th Asian Criminological Society Conference in 2021, he posed the question 'what's wrong with "penal populism"?' (Garland, 2021). For Garland, penal populism, while being an artifact of political instruments, is nevertheless rooted in sentiments felt by segments of the population. The problem of criminological experts has been that such penal populist sentiments have been largely brushed aside without seriously attempting to engage with these publics to make the case for criminological expertise.

In many ways, this follows a growing number of calls within the academy to engage in a type of public criminology (Hughes, 2007; Loader and Sparks, 2007). For Garland (2021), the recent success of public health experts in the COVID-19 epidemic contains many lessons for how criminologists may seek to do this by publicly exhibiting 'competence, wisdom and integrity' in order to 'inform and reassure an anxious public' and (re)gain the trust of the policy makers. This leads Garland to suggest that 'the real antidote to penal populism is the creation of a popular understanding of crime that has been brought into accordance with criminology's research findings'.

One way in which experts could contribute to such a goal is through public education about different types of policy frameworks and the harms of cannabis and drugs policy. Too often in cannabis policy debates, the lack of understanding about what depenalization, decriminalization or legal regulation actually means and how this is to be realized in policy measures is a source of public anxiety. Moreover, in cannabis and drugs policy, there is no silver bullet that will solve all problems – and so we must clearly and rationally explain the benefits and harms of particular policy frameworks.

Such endeavours also tie in to the call of political philosopher Michael Sandel (2010) for a (re)invigoration of a politics of the common good, one in which individuals operating across society think beyond their immediate environments to consider larger societal stakes. When a new problem arises, it ought to be the job of the criminological expert to do their utmost to calmly and straight-forwardly explain what different policy proposals mean for individuals and society.

In sum, in the context of calls for greater democratic legitimacy and transparency in decision-making, criminology and the social sciences cannot afford to sit idly by. We should actively strive towards providing rational and critical observations that engage with problems of concern to both the government and public, as well as revealing hidden issues and wider oppressive structures. This, of course, pertains not only to overtly punitive modalities of cannabis and illegal drugs control, but with shifts towards liberalization we should also be equally cautious of the effects of new structures and frameworks as well as who the new players are in cannabis regulation (Caulkins, 2014).

Reflections and future directions in comparative criminology

The above discussion has pointed to several ways in which criminological research and expertise may serve to contribute to better policy-making processes in cannabis control, but in conducting research, it is important to reflect on the means by which one arrived at a set of conclusions. In this final section of the book, the research methodology is reflected on and some thoughts for future directions in comparative criminology are offered.

A key question in evaluating and adapting conceptual and theoretical frameworks is whether they succeeded in comprehensively capturing the social phenomenon under question (Layder, 1998). Invariably, in the complex open systems of the social world, there cannot be full certainty or possibility that such tools are capable of explaining everything under their gaze, which therefore leaves space for competing accounts. For example, grand sociological theories, such as that presented in Garland's (2001) *The Culture of Control*, help account for many developments in crime control under late modern conditions, yet the counter-orthodox struggles and points of difference which are glossed over have been shown to be important in this research. They help demonstrate and explain the ways in which punitive policy may mellow out from national to subnational levels.

Thus, the research adapted and built on the framework of *The Culture of Control* through the identification of factors existing at national and subnational levels which mitigate the policy process as outlined above (for example, local political representation coupled with powers to shape policy initiatives). Yet it is important to stress that the findings presented in this book ought to be considered not as an objective truth but as a 'second best' representation that remains open to adaptation and change on the basis of further developed knowledge. In particular, while a range of cases beyond England & Wales and the Netherlands were also considered, these admittedly remain rather surface-level readings, and so further work is required to take these findings forward to empirically test and corroborate how such factors impact on the policy process in other areas of crime control and across different settings.

The same can also be said for the more middle-range framework of the multiple streams model that was adopted in this research (Kingdon, 1995). This was a useful device to capture the dynamic relations between different social actors and events that form part of the policy process. Importantly, the model allowed for a variety of processes to be captured in comparative perspective, highlighting differences between the more incremental style evidenced in the changes to *gedoogbeleid* in the Netherlands and the more reactive process which characterized the 2009 reclassification in England & Wales. Moreover, by taking into account the fluid and ever-changing possibilities of policy change, this allowed the model to consider broader social and structural influences and the choices of key individuals central to the developments.

However, we must recognize that in utilizing such analytical tools, there is a need to be reflective over how the research managed to adapt the models and concepts and to suggest ways to refine and adjust such tools (Layder, 1998). This is particularly relevant to the use of the multiple streams model in comparative work, as it was originally developed in relation to the US political system.

One way the research adapted and built on this model relates to the concept of the national mood. At face value, this seemed to indicate a homogenous societal feeling about an issue. However, the findings of this research indicated multiple moods regarding the issue of concern. In this sense, it is more useful to think of how, and why, particular representations are taken up and projected as a dominant feeling. This also relates to the concept of a window of opportunity, which, it has been argued, is not automatically opened in a logical and coherent way which accords with an objective notion of a problem; rather that it can be forced open with issues used by influential actors and agencies to question rulers and strengthen positions of power. Thus, actors, groups and networks seek to improve their standings and progress their belief systems and ideological agendas through projecting a collective national mood.

The research overtly adopted a broad interpretation of the multiple streams model, but there needs to be greater attention to what particular concepts mean in different political settings. For example, organized political forces covers a vast array of individuals and groups, which differs considerably across national jurisdictions. While the concept was useful to convey the broad mobilization of collective interests to advocate for policy change, questions remain over the organization of such forces and the constitution of such networks.

Moreover, there are aspects of the research which could have been done differently or which require further attention. A clear example of this is the somewhat clunky conceptualization of the subnational level of governance, especially concerning the partially devolved setting of Wales. Thus, further consideration is needed of how structures of governance may be conceptualized across varying geopolitical settings.

Relatedly, within criminology as a whole, there is a tendency to treat the somewhat disparate collection of states that comprise the United Kingdom as a single political entity. But as this research, among others, has also demonstrated, divergence does exist between Westminster and Cardiff (Brewster and Jones, 2019; Jones, 2020), and we can expect similar patterns in Edinburgh and Belfast regarding drugs control. A striking feature of contemporary British society is the perceived dearth of democratic legitimacy ingrained in the Westminster political elite and the desire for further decentralization, devolution and, particularly in the case of Scotland, independence. As the configuration of power shifts, alternatives to current regimes may become more feasible. Thus, as Stenson and Edwards (2004: 219) suggest, there is a 'need for further accounts of the uneven ways in which political rationalities and government technologies are configured in different localities by competing coalitions of actors', as exemplified in Goldson and Hughes' (2010) work on 'intra-system' diversification in the area of youth justice.

However, we should be hesitant to presume that, for example, because the Welsh context currently exhibits a more sympathetic perspective than England concerning crime and substance misuse, it should continue doing so following the transferral of more powers. With more power comes more responsibility, and more accountability to the public. As McAra (2006: 142) note regarding developments in Scottish youth justice, 'carrying the weight of political expectation' has also coincided with a process of 'de-tartanization' whereby politicians face similar pressures to those found in Westminster, because they have added responsibilities and are more accountable to the public, thus falling prey to perceived calls for more punitive measures from the media and public.

In addition, while the research was useful in demonstrating convergence and divergence through the use of a 'critical' case site in each jurisdiction, there are further questions about whether the tendencies found in each subnational site are representative across subnational sites as a whole. In other words, are the approaches in Cardiff or Utrecht indicative of the Cardiff-'ness' or Utrecht-'ness' of these contexts, or are they non-specific conditions of current responses? As such, comparisons of multiple subnational case sites within a single national context are required to further our understanding of such issues.

The need to refine criminological expertise on sites of the local also points to an important aspect which remained largely hidden in this research. As the primary focus of this book was processes of policy *making*, rather than policy implementation or outcomes, this leaves considerable space to explore in further depth the dynamics that emerge between the different policy levels of talk, decisions and action (Pollitt, 2001). In this sense, how formal organizations and actors on the ground, along with how non-state actors – such as unregulated CSCs or 'dark net' marketplaces – themselves participate in cannabis control are crucial to grasping a better understanding of the sorts of agendas, dispositions and mechanisms of different cannabis policies (van Hout and Bingham, 2014; Decorte, 2015; Decorte et al, 2017). As alluded to in Chapter 8, there are apparent differences in how different types of cannabis offences are processed by the criminal justice system, with possession 'offenders' more likely to be diverted away from incarceration. While on the whole the findings suggest a mellowing out of punitive policies, it is entirely possible that in some subnational spheres, more punitive responses to cannabis are also employed. For example, the use of stop-and-search in London for low-level drug offences is well noted (Eastwood et al, 2013).

The suggested move away from a state-centric crimino-logic also alerts us to the significance of taking account of structures existing above the state. Of course, this level has not been ignored in this research, but there was not the same level of in-depth examination, either at the European or global level, of how this shapes the policy process. Given that international conventions and agreements do exert considerable influence on individual nation states, research examining movements at this level are of central importance in seeing how future windows of opportunity may open or be blocked from imagining alternative approaches (see Room et al, 2008; Transnational Institute, 2014; Collins, 2018; Sischy and Blaustein, 2018).

In sum, what these points allude to is the need to further disentangle questions of context-dependency and context-independency. In this respect, Edwards' (2016) 'multi-centred governance' framework provides one promising way forward, through its focus on substantive relations of governance – and the sorts of dispositions and resources of policy actors that constitute and frame such relations – as well as the 'circuits of power' which traverse through different passage points.

Finally, in thinking about future programmes of comparative criminological research, particularly concerning cannabis and illegal drug policy, there are two further reflections, important for both the author and the wider criminological community.

First, the Anglocentrism of much of criminology needs urgent attention. While attempts to 'decolonise criminology' and draw attention to non-Western criminologies have started to make some progress in recent years (see Carrington et al, 2016; Liu, 2016; Blagg and Anthony, 2019), in studies of drug policy at least, it remains the case that academics in, and who focus on, Australasia, North America and the United Kingdom still dominate discussions. Notwithstanding the efforts of associations such as The International Society for the Study of Drug Policy, which is actively attempting to include academics from a diverse range of backgrounds, there is still a long way to go. Particularly in respect of the continents of Africa and Asia, which, combined, contain over 75 per cent of the world's population, representation of incredibly diverse countries at conferences and in journal articles remains minimal.

Second, and given the attention afforded to the work of David Garland in this monograph, it is perhaps fitting to finish by highlighting one particularly noteworthy aspect of his speech at the 12th Asian Criminological Society Conference in 2021: there is a lack of value diversity in academic criminology, which reduces the quality of academic debate (Garland, 2021). From the author's experience, this holds true in the sphere of drug policy, where there is an overwhelming tendency to support alternatives to prohibition and channel research resources to those contexts where liberalizing reforms are introduced. This is not to dispute the justness of such tendencies, but, and in line with the previous point, the field as a whole would be immensely enriched by a more diverse consideration of cases that challenge and question dominant paradigms of thought.

In summary, this book has sought to exemplify the worth of the sociological (and criminological) imagination in explaining contemporary responses to the control of cannabis through an examination of policy-making processes. Through an inter and intra-national comparison, it has been possible to generate a more detailed understanding of how and why patterns of convergence and divergence exist in policy processes by identifying a series of conditions and mechanisms which facilitate as well as frustrate adaptive and non-adaptive strategies of control. At a time when responses to cannabis are rapidly evolving across the globe, capturing the inherent complexities and messiness that allow for policy to be adapted, resisted, reworked or even subverted in preference of alternative values and policy directions is vital to contribute to debates around how cannabis-related acts are governed, and on what processes governance is, and ought to be, based.

Appendix

Table 1: Summary of participants

Type	England & Wales		The Netherlands	
	National	**Subnational**	**National**	**Subnational**
Academic/researcher[a]	8	0	8	0
(advisory committee)	(3)		(4)	
Non-governmental organization[b]	3	1	4	1
Politician	1	2	1	5
Political advisor	0	0	0	3
Civil service[c, d]	2	3	4	0
(advisory committee)	(1)		(3)	
Police[e]	4	3	3	1
Public Prosecutor's Office	0	0	4	1
Subtotal	18	9	24	11
Total	27		35	

[a] Includes a broad group of academics and researchers operating in the fields of social sciences/criminology, health and media studies.

[b] Includes representatives of think tanks and third sector drug agencies.

[c] In the Netherlands, this includes representatives of the Ministry of Health, Welfare and Sport; the Ministry of Justice and Security; and the Public Prosecutor's Office. In England & Wales, this includes representatives of the Home Office.

[d] Includes individuals working for the local authority at subnational level.

[e] At the national level, in England & Wales this refers to current and former representatives of the Association of Chief Police Officers, and in the Netherlands this refers to current and former representatives of the National Police Services Agency and the Dutch Police Union.

Table 2: Participant classification for in-text references

Code	Explanatory information
EW/NL	England & Wales/the Netherlands
A	Academic/researcher
AC (CJ, H)	Advisory committee (criminal justice, health)
NGO	Non-governmental organization
P	Politician/political figure
PA	Political advisor
CS	Civil service
POL	Police
PP	Public Prosecutor's Office

Table 3: Example interview schedule (police, subnational level, the Netherlands)

Section 1 The police and cannabis policy in Utrecht	1.1 Background information 1.2 What are the problems with cannabis in Utrecht, if any? 1.3 How are decisions made on cannabis policy at a local level? (Probe: relationship between police, prosecution service and mayor) 1.4 What factors influence these decisions? (Probe: political representation) 1.5 Where does cannabis lie in police priorities? (Probe: cultivation vs possession) 1.6 What is the role of the police in Utrecht's soft drugs policy? (Probe: checking coffeeshops; back door) 1.7 How are decisions regarding police resources/priorities decided? 1.8 What is the (potential) impact of the nationalization of the police? (Probe: national vs local agenda setting; accountability)
Section 2 Revisions to coffeeshop criteria	2.1 What was the reaction from Utrecht to the policy measures announced in 2011? Why? 2.2 What was the reaction from Utrecht to the revised policy measures announced in 2012? Why? 2.3 What is the relationship between national and local levels of policy making? (Probe: How much room for manoeuvre is given? Why?) 2.4 How have the new policy measures been put into local policy?
Section 3 Ongoing developments	3.1 How will the introduction of the THC [tetrahydrocannabinol] measure be put into local policy? (Probe: what is the position of the police towards this?) 3.2 What is the situation regarding Social Cannabis Club Domstad? (Probe: What is the position of the police?) 3.3 What do developments in cannabis policy over the last few years say about the nature of Dutch drugs policy?

Table 4: Overview of political party perspectives on cannabis policy in the Rutte I (2010–12) and Rutte II (2012–17) coalition governments

People's Party for Freedom and Democracy (VVD)	The People's Party for Freedom and Democracy (Volkspartij voor Vrijheid en Democratie – VVD) is a centre-Right party that strongly supports libertarian values (for example, the party supports pro-euthanasia and pro-abortion views), but has increasingly attempted to redefine itself as the law and order party. With regard to cannabis and other drugs, this has brought to light a glaring divide and ambivalence within the party. Liberal notions relating to free trade and consumption are counterbalanced with a strong priority on safety (and security), which has become a "main political issue" (NL-A-NGO2).
Christian Democratic Appeal (CDA)	Christian Democratic Appeal (Christen Democratisch Appel – CDA) is a centre-Right party. It is traditionally against liberal reforms to cannabis policy, instead advocating measures that reduce the numbers and visibility of coffeeshops, attempting to instil a moral perspective that the consumption of cannabis should be de-normalized on the basis that it limits meaningful participation in society.
Party for Freedom (PVV)	The Party for Freedom (Partij voor de Vrijheid – PVV) is a populist Right-wing party that adopts a tough position on issues such as immigration and law and order. It also has a strong law enforcement focus and supports clear policy measures to tackle crime, even adopting the US-style rhetoric of 'three strikes and you're out' (see PVV, 2010). Moreover, the PVV is distinctly against *gedoogbeleid* as a way of responding to problems. In the realm of drugs, this translates into a disdain for distinguishing between hard and soft drugs. The party's approach to cannabis concentrates on how to tackle drug-related crime.
Labour Party (PvdA)	The Labour Party (Partij van de Arbeid – PvdA) is a centre-Left party that favours cannabis policy proposals focusing on better regulation of coffeeshops, as opposed to a tougher and more repressive approach. The party views coffeeshops as providing a beneficial way to separate markets. The PvdA approaches the issue from a health-led harm reduction perspective, and while firmly agreeing with other political parties that cannabis has become a more harmful substance, it believes that state regulation of the problem would lead to better quality control.

Notes

Chapter 1

1 The study was granted ethical approval by Cardiff University's School of Social Sciences Research Ethics Committee.

2 National governing coalitions in the Netherlands are named after the prime minister. In this case, 'Rutte I' refers to the first cabinet under the leadership of Mark Rutte.

3 An issue worth addressing from an analytical point of view is that there are two clear policy 'moments' being analysed in the Netherlands (changes under Rutte I and Rutte II, due to trials and planned introduction dates) but only one in England & Wales. However, given that the changes undertaken in Rutte II were inseparable from those of Rutte I, they were considered as the same 'movement'.

Chapter 2

1 There are several types of cannabis plant. Here, the focus is mainly on those forms that are directly consumed, as opposed to those which are used in agricultural and industrial applications.

2 For contrasting discussions on the role of British colonial interests and domestic interests in advancing cannabis prohibition in Egypt, readers are referred to Mills (2003) and Kozma (2011).

3 The CND is comprised of representatives from United Nations member states. The purpose of the CND is to supervise the application of drug control treaties and to vote on recommendations by WHO regarding the scheduling of controlled substances.

4 The schedules classify substances according to their risk of addiction and abuse as well as their medical benefits, with different levels of control applying to different schedules. Schedule I substances are considered to have addictive properties with a serious risk of abuse; Schedule II substances have the lowest risk of abuse and are normally used for medical purposes; Schedule III relates to preparations of Schedule II substances; and Schedule IV lists the most dangerous substances, already in Schedule I, which are considered to be particularly harmful with little medical benefit. Accordingly, Schedule I and IV substances are subject to the strictest controls while Schedule II and III substances are given greater leniency.

5 The INCB was established under the terms of the 1961 UN Single Convention on Narcotic Drugs. It is a quasi-judicial monitoring body for the implementation of drug control treaties.

Chapter 3

1 Hereafter the 'United Kingdom' is used for the purposes of this section.

2 The historical ideologies of these two parties are vastly more complex than can be presented here. See Moran (2005).

3 The polder model refers to the historical necessity for people of different socio-economic backgrounds to put aside differences to solve common problems, most notably that of protecting 'polders' - land reclaimed from the sea - from flooding.

4 Underage clients were those under 18, or under 16 in some municipalities. See Pakes (2005).

5 At the time, only drug offences that carried a maximum custodial sentence of five years or more were an 'arrestable offence'. As possession of a Class C substance had a maximum sentence of two years, this meant it was non-arrestable.

6 'County lines' refers to 'the migratory practices of drug supply networks who … travel out from their native major urban conurbations to establish retail operations in provincial satellite areas' (Spicer, 2021:19).

7 The 'Dutch disease' refers to how profits from newly discovered natural gas were used to fund the large welfare system. As Andeweg and Irwin (2005:191) note, '[t]his meant that an income source that would eventually dry up was being used not to improve economic infrastructure, but for welfare benefits'. However, not even natural gas sales were enough to pay for welfare programmes, leading to a budget deficit.

8 'Nuisance' refers to a collection of public order incivilities. With regards to coffeeshops, this relates mainly to parking, noise and loitering, but can also include drug dealing and other illicit activities located around the vicinity of coffeeshops.

Chapter 4

1 EW-POL1: Former Chief Constable and ACPO Lead on Drugs

2 EW-POL1: Former Chief Constable and ACPO Lead on Drugs

3 EW-A5: Academic Expert in Criminology

4 EW-POL4: Former Chief Constable and ACPO Lead on Drugs

5 EW-A3: Academic and Former BBC Home Affairs Correspondent

6 EW-NGO1: Former UKBA and Member of National Drug Prevention Alliance

7 EW-A1: Academic Expert in Criminology

8 EW-A-AC-H1: Former Chair of the ACMD

9 EW-A3: Academic and Former BBC Home Affairs Correspondent

10 EW-A2: Academic Expert in Criminology and Former Home Office Researcher

11 EW-A1: Academic Expert in Criminology

12 EW-A1: Academic Expert in Criminology

13 EW-POL5: Former Chief Constable

14 EW-NGO1: Former UKBA and Member of National Drug Prevention Alliance

15 EW-POL4: Former Chief Constable and ACPO Lead on Drugs

16 NL-PP3: Policy Worker, Public Prosecutor's Office, Limburg

17 NL-PP2: Public Prosecutor, Limburg

18 NL-A-AC-CJ: Academic Expert in Criminology and Member of van de Donk Committee

19 NL-POL1: Former Chief of Police and President of the Police Union

20 NL-A-AC-CJ: Academic Expert in Criminology and Member of van de Donk Committee

21 NL-A-AC-CJ: Academic Expert in Criminology and Member of van de Donk Committee

22 NL-P2: VVD Politician, Utrecht

23 NL-A-NGO3: Independent Research Organization

24 NL-POL1: Former Chief of Police and President of the Police Union

25 NL-POL3: Police Officer, KLPD

26 NL-A-NGO1: Independent Research Organization and Drugs Worker; NL-POL2: Police Officer, Organized Cannabis Cultivation Taskforce

[27] NL-A-AC-H1: Academic Expert in Health and Member of van de Donk Committee
[28] NL-A-NGO1: Independent Research Organization and Drugs Worker
[29] NL-P4: CDA Politician, Utrecht
[30] NL-A-NGO3: Independent Research Organization
[31] NL-CS-AC-H1: Senior Civil Servant in Ministry of Health, Welfare and Sport and Member of Garretsen Committee
[32] NL-A-NGO3: Independent Research Organization

Chapter 5

[1] EW-A1: Academic Expert in Criminology
[2] EW-A3: Academic and Former BBC Home Affairs Correspondent
[3] EW-P1: Senior Political Figure
[4] EW-POL1: Former Chief Constable and ACPO Lead on Drugs
[5] EW-NGO-AC: Independent Drugs Policy Organization and Former ACMD Member
[6] EW-A1: Academic Expert in Criminology
[7] EW-A4: Academic Expert in Criminology
[8] EW-P2: Labour MP, South Wales
[9] EW-NGO2: Third Sector Organization
[10] EW-NGO-AC: Independent Drugs Policy Organization and Former ACMD Member
[11] NL-A-AC-CJ: Academic Expert in Criminology and Member of van de Donk Committee
[12] NL-A2: Academic Expert in Criminology
[13] NL-A3: Academic Expert in Criminology
[14] NL-A-NGO3: Independent Research Organization
[15] NL-A1: Academic Expert in Social Sciences
[16] NL-A2: Academic Expert in Criminology
[17] NL-CS-AC-H1: Senior Civil Servant in Ministry of Health, Welfare and Sport and Member of Garretsen Committee
[18] NL-PP4: Policy Worker, Public Prosecutor's Office
[19] NL-A3: Academic Expert in Criminology
[20] NL-A-CS: Research and Documentation Centre Researcher
[21] NL-A-AC-CJ: Academic Expert in Criminology and Member of van de Donk Committee
[22] NL-A-AC-CJ: Academic Expert in Criminology and Member of van de Donk Committee
[23] NL-A-AC-CJ: Academic Expert in Criminology and Member of van de Donk Committee
[24] NL-A-AC-CJ: Academic Expert in Criminology and Member of van de Donk Committee
[25] NL-A-AC-H2: Academic Expert in Health and Member of Garretsen Committee
[26] NL-CS-AC-CJ: Senior Civil Servant in Ministry of Justice and Security and Member of van de Donk Committee
[27] NL-POL1: Former Chief of Police and President of Police Union
[28] NL-P1: D'66 Politician, House of Representatives
[29] NL-A3: Academic Expert in Criminology
[30] NL-A-CS: Research and Documentation Centre Researcher
[31] NL-PP4: Policy Worker, Public Prosecutor's Office
[32] For further details, see www.act.gov.au/cannabis/home

Chapter 6

[1] EW-CS-CJ2: Former Senior Home Office Civil Servant
[2] EW-A5: Academic Expert in Criminology
[3] EW-CS-CJ2: Former Senior Home Office Civil Servant
[4] EW-A5: Academic Expert in Criminology

5 EW-A-AC-H2: Former Chair of the ACMD
6 EW-NGO-AC: Independent Drugs Policy Organization and Former ACMD Member
7 EW-NGO-AC: Independent Drugs Policy Organization and Former ACMD Member
8 EW-CS-CJ: Former Senior Home Office Civil Servant
9 EW-A5: Academic Expert in Criminology
10 See McLaughlin (2002: 52–4) and Stenson (2002) for discussions of New Labour and middle England.
11 EW-CS-CJ2: Former Senior Home Office Civil Servant
12 EW-A3: Academic and Former BBC Home Affairs Correspondent
13 EW-A3: Academic and Former BBC Home Affairs Correspondent
14 See a piece in the *Daily Mail* (2008) entitled 'Gordon Brown made a brave and justified decision on cannabis', published one day after the reclassification announcement by Jacqui Smith in the House of Commons.
15 EW-NGO1: Former UKBA and Member of National Drug Prevention Alliance
16 EW-A1: Academic Expert in Criminology
17 EW-POL4: Former Chief Constable and ACPO Lead on Drugs
18 EW-NGO2: Third Sector Organization
19 NL-CS-AC-CJ: Senior Civil Servant in Ministry of Justice and Security and Member of van de Donk Committee
20 NL-A2: Academic Expert in Criminology
21 NL-P4: CDA Politician, Utrecht
22 NL-A-NGO2: Independent Research Organization
23 NL-POL1: Former Chief of Police and President of Police Union
24 NL-P4: CDA Politician, Utrecht
25 NL-A3: Academic Expert in Criminology
26 NL-CS-AC-CJ: Senior Civil Servant in Ministry of Justice and Security and Member of van de Donk Committee
27 NL-PA3: Policy Advisor to the Mayor, Utrecht
28 NL-A2: Academic Expert in Criminology
29 NL-CS-AC-CJ: Senior Civil Servant in Ministry of Justice and Security and Member of van de Donk Committee
30 NL-PA1: Political Advisor, Utrecht
31 NL-A1: Academic Expert in Social Sciences
32 NL-NGO2: Drugs Policy Reform Organization
33 NL-A2: Academic Expert in Criminology
34 NL-NGO2: Drugs Policy Reform Organization
35 NL-P2: VVD Politician, Utrecht
36 NL-PP1: Policy Worker, Public Prosecutor's Office
37 NL-PA3: Policy Advisor to the Mayor, Utrecht
38 NL-A-AC-H1: Academic Expert in Health and Member of van de Donk/Garretsen Committees
39 NL-A-AC-H1: Academic Expert in Health and Member of van de Donk/Garretsen Committees
40 Similar in this respect are the legalization reforms of Canada in 2018, which occurred with the support of only 35–40 per cent of the population (see Fischer et al, 2020).

Chapter 8

1 EW-P1: Senior Political Figure
2 EW-P1: Senior Political Figure
3 EW-NGO-AC: Independent Drugs Policy Organization and Former ACMD Member

4 EW-CS-H2: Substance Misuse Action Team, Cardiff
5 EW-POL-CS1: South Wales Police and Welsh Government
6 EW-P1: Senior Political Figure
7 EW-CS-H1: Substance Misuse Policy Worker, Cardiff and Welsh Government
8 EW-P1: Senior Political Figure
9 EW-P2: Labour MP, South Wales
10 EW-P1: Senior Political Figure
11 EW-POL3: Neighbourhood Team Supervisor, South Wales Police
12 EW-POL6: Police Constable, South Wales Police
13 EW-POL-CS2: South Wales Police, Welsh Government and ACPO Cymru
14 NL-CS-AC-CJ: Senior Civil Servant in Ministry of Justice and Security and Member of van de Donk Committee
15 NL-POL4: Utrecht Police
16 NL-P2: VVD Politician, Utrecht
17 NL-P4: CDA Politician, Utrecht
18 NL-PA4: D'66 Policy Advisor
19 NL-PA1: Policy Advisor, Utrecht
20 NL-P5: D'66 Alderperson, Utrecht
21 NL-P6: D'66 Politician, Utrecht
22 NL-P5: D'66 Alderperson, Utrecht
23 NL-PA3: Policy Advisor to the Mayor, Utrecht
24 NL-P3: PvdA Politician, Utrecht
25 NL-P2: VVD Politician, Utrecht
26 NL-P5: D'66 Alderperson, Utrecht
27 NL-P4: CDA Politician, Utrecht
28 Alderpersons are appointed by the municipal council, while mayors are appointed by the Ministry of Interior and Kingdom Relations, and validated by the Crown, with advice given by the local council.
29 NL-P5: D'66 Alderperson, Utrecht
30 NL-PP5: Policy Worker, Public Prosecutor's Office, Utrecht
31 NL-P5: D'66 Alderperson, Utrecht
32 NL-P2: VVD Politician, Utrecht
33 NL-P4: CDA Politician, Utrecht
34 NL-P5: D'66 Alderperson, Utrecht

Chapter 9

1 NL-A-AC-CJ: Academic Expert in Criminology and Member of the van de Donk Committee
2 NL-A1: Academic Expert in Social Sciences
3 NL-A-AC-H1: Academic Expert in Health and Member of van de Donk/Garretsen Committees
4 Especially given the resignation of eight ACMD members between late 2009 and early 2010 in protest over ministerial influence following Professor David Nutt's controversial sacking (see Laurence, 2010).

References

Aarts, K. and van der Kolk, H. (2007) 'The parliamentary election in the Netherlands, 22 November 2006', *Electoral Studies*, 26(4): 832–7.

Aarts, K. and van der Kolk, H. (2011) 'The Dutch parliamentary election of June 9, 2010', *Electoral Studies*, 30(3): 577–80.

ABC News (2007) 'Opposition calls for scrapping of "soft" cannabis laws' [Online], 24 March, Available at: https://www.abc.net.au/news/2007-03-25/opposition-calls-for-scrapping-of-soft-cannabis/2225300 [Accessed 17 August 2021].

Abel, S. and Casswell, S. (1998) 'Cannabis in New Zealand: Policy and prospects', *Social Policy Journal of New Zealand*, 10: 70–85.

Adams, J., de Vries, C. and Leiter, D. (2011) 'Subconstituency reactions to elite depolarization in the Netherlands: An analysis of the Dutch public's policy beliefs and partisan loyalties, 1986–98', *British Journal of Political Science*, 42(1): 81–105.

Advisory Committee Experiment Closed Cannabis Chain (the Netherlands) (2018) *An Experiment with a Closed Cannabis Chain*, Den Haag: Advisory Committee Experiment Closed Cannabis Chain.

Advisory Committee on Drug Dependency (UK) (1968) *Cannabis: Report by the Advisory Committee on Drug Dependence*, London: Home Office.

Advisory Committee on Drugs Policy (the Netherlands) (2009) *Geen Deuren maar Daden: Nieuwe Accenten in het Nederlands Drugsbeleid* [No Doors but Deeds: New Emphasis in Dutch Drugs Policy], Den Haag: Rijksoverheid.

Advisory Council on the Misuse of Drugs (ACMD) (UK) (2002) *The Classification of Cannabis under the Misuse of Drugs Act 1971*, London: Home Office.

Advisory Council on the Misuse of Drugs (ACMD) (UK) (2006) *Further Consideration of the Classification of Cannabis under the Misuse of Drugs Act 1971*, London: Home Office.

Advisory Council on the Misuse of Drugs (ACMD) (UK) (2008) *Cannabis: Classification and Public Health*, London: Home Office.

African Union (2019) *Plan of Action on Drug Control and Crime Prevention, 2019–2023*, Addis Ababa: African Union.

Al-Shazly, F. and Tinasti, K. (2016) 'Incarceration or mandatory treatment: Drug use and the law in the Middle East and North Africa', *International Journal of Drug Policy*, 31: 172–7.

Allen, G. and Tunnicliffe, R. (2021) *Drug Crime: Statistics for England and Wales*, London: House of Commons Library.

Almond, G. and Verba, S. (1989) *The Civic Culture: Political Attitudes and Democracy in Five Nations*, Newbury Park, CA: Sage.

Andeweg, R. (2008) 'Coalition politics in the Netherlands: From accommodation to politicization', *Acta Politica*, 43(2–3): 254–77.

Andeweg, R. and Irwin, G. (2005) *Governance and Politics of the Netherlands* (2nd edn), Houndmills: Palgrave.

Andreas, P. and Nadelmann, E. (2006) *Policing the Globe: Criminalization and Crime Control in International Relations*, New York: Oxford University Press.

Arana, X. (2019) *Cannabis Regulation in Europe: Country Report Spain*, Amsterdam: Transnational Institute.

Arana, X. and Pares, O. (2020) 'Cannabis social clubs in Spain', in T. Decorte, S. Lenton and C. Wilkins (eds) *Legalizing Cannabis: Experiences, Lessons and Scenarios*, Abingdon: Routledge, pp 307–22.

Arseneault, L., Cannon, M., Poulton, R., Murray, R., Caspi, A. and Moffitt, T. (2002) 'Cannabis use in adolescence and risk for adult psychosis: Longitudinal prospective study', *British Medical Journal*, 325(7374): 1212–13.

Association of Chief Police Officers (ACPO) (UK) (2003) *Cannabis Enforcement Guidance*, London: ACPO.

Association of Chief Police Officers (ACPO) (UK) (2009) *ACPO Guidance on Cannabis Possession for Personal Use: Revised Intervention Framework*, London: ACPO.

Association of Chief Police Officers (ACPO) (UK) (2010) *Findings from the UK National Problem Profile: Commercial Cultivation of Cannabis*, London: ACPO.

Association of Southeast Asian Nations (ASEAN) (2017) *The ASEAN Work Plan on Securing Communities against Illicit Drugs, 2016–2025*, Jakarta: ASEAN.

ATA-Net (2021) 'Dai Ichi tiichin: "Taima: Kinjirareta Rekishi to Iryo e no Mirai"' [The first teach-in: 'Cannabis: A forbidden history and the future for medicine'] [Online], Available at: https://ata-net.jp/joint/joint-thachin/joint-thachin1 [Accessed 14 June 2021].

Australian Associated Press (2007) 'Scrap Labor's "soft" cannabis laws: Omodei' [Online], Available at: www.proquest.com [Accessed 17 August 2021].

Australian Associated Press (2011) 'WA called Australia's "cannabis capital"' [Online], Available at: www.proquest.com [Accessed 17 August 2021].

Australian Associated Press (2019) 'Australian Capital Territory votes to legalise cannabis for personal use', *The Guardian* [Online], 25 September, Available at: https://www.theguardian.com/australia-news/2019/sep/25/cannabis-set-to-be-legalised-in-australian-capital-territory-for-personal-use [Accessed 17 August 2021].

Bakema, W. and Secker, I. (1988) 'Ministerial expertise and the Dutch case', *European Journal of Political Research*, 16(2): 153–70.

Baker, K. (1993) *The Turbulent Years: My Life in Politics*, London: Faber & Faber.

Ballotpedia (2021) '2020 marijuana legalization and marijuana-related ballot measures' [Online], Available at: https://ballotpedia.org/2020_marijuana_legalization_and_marijuana-related_ballot_measures#Summary_of_campaign_contributions [Accessed 10 August 2021].

Ballotta, D., Bergeron, H. and Hughes, B. (2008) 'Cannabis control in Europe', in S. Sznitman, B. Olsson and R. Room (eds) *A Cannabis Reader: Global Issues and Local Experiences*, Lisbon: European Monitoring Centre for Drugs and Drug Addiction, pp 97–118.

Bardach, E. (2005) *Practical Guide for Policy Analysis: The Eightfold Path to More Effective Problem Solving* (2nd edn), Washington, DC: CQ Press.

Barrett, D. (2019) 'Canada, cannabis and the relationship between UN child rights and drug control treaties', *International Journal of Drug Policy*, 71: 29–35.

Bauman, Z. (1998) *Globalization: The Human Consequences*, Cambridge: Polity Press.

BBC News (2008) 'PM "to send message" on cannabis' [Online], 29 April, Available at: http://news.bbc.co.uk/1/hi/uk_politics/7372876.stm [Accessed 10 November 2014].

BBC News (2021) 'Drug consumption rooms are a "distraction" says UK Minister' [Online], 27 February, Available at: https://www.bbc.com/news/uk-scotland-51644786 [Accessed 22 September 2021].

Beck, U. (2000) *The Brave New World of Work*, Cambridge: Polity Press.

Beeching, J. (1977) *The Chinese Opium Wars*, San Diego: Harcourt Brace Jovanovich.

Belackova, V., Tomkova, A. and Zabransky, T. (2016) 'Qualitative research in Spanish cannabis social clubs: "The moment you enter the door, you are minimising the risks"', *International Journal of Drug Policy*, 34: 49–57.

Belackova, V., van de Ven, K. and Roubalova, M. (2020) '"More than just counting the plants": Different home cannabis cultivation policies, cannabis supply contexts and approaches to their evaluation', in T. Decorte, S. Lenton and C. Wilkins (eds) *Legalizing Cannabis: Experiences, Lessons and Scenarios*, Abingdon: Routledge, pp 154–79.

Berridge, V. (1981) *Opium and the People*, London: Allen Lane.

Berry, M. (2002) 'Validity and reliability issues in elite interviews', *Political Science and Politics*, 35(4): 679–82.

Bewley-Taylor, D.R. and Jelsma, M. (2012) '*The limits of latitude: The UN drug control conventions*', *Transnational Institute and International Drug Policy Consortium* [Online], Available at: https://www.tni.org/en/publication/the-limits-of-latitude [Accessed 4 June 2021].

Bhaskar, R. (1986) *Scientific Realism and Human Emancipation*, London: Routledge.

Bieleman, B. and Goeree, P. (2001) *Coffeeshops in Nederland: Aantallen en Gemeentelijk Beleid in 2000* [Coffeeshops in the Netherlands: Number and Municipal Policies in 2000], Groningen: Intraval.

Bieleman, B., Nijkamp, R. and Bak, T. (2012) *Coffeeshops in Nederland 2011: Aantallen Coffeeshops en Gemeentelijk Beleid 1999–2011* [Coffeeshops in the Netherlands 2011: Number and Municipal Policies 1999–2011], Groningen: Intraval.

Blagg, H. and Anthony, T. (2019) *Decolonising Criminology: Imagining Justice in a Postcolonial World*, London: Palgrave Macmillan.

Blom, J. (2000) 'Pillarisation in perspective', *West European Politics*, 23(3): 153–64.

Boekhout van Solinge, T. (1999) 'Dutch drug policy in a European context', *Journal of Drug Issues*, 29(3): 511–28.

Bogdanor, V. (1999) *Devolution in the United Kingdom*, Oxford: Oxford University Press.

Booker, C., Wyden, R. and Shumer, C. (2021) *Cannabis Administration and Opportunity Act: Discussion Draft*, Washington, DC: United States Senate.

Boone, M. (2011) 'Judicial rehabilitation in the Netherlands: Balancing between safety and privacy', *European Journal of Probation*, 3(1) 63–78.

Booth, M. (2003) *Cannabis: A History*, London: Doubleday.

Brewster, D. (2017) 'Culture(s) of control: Political dynamics in cannabis policy in England & Wales and the Netherlands', *European Journal of Drug Policy*, 14(5): 566–85.

Brewster, D. (2018a) 'A critical assessment of indications of the national prevalence of illegal drug use in Japan', *Contemporary Drug Problems*, 45(4): 425–40.

Brewster, D. (2018b) 'The structured ambivalence of cannabis control in England & Wales', *International Journal of Drug Policy*, 53: 125–32.

Brewster, D. (2020) 'Crime control in Japan: Exceptional, convergent or what else?', *The British Journal of Criminology*, 60(6): 1547–66.

Brewster, D. and Jones, R. (2019) 'Distinctly divergent or hanging onto English coat-tails? Drug policy in post-devolution Wales', *Criminology & Criminal Justice*, 19(3): 364–81.

Brunsson, N. (1993) 'Ideas and actions: Justification and hypocrisy as alternatives to control', *Accounting, Organizations and Society*, 18(6): 489–506.

Bryant, C. (1981) 'Depillarisation in the Netherlands', *The British Journal of Sociology*, 32(1): 56–74.

Burris, S., Drahos, P. and Shearing, C. (2005) 'Nodal governance', *Australian Journal of Legal Philosophy*, 30: 30–58.

Buruma, Y. (2007) 'Dutch tolerance: On drugs, prostitution, and euthanasia', in M. Tonry and C. Bijleveld (eds) *Crime and Justice in the Netherlands*, Crime and Justice, Vol 35, Chicago: University of Chicago Press, pp 73–113.

Cabinet Office (UK) (1999) *Modernising Government*, Cm 4310, London: The Stationery Office.

Cabinet Office Strategy Unit (UK) (2004) *Alcohol Harm Reduction Strategy for England*, London: Cabinet Office.

Cambron, C., Guttmannova, K. and Fleming, C. (2017) 'State and national contexts in evaluating cannabis laws: A case study of Washington State', *Journal of Drug Issues*, 47(1): 74–90.

Canadian Centre on Substance Use and Addiction (2020) 'Cannabis (Canadian drug summary)' [Online], Available at: https://www.ccsa.ca/cannabis-canadian-drug-summary [Accessed 5 July 2021].

Carrington, K., Hogg, R. and Sozzo, M. (2016) Southern criminology. *The British Journal of Criminology*, 56: 1-20.

Casey, L. (2008) *Engaging Communities in Fighting Crime*, London: Cabinet Office.

Castells, M. (2001) *The Internet Galaxy*, Oxford: Oxford University Press.

Caulkins, J. (2014) 'Nonprofit motive', *Washington Monthly* [Online], 2 March, Available at: https://washingtonmonthly.com/magazine/marchaprilmay-2014/nonprofit-motive/ [Accessed 16 September 2015].

Caulkins, J., Kilmer, B., Kleiman, M., MacCoun, R., Midgette, G., Oglesby, P., Pacula, R. and Reuter, P. (2015) *Considering Marijuana Legalization: Insights for Vermont and Other Jurisdictions*, Santa Monica, CA: RAND Corporation.

Central Committee on the Treatment of Heroin Addicts (2002) *Medical Co-Prescription of Heroin: Two Randomized Control Trials*. Utrecht: Central Committee on the Treatment of Heroin Addicts.

Chandler, J. (2001) *Local Government Today* (3rd edn), Manchester: Manchester University Press.

Chaney, P., Hall, T. and Pithouse, A. (2001) 'New governance – new democracy?', in P. Chaney, T. Hall and A. Pithouse (eds) *New Governance – New Democracy? Post-Devolution Wales*, Cardiff: University of Wales Press, pp 1–17.

Chatwin, C. (2007) 'Multi-level governance: The way forward for European illicit drug policy?', *International Journal of Drug Policy*, 18(6): 494–502.

Chatwin, C. (2013) 'A critical evaluation of the European drug strategy: Has it brought added value to drug policy making at the national level?', *International Journal of Drug Policy*, 24(3): 251–6.

Christie, N. (2000) *Crime Control as Industry* (3rd edn), London: Routledge.

City of Utrecht (2013) Utrecht Gemeenteblad, 350, 12 July 2013, Utrecht: Gemeente Utrecht.

City of Utrecht Municipal Executive (2011) *Brief Wetenschappelijke Experimenten Cannabisbeleid* [Letter on Scientific Experiments with Cannabis Policy], Utrecht: College van Burgermeester en Wethouders.

Cohen, S. (1972) *Folk Devils and Moral Panics: The Creation of Mods and Rockers*, London: MacGibbon and Gee.

Cohen, S. (1985) *Visions of Social Control: Crime, Punishment and Classification*, Cambridge: Polity Press.

Cole, A. and John, P. (2001) *Local Governance in England and France*, London: Routledge.

Collins, J. (2018) 'Rethinking "flexibilities" in the international drug control system: Potential, precedents and models for reforms', *International Journal of Drug Policy*, 60: 107–14.

Collins, J. (2020) 'A brief history of cannabis and the drug conventions', *AJIL Unbound*, 114: 279–84.

Commission on Narcotic Drugs (CND) (2019) *Ministerial Declaration on Strengthening our Actions at the National, Regional and International Levels to Accelerate the Implementation of Our Joint Commitments to Address and Counter the World Drug Problem*, Vienna: Commission on Narcotic Drugs.

Commission on Narcotic Drugs (CND) (2020) 'Press statement – 2 December 2020: CND votes on recommendations for cannabis and cannabis-related substances' [Online], Available at: https://www.unodc.org/documents/commissions/CND/CND_Sessions/CND_63Reconvened/press_statement_CND_2_December.pdf [Accessed 22 June 2021].

Conrad, P. and Schneider, J.W. (1992) *Deviance and Medicalization: From Badness to Sickness*, Philadelphia, PA: Temple University Press.

Cox, C. (2018) 'The Canadian Cannabis Act legalizes and regulates recreational cannabis use in 2018', *Health Policy*, 122(3): 205–9.

Crépault, J.F., Rehm, J. and Fischer, B. (2016) 'The *Cannabis Policy Framework* by the Centre for Addiction and Mental Health: A proposal for a public health approach to cannabis policy in Canada', *International Journal of Drug Policy*, 34: 1–4.

Croydon, S. (2016) *The Politics of Police Detention in Japan: Consensus of Convenience*, Oxford: Oxford University Press.

Cruz, J., Queirolo, R. and Boidi, M. (2016) 'Determinants of public support for marijuana legalization in Uruguay, the United States, and El Salvador', *Journal of Drug Issues*, 46(4): 308–25.

Cruz, J., Boidi, M. and Queirolo, R. (2017) 'The status of support for cannabis regulation in Uruguay 4 years after reform: Evidence from public opinion surveys', *Drug and Alcohol Review*, 37(S1): S429–S434.

Cruz, J., Boidi, M. and Queirolo, R. (2018) 'Saying no to weed: Public opinion towards cannabis legalisation in Uruguay', *Drugs: Education, Prevention and Policy*, 25(1): 67–76.

Cullen, F. (2013) 'Rehabilitation: Beyond nothing works', *Crime and Justice*, 42(1): 299–376.

Daalder, H. (1955) 'Parties and politics in the Netherlands', *Political Studies*, 3(1): 1–16.

Daalder, H. (1966) 'The Netherlands', in R. Dahl (ed) *Political Oppositions in Western Democracies*, New Haven, CT: Yale University Press, pp 188–236.

Daalder, H. (1987) 'The Dutch party system: From segmentation to polarization – and then?', in H. Daalder (ed) *Party Systems in Denmark, Austria, Switzerland, the Netherlands and Belgium*, London: Pinter, pp 193–284.

Daily Mail (2008) 'Gordon Brown made a brave and justified decision on cannabis' [Online], 7 May, Available at: http://dailym.ai/WukHHa [Accessed 15 January 2014].

Davenport, S. and Pardo, B. (2016) 'The Dangerous Drugs Act Amendment in Jamaica: Reviewing goals, implementation, and challenges', *International Journal of Drug Policy*, 37: 60–9.

de Bruin, D., Dijkstra, M. and Breeksema, J. (2008) *Coffeeshops in Nederland 2007: Naleving en Handhaving van Coffeeshopregels* [Coffeeshops in the Netherlands 2007: Compliance and Enforcement of Coffeeshop Regulations], Utrecht: Stichting CVO.

de Kort, M. (1994) 'A short history of drugs in the Netherlands', in E. Leuw and I. Marshall (eds) *Between Prohibition and Legalization: The Dutch Experiment in Drug Policy*, Amsterdam: Kugler, pp 3–22.

Deacon, R. and Sandry, A. (2007) *Devolution in the United Kingdom*, Edinburgh: Edinburgh University Press.

Decorte, T. (2015) 'Cannabis social clubs in Belgium: Organizational strengths and weaknesses, and threats to the model', *International Journal of Drug Policy*, 26(2): 122–30.

Decorte, T. and Potter, G. (2015) 'The globalisation of cannabis cultivation: A growing challenge', *International Journal of Drug Policy*, 26(3): 221–5.

Decorte, T., Pardal, M., Queirolo, R., Boidi, M., Aviles, C. and Pares, O. (2017) 'Regulating cannabis social clubs: A comparative analysis of legal and self-regulatory practices in Spain, Belgium and Uruguay', *International Journal of Drug Policy*, 43: 44–56.

Decorte, T., Lenton, S. and Wilkins, C. (2020a) 'Introduction', in T. Decorte, S. Lenton and C. Wilkins (eds) *Legalizing Cannabis: Experiences, Lessons and Scenarios*, Abingdon: Routledge, pp 1–8.

Decorte, T., Lenton, S. and Wilkins, C. (eds) (2020b) *Legalizing Cannabis: Experiences, Lessons and Scenarios*, Abingdon: Routledge.

Department of Health (UK) (2011) *United Kingdom Drug Situation: Annual Report to the European Monitoring Centre for Drugs and Drug Addiction (EMCDDA), 2011*, London: Department of Health.

Department of Justice (Canada) (2021) 'Cannabis legalization and regulation' [Online], Available at: https://www.justice.gc.ca/eng/cj-jp/cannabis/ [Accessed 7 June 2021].

Department of Justice (US) (2013) 'Guidance regarding marijuana enforcement' [Online], 29 August, Available at: https://www.justice.gov/iso/opa/resources/3052013829132756857467.pdf [Accessed 28 June 2021].

Devroe, A., Edwards, A. and Ponsaers, P. (eds) (2017) *Policing European Metropolises: The Politics of Security in City-Regions*, London: Routledge.

Downes, D. (1982) 'The origins and consequences of Dutch penal policy since 1945: A preliminary analysis', *The British Journal of Criminology*, 22(4): 325–62.

Downes, D. (1988) *Contrasts in Tolerance: Post-War Penal Policy in the Netherlands and England and Wales*, Oxford: Clarendon Press.

Downes, D. and van Swaaningen, R. (2007) 'The road to dystopia? Changes in the penal climate of the Netherlands', in M. Tonry and C. Bijleveld (eds) *Crime and Justice in the Netherlands*, Crime and Justice, Vol 35, Chicago: University of Chicago Press, pp 31–72.

Drakeford, M. and Gregory, L. (2011) 'Governance and social policy in a devolved Wales', in C. Williams (ed) *Social Policy for Social Welfare Practice in a Devolved Wales* (2nd edn), Birmingham: Venture Press, pp 21–34.

Drug and Alcohol Office (Western Australia) (2007) *Statutory Review: Cannabis Control Act 2003. Report to the Minister for Health: Technical Report*, Perth: Drug and Alcohol Office.

Drug and Alcohol Office (Western Australia) (2011) *Cannabis Laws in Western Australia* [Online], Available at: https://www.mhc.wa.gov.au/media/1227/cannabis-laws-in-western-australia-a5-booklet.pdf [Accessed 17 August 2021].

Easton, D. (1965) *A Systems Analysis of Political Life*, New York: John Wiley and Sons.

Eastwood, N. (2020) 'Cannabis decriminalization policies across the globe', in T. Decorte, S. Lenton and C. Wilkins (eds) *Legalizing Cannabis: Experiences, Lessons and Scenarios*, Abingdon: Routledge, pp 133–53.

Eastwood, N., Shiner, M. and Bear, D. (2013) *The Numbers in Black and White: Ethnic Disparities in the Policing and Prosecution of Drug Offences in England and Wales*, London: Release.

Edwards, A. (2016) 'Multi-centred governance and circuits of power in liberal modes of security', *Global Crime*, 17(3–4): 240–63.

Edwards, A. and Hughes, G. (2005) 'Comparing the governance of safety in Europe: A geo-historical approach', *Theoretical Criminology*, 9(3): 345–63.

Edwards, A. and Hughes, G. (2012) 'Public safety regimes: Negotiated orders and political analysis in criminology', *Criminology & Criminal Justice*, 12(4): 433–58.

Edwards, A., Hughes, G. and Lord, N. (2013a) 'Crime prevention and public safety in Europe: Challenges for comparative criminology', in S. Body-Gendrot, M. Hough, K. Kerezsi, R. Levy and S. Snacken (eds) *The Routledge Handbook of European Criminology*, London: Routledge, pp 368–84.

Edwards, A., Hughes, G. and Lord, N. (2013b) 'Urban security in Europe: Translating a concept in public criminology', *European Journal of Criminology*, 10(3): 260–83.

El-Khoury, J., Khalil, R.B., Nemer, A. and Richa, S. (2020) 'Legalizing medical cannabis in Lebanon: The complex interface between medicine, law, ethics, and economics', *Cannabis and Cannabinoid Research* [Online], Available at: https://doi.org/10.1089/can.2020.0108 [Accessed 15 September 2021].

Eligh, J. (2019) *The Evolution of Illicit Drug Markets and Drug Policy in Africa*, Geneva: The Global Initiative against Transnational Organised Crime.

Estrada, F. (2004) 'The transformation of the politics of crime in high crime societies', *European Journal of Criminology*, 1(4): 419–43.

European Monitoring Centre for Drugs and Drug Addiction (2014) *European Drug Report: Trends and Developments*, Lisbon: European Monitoring Centre for Drugs and Drug Addiction.

European Union (EU) (2013) *European Union Drug Strategy, 2013–2020*, Luxembourg: General Secretariat of the EU Council.

Evans, J. and Hayne, J. (2019) 'Canberra's cannabis legalisation faces several hurdles, here's what's being proposed', *ABC News* [Online], 20 February, Available at: https://www.abc.net.au/news/2019-02-20/canberras-cannabis-laws-explained/10830170 [Accessed 17 August 2021].

Evans, J., Jones, R. and Musgrove, N. (2021) '"Dragonisation" revisited: A progressive criminal justice policy in Wales?', *Criminology & Criminal Justice* [Online], Available at: https://doi.org/10.1177/1748895821990428 [Accessed 2 May 2021].

Expert Committee on the List System of the Opium Act (the Netherlands) (2011) *Drugs in Lijsten* [Drugs in Lists], Den Haag: Rijksoverheid.

Farrell, G., Tilley, N. and Tseloni, A. (2014) 'Why the crime drop?', *Crime and Justice*, 43(1): 421–90.

Feeley, M. and Simon, J. (1994) 'Actuarial justice: The emerging new criminal law', in D. Nelken (ed) *The Futures of Criminology*, London: Sage, pp 173–201.

Fetherston, J. and Lenton, S. (2007) *Effects of the Western Australian Cannabis Infringement Notice Scheme on Public Attitudes, Knowledge and Use*, Perth: The National Drug Research Institute.

Fischer, B. and Bullen, C. (2020) 'Emerging prospects for non-medical cannabis legalisation in New Zealand: An initial view and contextualization', *International Journal of Drug Policy*, 76: 102632. https://doi.org/10.1016/j.drugpo.2019.102632

Fischer, B. and Hall, W. (2021) 'New Zealand's failed cannabis legalization referendum – implications for cannabis policy reform', *The Lancet Regional Health – Western Pacific*, 7: 100080. https://doi.org/10.1016/j.lanwpc.2020.100080

Fischer, B., Erickson, P. and Smart, R. (1996) 'The new Canadian drug law: One step forward, two steps backward', *International Journal of Drug Policy*, 7(3): 172–9.

Fischer, B., Ala-Leppilampi, K., Single, E. and Robins, A. (2003) 'Cannabis law reform in Canada: Is the "saga of promise, hesitation and retreat" coming to an end?', *Canadian Journal of Criminology and Criminal Justice*, 45(3): 265–98.

Fischer, B., Kuganesan, S. and Room, R. (2015) 'Medical marijuana programs: Implications for cannabis control policy – observations from Canada', *International Journal of Drug Policy*, 26(1): 15–19.

Fischer, B., Rehm, J. and Crépault, J.F. (2016) 'Realistically furthering the goals of public health by cannabis legalization with strict regulation: Response to Kalant', *International Journal of Drug Policy*, 34: 11–16.

Fischer, B., Russell, C. and Boyd, N. (2020) 'A century of cannabis control in Canada: A brief overview of history, context and policy frameworks from prohibition to legalization', in T. Decorte, S. Lenton and C. Wilkins (eds) *Legalizing Cannabis: Experiences, Lessons and Scenarios*, Abingdon: Routledge, pp 89–115.

Forsyth, J. (2021) 'Don't bet on Boris Johnson decriminalising cannabis', *The Times* [Online], 9 April, Available at: https://bit.ly/3hX1idr [Accessed 10 March 2022].

Franke, H. (1990) 'Dutch tolerance: Facts and fables', *The British Journal of Criminology*, 30(1): 81–93.

Freidson, E. (1970) *Profession of Medicine: A Study of the Sociology of Applied Knowledge*, New York: Dodd, Mead & Company.

Friedman, J. (1986) 'The world city hypothesis', *Development and Change*, 17(1): 69–83.

Friman, H.R. (1991) 'The United States, Japan, and the international drug trade: Troubled partnership', *Asian Survey*, 31(9): 875–90.

Gamella, J. and Jimenez Rodrigo, M. (2004) 'A brief history of cannabis policies in Spain (1968–2003)', *Journal of Drug Issues*, 34(4): 623–59.

Garland, D. (1996) 'The limits of the sovereign state: Strategies of crime control in contemporary society', *The British Journal of Criminology*, 36(4): 445–71.

Garland, D. (2001) *The Culture of Control*, Oxford: Oxford University Press.

Garland, D. (2004) 'Beyond the culture of control', *Critical Review of International Social and Political Philosophy*, 7(2): 160–89.

Garland, D. (2018) 'Theoretical advances and problems in the sociology of punishment', *Punishment & Society*, 20(1): 8–33.

Garland, D. (2021) 'What's wrong with "penal populism"? Politics, the public, and penological expertise', 12th Annual Asian Criminological Society Conference, Kyoto.

Garland, D. and Sparks, R. (2000) 'Criminology, social theory and the challenge of our times', *The British Journal of Criminology*, 40(2): 189–204.

Garretsen, H. (2010) 'The Dutch and their drugs: The end of an era? Reflections on Dutch policies towards tobacco, alcohol and illegal drugs', *Drugs: Education, Prevention and Policy*, 17(5): 485–95.

Garvey, T. and Yeh, B. (2014) *State Legalization of Recreational Marijuana: Selected Legal Issues*, Washington, DC: Congressional Research Service.

Gayle, D. (2015) 'Durham police stop targeting pot smokers and small-scale growers', *The Guardian* [Online], 22 July, Available at: https://www.theguardian.com/society/2015/jul/22/durham-police-stop-targeting-pot-smokers-and-small-scale-growers [Accessed 22 September 2021].

Giddens, A. (1998) *The Third Way: The Renewal of Social Democracy*, Cambridge: Polity Press.

Global Commission on Drug Policy (2011) *War on Drugs: Report of the Global Commission on Drug Policy*, Geneva: GCDP.

Global Commission on Drug Policy (2014) *Taking Control: Pathways to Drug Policies That Work*, Geneva: GCDP.

Goldson, B. and Hughes, G. (2010) 'Sociological criminology and youth justice: Comparative policy analysis and academic intervention', *Criminology & Criminal Justice*, 10(2): 211–30.

Gordon, A. (2016) 'Vision for Jamaica's new legal ganja industry', *Jamaica Observer* [Online], 18 June, Available at: https://www.jamaicaobserver.com/columns/Vision-for-Jamaicas-new-legal-ganja-industry/ [Accessed 28 June 2021].

Grapendaal, M., Groen, P. and van der Heide, W. (1997) *Duur en Volume: Ontwikkeling van de Onvoorwaardelijke Vrijheidsstraf tussen 1985 en 1995; Feiten en Verklaringen* [Duration and Volume: Development of Unconditional Custody between 1985 and 1995; Facts and Statements], The Hague: Ministry of Justice/WODC.

Greenfield, V. and Paoli, L. (2012) 'If supply-oriented drug policy is broken, can harm reduction help fix it? Melding disciplines and methods to advance international drug-control policy', *International Journal of Drug Policy*, 23(1): 6–15.

Greenfield, V. and Paoli, L. (2013) 'A framework to assess the harms of crimes', *The British Journal of Criminology*, 53(5): 864–85.

Hain, P. (1999) 'Meet Blair, the libertarian socialist', *New Statesman*, 12 March, pp 25–6. London: New Statesman.
Hallsworth, S. and Lea, J. (2011) 'Reconstructing Leviathan: Emerging contours of the security state', *Theoretical Criminology*, 15(2): 141–57.
Hamai, K. and Ellis, T. (2006) 'Crime and criminal justice in modern Japan: From re-integrative shaming to popular punitivism', *International Journal of the Sociology of Law*, 34(3): 157–78.
Hanson, V. (2020) 'Cannabis policy reform: Jamaica's experience', in T. Decorte, S. Lenton and C. Wilkins (eds) *Legalizing Cannabis: Experiences, Lessons and Scenarios*, Abingdon: Routledge, pp 375–89.
Hardwick, D. and King, L. (2008) *Home Office Cannabis Potency Study 2008*. London: Home Office.
Hatton, B. (2022) 'Starmer against changing drug laws as London considers reducing cannabis arrests', *The Independent* [Online], 4 January, Available at: https://bit.ly/3tNM0NB [Accessed 10 March 2022].
Hillyard, P., Sim, J., Tombs, S. and Whyte, D. (2004) 'Leaving a "stain upon the silence": Contemporary criminology and the politics of dissent', *The British Journal of Criminology*, 44(3): 369–90.
HM Government (UK) (2017) *2017 Drug Strategy*, London: HM Government.
HM Inspectorate of Constabulary (UK) (2013) *Crime Recording in Kent*, London: HMIC.
Home Affairs Committee (UK) (2002) *The Government's Drug Policy: Is It Working?* London: House of Commons.
Home Office (UK) (1995) *Tackling Drugs Together*, London: Home Office.
Home Office (UK) (1998) *Tackling Drugs to Build a Better Britain: The Government's Ten-Year Strategy for Tackling Substance Misuse*, London: Home Office.
Home Office (UK) (2002a) *The Government's Drug Policy: Is It Working? The Government Reply to the Third Report from the Home Affairs Committee*, London: Home Office.
Home Office (UK) (2002b) *Updated Drug Strategy 2002*, London: Home Office.
Home Office (UK) (2004) *Tackling Drugs: Changing Lives – Keeping Communities Safe from Drugs. Drug Strategy Progress Report 2004*, London: Home Office.
Home Office (UK) (2008a) *Drugs: Protecting Families and Communities*, London: Home Office.
Home Office (UK) (2008b) *Explanatory Memorandum to the Misuse of Drugs Act 1971 (Amendment) Order 2008*, London: Home Office.
Home Office (UK) (2008c) *Government Response to the Recommendations Made by the Advisory Council on the Misuse of Drugs in its Report Cannabis: Classification and Public Health*, London: Home Office.
Home Office (UK) (2009) *Home Office Circular 001/2009 – Controlled Drugs: Reclassification of Cannabis*, London: Home Office.

Home Office (UK) (2012a) *Crimes Detected in England and Wales 2011/12*, London: Home Office.

Home Office (UK) (2012b) *Drug Misuse Declared: Findings from the 2011–12 Crime Survey for England and Wales*, London: Home Office.

Home Office (UK) (2013) *Drug Misuse: Findings from the 2012/13 Crime Survey for England and Wales*, London: Home Office.

Home Office (UK) (2014) *Drugs: International Comparators*, London: Home Office.

Hope, T. (2009) 'The illusion of control: A response to Professor Sherman', *Criminology & Criminal Justice*, 9(2): 125–34.

Hough, M. (2013) 'Procedural justice and professional policing in times of austerity', *Criminology & Criminal Justice*, 13(2): 181–97.

House of Commons (UK) (2000) *Cannabis*, London: House of Commons.

House of Commons (UK) (2007) Hansard 463(126), 18 July, London: House of Commons.

House of Commons (UK) (2008a) Hansard 475(89), 7 May, London: House of Commons.

House of Commons (UK) (2008b) Hansard 482(162), 12 November, London: House of Commons.

House of Commons (UK) (2009) *Communities and Local Government Select Committee – Sixth Report of Session 2008–09: The Balance of Power: Central and Local Government*, London: House of Commons.

House of Lords (UK) (1953) Hansard 182, 20 May, London: House of Lords.

House of Representatives of the States General (the Netherlands) (1995) *Drugs Policy in the Netherlands: Continuity and Change*, The Hague: Ministry of Health, Welfare and Sport.

House of Representatives of the States General (the Netherlands) (2006) *Notitie Integrale Aanpak Hennepteelt* [Note Integral Approach to Cannabis Cultivation], The Hague: Tweede Kamer der Staten-Generaal.

House of Representatives of the States General (the Netherlands) (2011a) Vergaderjaar [Session Year] 2010–11, 24 077 (259), The Hague: Tweede Kamer der Staten-Generaal.

House of Representatives of the States General (the Netherlands) (2011b) Vergaderjaar [Session Year] 2011–12, 24 077 (265), The Hague: Tweede Kamer der Staten-Generaal.

House of Representatives of the States General (the Netherlands) (2011c) Vergaderjaar [Session Year] 2011–12, 24 077 (267), The Hague: Tweede Kamer der Staten-Generaal.

House of Representatives of the States General (the Netherlands) (2012) Vergaderjaar [Session Year] 2012–13, 24 077 (293), The Hague: Tweede Kamer der Staten-Generaal.

Hughes, C. (2020) 'The Australian experience and opportunities for cannabis law reform', in T. Decorte, S. Lenton and C. Wilkins (eds) *Legalizing Cannabis: Experiences, Lessons and Scenarios*, Abingdon: Routledge, pp 337–74.

Hughes, C. and Stevens, A. (2010) 'What can we learn from the Portuguese decriminalization of illicit drugs?', *The British Journal of Criminology*, 50(6): 999–1022.

Hughes, C. and Stevens, A. (2012) 'A resounding success or disastrous failure: Re-examining the interpretation of evidence on the Portuguese decriminalisation of illicit drugs', *Drug and Alcohol Review*, 31(1): 101–13.

Hughes, C., Seear, K., Ritter, A. and Mazerolle, L. (2019) *Criminal Justice Responses Relating to Personal Use and Possession of Illicit Drugs: The Reach of Australian Drug Diversion Programs and Barriers and Facilitators to Expansion*, Drug Policy Modelling Program, Monograph 27, Sydney: National Drug and Alcohol Research Centre, UNSW Sydney.

Hughes, G. (2007) *The Politics of Crime and Community*, Basingstoke: Palgrave Macmillan.

Hutchinson, S. (2006) 'Countering catastrophic criminology', *Punishment & Society*, 8(4): 443–67.

Inatsugu, H. (2011) 'The system of bureaucrats in Japan', in T. Inoguchi and P. Jain (eds) *Japanese Politics Today: From Karaoke to Kabuki Democracy*, New York: Palgrave Macmillan, pp 29–50.

International Drug Policy Consortium (2019) *10 Years of Drug Policy in Asia: How Far Have We Come?* London: International Drug Policy Consortium.

International Narcotics Control Board (INCB) (2013) *Uruguay is Breaking the International Conventions on Drug Control with the Cannabis Legislation Approved by Its Congress* [Online], Available at: https://incb.org/documents/Publications/PressRelease/PR2013/press_release_111213.pdf [Accessed 6 July 2021].

Irwin, G. and van Holsteyn, J. (2004) 'The 2002 and 2003 parliamentary elections in the Netherlands', *Electoral Studies*, 23(3): 551–7.

Jansen, A. (1994) 'The development of a "legal" consumers market for cannabis: The "coffee shop" phenomenon', in E. Leuw and I. Marshall (eds) *Between Prohibition and Legalization: The Dutch Experiment in Drug Policy*, Amsterdam: Kugler, pp 169–81.

Jarvis, G. and Parker, H. (1989) 'Young heroin users and crime: How do the "new users" finance their habits?', *The British Journal of Criminology*, 29(2): 175–85.

Johnson, D. (2002) *The Japanese Way of Justice: Prosecuting Crime in Japan*, Oxford: Oxford University Press.

Joint United Nations Programme on HIV/AIDS (UNAIDS) (2015) *A Public Health and Rights Approach to Drugs*, Geneva: UNAIDS.

Jones, E. (2002) 'Politics beyond accommodation? The May 2002 Dutch parliamentary elections', *Dutch Crossing*, 6(1): 61–78.

Jones, R. (2020) 'Criminology and criminal justice in post-devolution Wales', *European Journal of Criminology*, [Online], Available at: https://doi.org/10.1177/1477370820916447 [Accessed 2 May 2021].

Jones, S., Porter, R. and Bishop, C. (2017) 'The implementation of medical ganja in Jamaica', *International Journal of Drug Policy*, 42: 115–17.

Jones, T. (1995) *Policing and Democracy in the Netherlands*, London: Policy Studies Institute.

Jones, T. (2012) 'Governing security: Pluralization, privatization, and the polarization in crime control and policing', in M. Maguire, R. Morgan and R. Reiner (eds) *The Oxford Handbook of Criminology* (5th edn), Oxford: Oxford University Press, pp 743–68.

Jones, T. and Newburn, T. (2007) *Policy Transfer and Criminal Justice: Exploring US Influence over British Crime Control Policy*, Maidenhead: Open University Press.

Jones, T., van Steden, R. and Boutellier, H. (2009) 'Pluralisation of policing in England & Wales and the Netherlands: Exploring similarity and difference', *Policing and Society*, 19(3): 282–99.

Junger-Tas, J. and Junger, M. (2007) 'The Dutch criminological enterprise', in M. Tonry and C. Bijleveld (eds) *Crime and Justice in the Netherlands*, Crime and Justice, Vol 35, Chicago: University of Chicago Press, pp 115–62.

Kalant, H. (2016) 'A critique of cannabis legalization proposals in Canada', *International Journal of Drug Policy*, 34: 5–10.

Kandel, D. (1975) 'Stages in adolescent involvement in drug use', *Science*, 190(4217): 912–14.

Kelsall, D. (2017) 'Cannabis legislation fails to protect Canada's youth', *Canadian Medical Association Journal*, 189(21): E737–E738.

Kelsey, R. (2018) 'Police leader urges for new approach on cannabis', *BBC News* [Online], 12 September, Available at: https://www.bbc.com/news/uk-45288789 [Accessed 2 March 2022].

Keman, H. and Krouwel, A. (2007) 'The rise of a new political class: Emerging new parties and the populist challenge', *The NET Journal of Political Science*, 5(1): 75–94.

Keyzer, P. (2020) 'How section 90 of the *Constitution* makes cannabis law reform less likely in Australia', *Alternative Law Journal*, 45(4): 247–53.

Kilmer, B., Kruithof, K., Pardal, M., Caulkins, J. and Rubin, J. (2013) *Multinational Overview of Cannabis Production Regimes*, Cambridge: RAND Europe.

Kingdon, J. (1995) *Agendas, Alternatives and Public Policies* (2nd edn), New York: Harper Collins.

Korf, D. (2002) 'Dutch coffee shops and trends in cannabis use', *Addictive Behaviors*, 27(6): 851–66.

Korf, D. (2008) 'An open front door: The coffee shop phenomenon in the Netherlands', in S. Sznitman, B. Olsson and R. Room (eds) *A Cannabis Reader: Global Issues and Local Experiences*, Monograph Series 8, Volume 1, Lisbon: European Monitoring Centre for Drugs and Drug Addiction, pp 137–54.

Korf, D. (2020) 'Coffeeshops in the Netherlands: Regulating the front door and the back door', in T. Decorte, S. Lenton and C. Wilkins (eds) *Legalizing Cannabis: Experiences, Lessons and Scenarios*, Abingdon: Routledge, pp 285–306.

Korf, D., Riper, H. and Bullington, B. (1999) Windmills in their minds? Drug policy and drug research in the Netherlands. *Journal of Drug Issues*, 29(3): 451–472.

Kozma, L. (2011) 'Cannabis prohibition in Egypt, 1880–1939: From local ban to League of Nations diplomacy', *Middle Eastern Studies*, 47(3): 443–60.

Kreulen, E. (2019) 'De proef met legal wiethandel dreigt te stoppen, want er is te weinig animo' [Trial of legal cannabis trade threatens to end as there is too little enthusiasm], *Trouw* [Online], 31 May, Available at: https://www.trouw.nl/nieuws/de-proef-met-legale-wiethandel-dreigt-te-stoppen-want-er-is-te-weinig-animo~b41de243/ [Accessed 11 August 2021].

Lancione, S., Wade, K., Windle, S.B., Filion, K.B., Thombs, B.D. and Eisenberg, M.J. (2020) 'Non-medical cannabis in North America: An overview of regulatory approaches', *Public Health*, 178: 7–14.

Laurance, J. (2010) 'Drug ban chaos after resignation of advisor' [Online], 3 April, Available at: http://ind.pn/1tMLzQq [Accessed 4 August 2014].

Layder, D. (1998) *Sociological Practice: Linking Theory and Social Research*, London: Sage.

Lea, J. and Young, J. (1984) *What Is to Be Done about Law and Order?* London: Penguin.

Lee, M. and South, N. (2008) 'Drugs policing', in T. Newburn (ed) *The Handbook of Policing* (2nd edn), London: Routledge, pp 497–521.

Legislative Assembly for the Australian Capital Territory (2018a) *Drugs of Dependence (Personal Cannabis Use) Amendment Bill 2018: Explanatory Statement*, Canberra: Legislative Assembly for the Australian Capital Territory.

Legislative Assembly for the Australian Capital Territory (2018b) Hansard, 2018 Week 13, 28 November, Canberra: Legislative Assembly for the Australian Capital Territory.

Legislative Assembly for the Australian Capital Territory (2019) *Government Response to Standing Committee on Health, Ageing and Community Services Inquiry into the Drugs of Dependence (Personal Cannabis) Amendment Bill 2018 Private Members Bill*, Canberra: Legislative Assembly for the Australian Capital Territory.

Lenton, S. (2004) 'Pot, politics and the press – reflections on cannabis law reform in Western Australia', *Drug and Alcohol Review*, 23(2): 223–33.

Lenton, S. and Allsop, S. (2010) 'A tale of CIN – the Cannabis Infringement Notice scheme in Western Australia', *Addiction*, 105(5): 808–16.

Leon, K. and Weitzer, R. (2014) 'Legalizing recreational marijuana: Comparing ballot outcomes in four states', *Journal of Qualitative Criminal Justice and Criminology*, 2(2): 193–218.

Leuw, E. (1994) 'Initial construction and development of the official Dutch drug policy', in E. Leuw and I. Marshall (eds) *Between Prohibition and Legalization: The Dutch Experiment in Drug Policy*, Amsterdam: Kugler, pp 23–40.

Leveson Inquiry (2012) *Transcript of Morning Hearing*, 11 June 2012, London: Leveson Inquiry.

Levi-Faur, D. and Jordana, J. (2005) 'Regulatory capitalism: Policy irritants and convergent divergence', *The Annals of the American Academy of Political and Social Science*, 598(2): 191–7.

Lijphart, A. (1968) *The Politics of Accommodation: Pluralism and Democracy in the Netherlands*, Berkeley: University of California Press.

Lijphart, A. (1977) *Democracy in Plural Societies: A Comparative Exploration*, New Haven, CT: Yale University Press.

Lijphart, A. (1989) 'From the politics of accommodation to adversarial politics in the Netherlands', *West European Politics*, 12(1): 139–53.

Lindblom, C.E. (1959) 'The science of "muddling through"', *Public Administration Review*, 19(2): 79–88.

Lindblom, C.E. (1979) 'Still muddling, not yet through', *Public Administration Review*, 39(6): 517–26.

Lipsky, M. (2010) *Street-Level Bureaucracy: Dilemmas of the Individual in Public Services*, New York: Russell Sage Foundation.

Liu, J. (2016) 'Asian paradigm theory and access to justice', *Journal of Contemporary Criminal Justice*, 32(3): 205–24.

Loader, I. (2006) 'Fall of the "platonic guardians": Liberalism, criminology and political responses to crime in England and Wales', *The British Journal of Criminology*, 46(4): 561–86.

Loader, I. and Sparks, R. (2004) 'For an historical sociology of crime policy in England and Wales since 1968', *Critical Review of International Social and Political Philosophy*, 7(2): 5–32.

Loader, I. and Sparks, R. (2007) 'Contemporary landscapes of crime, order, and control: Governance, risk, and globalization', in M. Maguire, R. Morgan and R. Reiner (eds) *The Oxford Handbook of Criminology* (4th edn), Oxford: Oxford University Press, pp 78–101.

Loughlin, J. (2001) *Subnational Democracy in the European Union: Challenges and Opportunities*, Oxford: Oxford University Press.

MacCoun, R. and Reuter, P. (1997) 'Interpreting Dutch cannabis policy: Reasoning by analogy in the legalization debate', *Science*, 278(5335): 47–52.

MacCoun, R. and Reuter, P. (2001) *Drug War Heresies: Learning from Other Vices, Times and Places*, Cambridge: Cambridge University Press.

MacGregor, S. (2006) '"*Tackling Drugs Together*" and the establishment of the principle that "treatment works"', *Drugs: Education, Prevention and Policy*, 13(5): 399–408.

Marks, A. (2019) 'Defining "personal consumption" in drug legislation and Spanish cannabis clubs', *International and Comparative Law Quarterly*, 68(1): 193–223.

Matthews, R. (2002) 'Crime and control in late modernity', *Theoretical Criminology*, 6(2): 217–26.

May, T., Warburton, H., Turnbull, P.J. and Hough, M. (2002) *Times They Are A-Changing: Policing of Cannabis*, York: Joseph Rowntree Foundation.

May, T., Duffy, M., Warburton, H. and Hough, M. (2007) *Policing Cannabis as a Class C Drug: An Arresting Change?* York: Joseph Rowntree Foundation.

McAra, L. (2006) 'Welfare in crisis? Key developments in Scottish youth justice', in J. Muncie and B. Goldson (eds) *Comparative Youth Justice*, London: Sage, pp 127–45.

McAuley, A., Aucott, L. and Matheson, C. (2015) 'Exploring the life-saving potential of naloxone: A systematic review and descriptive meta-analysis of take home naloxone (THN) programmes for opioid users', *International Journal of Drug Policy*, 26(12): 1183–8.

McLaughlin, E. (2002) 'Same bed, different dreams: Postmodern reflections on crime prevention and community safety', in G. Hughes and A. Edwards (eds) *Crime Control and Community: The New Politics of Public Safety*, Cullompton: Willan, pp 46–62.

Mead, A. (2019) 'Legal and regulatory issues governing cannabis and cannabis-derived products in the United States', *Frontiers in Plant Science*, 10: 697. doi: 10.3389/fpls.2019.00697

Measham, F. and Shiner, M. (2009) 'The legacy of "normalisation": The role of classical and contemporary criminological theory in understanding young people's drug use', *International Journal of Drug Policy*, 20(6): 502–8.

Measham, F. and South, N. (2012) 'Drugs, alcohol, and crime', in M. Maguire, R. Morgan and R. Reiner (eds) *The Oxford Handbook of Criminology* (5th edn), Oxford: Oxford University Press, pp 686–716.

Mennes, R., Pieper, R., Schoonbeek, I. and Bieleman, B. (2021) *Coffeeshops in Nederland 2020: Aantallen Coffeeshops en Gemeentelijk Beleid 1999–2020* [Coffeeshops in the Netherlands 2020: The Number of Coffeeshops and Municipal Policy 1999–2020], Groningen: Breuer Onderzoek & Intraval Advies.

Metropolitan Police Authority (2002) *The Lambeth Cannabis Warning Pilot Scheme*, London: Metropolitan Police Authority.

Mikos, R. (2009) 'On the limits of supremacy: Medical marijuana and the states' overlooked power to legalize federal crime', *Vanderbilt Law Review*, 62(5): 1419–82.

Mills, J. (2003) *Cannabis Britannica*, Oxford: Oxford University Press.

Mills, J. (2012) 'Science, diplomacy and cannabis: The evidence base and the international drugs regulatory system, 1924–1961', in J. Collins (ed) *Governing the Global Drug Wars*, London: LSE, pp 25–30.

Mills, J. (2013) *Cannabis Nation: Control and Consumption in Britain, 1928–2008*, Oxford: Oxford University Press.

Ministry of Health (UK) (1926) *Report of the Departmental Committee on Morphine and Heroin Addiction*, London: HMSO.

Ministry of Health, Labour and Welfare (Japan) (2021) *Taimato no Yakubutsutaisaku no Arikata Kentokai* [Investigative Commission on Measures against Cannabis] [Online], Available at: https://www.mhlw.go.jp/stf/shingi/other-syokuhin_436610_00005.html [Accessed 14 June 2021].

Ministry of Health, Welfare and Sport (the Netherlands) (2003) *Drug Policy in the Netherlands: Basic Principles and Enforcement in Practice*, The Hague: Ministry of Health, Welfare and Sport.

Ministry of Justice (Japan) (2020) *Hanzai Hakusho* [Crime White Paper], Tokyo: Ministry of Justice.

Ministry of Justice (the Netherlands) (1985) *Society and Crime: A Policy Plan for the Future*, The Hague: Ministry of Justice.

Ministry of Justice (the Netherlands) (1990) *Law in Motion: A Policy Plan for Justice in the Years Ahead*, The Hague: Ministry of Justice.

Ministry of Justice (UK) (2021) 'Prison population figures, 2021' [Online], Available at: https://www.gov.uk/government/statistics/prison-population-figures-2021 [Accessed 2 September 2021].

Monaghan, M. (2011) *Evidence Versus Politics: Exploiting Research in UK Drug Policy Making?* Bristol: Policy Press.

Moran, M. (2005) *Politics and Governance in the UK*, Basingstoke: Palgrave Macmillan.

MORI (2002) *Policing the Possession of Cannabis: Residents' Views on the Lambeth Experiment*, London: MORI/Police Foundation.

Morris, Z. (2009) 'The truth about interviewing elites', *Politics*, 29(3): 209–17.

Mosher, C. and Akins, C. (2020) 'Recreational marijuana legalization in Washington State', in T. Decorte, S. Lenton and C. Wilkins (eds) *Legalizing Cannabis: Experiences, Lessons and Scenarios*, Abingdon: Routledge, pp 62–88.

Mravcik, V. (2015) '(De)criminalisation of the possession of drugs for personal use – a view from the Czech Republic', *International Journal of Drug Policy*, 26(7): 705–7.

Mwenda, L., Ahmad, M. and Kumari, K. (2005) *Seizures of Drugs in England and Wales, 2003*, London: Home Office.

Nagayoshi, H. (2019) *Taima: Kinjirareta Rekishi to Iryo e no Mirai* [Cannabis: A Forbidden History and the Future for Medicine], Tokyo: Cosmic Publishing.

Nakamura, T. (2002) *A Declining Technocratic Regime: Bureaucracy, Political Parties and Interest Groups in Japan, 1950–2000*, Democracy, Governance and Human Rights Programme Paper Number 9, Geneva: United Nations Research Institute for Social Development.

National Assembly for Wales (2000) *Tackling Substance Misuse in Wales: A Partnership Approach*, Cardiff: National Assembly for Wales.

National Conference of State Legislatures (US) (2021) 'State medical marijuana laws', [Online], 14 June, Available at: https://www.ncsl.org/research/health/state-medical-marijuana-laws.aspx [Accessed 19 May 2021].

National Police Agency (Japan) (2021) *Keisatsu Hakusho* [The Police White Paper], Tokyo: National Police Agency.

National Police Services Agency (the Netherlands) (2008) *Het Groene Goud* [The Green Gold], Zoetermeer: KLPD.

National Police Services Agency (the Netherlands) (2012a) *Georganiseerde Hennepteelt: Criminaliteitsbeeldanalyse 2012* [Organized Cannabis Cultivation: Crime Image Analysis 2012], Zoetermeer: KLPD.

National Police Services Agency (the Netherlands) (2012b) *Nationaal Dreigingsbeeld 2012: Georganiseerde Criminaliteit* [National Threat Assessment 2012: Organized Crime], Zoetermeer: KLPD.

Ndlovu, R. (2020) 'Zimbabwe $1.25 billion plan sees cannabis as biggest cash crop', *Bloomberg* [Online], 30 November, Available at: https://www.bloomberg.com/news/articles/2020-11-30/zimbabwe-1-25-billion-plan-sees-cannabis-as-biggest-cash-crop [Accessed 24 September 2021].

Newburn, T. (1991) *Permission and Regulation: Law and Morals in Post-War Britain*, London: Routledge.

Niesink, R. and Rigter, S. (2013) *THC-Concentraties in Wiet, Nederwiet en Hasj in Nederlandse Coffeeshops* [THC Concentrations in Weed, Dutch Weed and Hashish in Dutch Coffeeshops], Utrecht: Trimbos Instituut.

Nutt, D., King, L., Saulsbury, W. and Blakemore, C. (2007) 'Development of a rational scale to assess the harm of drugs of potential misuse', *The Lancet*, 369(9566): 1047–53.

Nutt, D., King, L. and Phillips, L. (2010) 'Drug harms in the UK: A multicriteria decision analysis', *The Lancet*, 376(9752): 1558–65.

O'Malley, P. (2000) 'Criminologies of catastrophe? Understanding criminal justice on the edge of the new millennium', *The Australian and New Zealand Journal of Criminology*, 33(2): 153–67.

O'Malley, P. (2002) 'Review symposium: The culture of control', *Punishment & Society*, 4(2): 259–61.

Obradovic, I. (2021) 'From prohibition to regulation: A comparative analysis of the emergence and related outcomes of new legal cannabis policy models (Colorado, Washington State and Uruguay)', *International Journal of Drug Policy*, 91:102590. doi: 10.1016/j.drugpo.2019.11.002

Office for National Statistics (UK) (2020) 'Drug misuse in England and Wales: Year ending March 2020' [Online], 9 December, Available at: https://www.ons.gov.uk/peoplepopulationandcommunity/crimeandjustice/articles/drugmisuseinenglandandwales/yearendingmarch2020#overall-trends-in-drug-misuse [Accessed 2 September 2021].

Office of the Attorney General (US) (2018) 'Marijuana enforcement' [Online], 4 January, Available at: https://www.justice.gov/opa/press-release/file/1022196/download [Accessed 28 June 2021].

Office of the High Commissioner for Human Rights (1989) 'Convention on the rights of the child' [Online], Available at: https://www.ohchr.org/en/professionalinterest/pages/crc.aspx [Accessed 5 July 2021].

Osborne, G. and Fogel, C. (2017) 'Perspectives on cannabis legalization among Canadian recreational users', *Contemporary Drug Problems*, 44(1): 12–31.

Osmond, J. (2007) *Building the Nation: Creating 'Internal Political Solidarity'*, Cardiff: Institute of Welsh Affairs.

Ossebaard, H. and van de Wijngaart, G. (1998) 'Purple haze: The remaking of Dutch drug policy', *International Journal of Drug Policy*, 9: 263–71.

Owen, J. (2007) 'Cannabis: An apology', *The Independent* [Online], 18 March, Available at: https://www.independent.co.uk/life-style/health-and-families/health-news/cannabis-an-apology-5332409.html [Accessed 10 January 2014].

Pacula, R. (2021) 'Commentary on Rychert and Wilkins (2021) "Why did New Zealand's referendum to legalise recreational cannabis fail?"', *Drug and Alcohol Review*, [Online], Available at: https://onlinelibrary.wiley.com/doi/10.1111/dar.13300 [Accessed 20 June 2021].

Pakes, F. (2000) 'League champions in mid table: On the major changes in Dutch prison policy', *The Howard Journal*, 39(1): 30–9.

Pakes, F. (2003) 'Tolerance and pragmatism in the Netherlands: Euthanasia, coffeeshops and prostitution in the "purple years", 1994–2002', *International Journal of Police Science and Management*, 5(4): 217–28.

Pakes, F. (2004) 'The politics of discontent: The emergence of a new criminal justice discourse in the Netherlands', *The Howard Journal*, 43(3): 284–98.

Pakes, F. (2005) 'Penalization and retreat: The changing face of Dutch criminal justice', *Criminal Justice*, 5(2): 145–61.

Paoli, L., Greenfield, V. and Zoutendijk, A. (2013) 'The harms of cocaine trafficking: Applying a new framework for assessment', *Journal of Drug Issues*, 43(4): 407–36.

Pardal, M., Queirolo, R., Alvarez, E. and Repetto, L. (2019) 'Uruguayan Cannabis Social Clubs: From activism to dispensaries?', *International Journal of Drug Policy*, 73: 49–57.

Pardo, B. (2014) 'Cannabis policy reforms in the Americas: A comparative analysis of Colorado, Washington, and Uruguay', *International Journal of Drug Policy*, 25(4): 727–35.

Pares, O. and Bouso, J. (2015) *Innovation Born of Necessity: Pioneering Drug Policy in Catalonia*, New York: Open Society Foundations.

Pares, O., Jubert-Cortiella, X., Olivares-Galvez, S., Diaz-Castellano, A., Jimenez-Garrido, D. and Bouso, J. (2019) 'Use and habits of the protagonists of the story: Cannabis social clubs in Barcelona', *Journal of Drug Issues*, 49(4): 607–24.

Parker, H. and Newcombe, R. (1987) 'Heroin use and acquisitive crime in an English community', *The British Journal of Sociology*, 38(3): 331–50.

Parker, H., Measham, F. and Aldridge, J. (1998) *Illegal Leisure: The Normalisation of Adolescent Recreational Drug Use*, London: Routledge.

Parry, C., Myers, B. and Caulkins, J. (2019) 'Decriminalisation of recreational cannabis in South Africa', *The Lancet*, 393(10183): 1804–5.

Partij voor de Vrijheid (PVV) (2010) *De agenda van hoop en optimism: Een tijd om te kiezen: PVV 2010-2015*. The Hague: Partij voor de Vrijheid.

Pennings, P. and Keman, H. (2008) 'The changing landscape of Dutch politics since the 1970s: A comparative exploration', *Acta Politica*, 43: 154–79.

Peters, G. (2005) 'The problem of policy problems', *Journal of Comparative Policy Analysis: Research and Practice*, 7(4): 349–70.

Police Foundation (2000) *Drugs and the Law: Report of the Independent Inquiry into the Misuse of Drugs Act 1971*, London: Police Foundation.

Pollitt, C. (2001) 'Convergence: The useful myth?', *Public Administration*, 79(4): 933–47.

Powell, M. (2000) 'New Labour and the third way in the British welfare state: A new and distinctive approach?', *Critical Social Policy*, 20(1): 39–60.

Pugh, M. (1994) *State and Society: British Political and Social History 1870–1992*, London: Edward Arnold.

Punay, E. (2020) 'Medical Marijuana Bill filed', *PhilStar* [Online], 11 December, Available at: https://www.philstar.com/headlines/2020/12/11/2062949/medical-marijuana-bill-filed [Accessed 10 August 2021].

Queirolo, R. (2020) 'Uruguay: The first country to legalize cannabis', in T. Decorte, S. Lenton and C. Wilkins (eds) *Legalizing Cannabis: Experiences, Lessons and Scenarios*, Abingdon: Routledge, pp 116–30.

Quintas, J. and Arana, X. (2017) 'Decriminalization: Different models in Portugal and Spain', in E. Savona, M. Kleiman and F. Calderoni (eds) *Dual Markets: Comparative Approaches to Regulation*, Cham: Springer International Publishing, pp 121–43.

Radler, R. (2021) 'The Biden administration's expected criminal enforcement stance on marijuana', *JD Supra* [Online], 2 February, Available at: https://www.jdsupra.com/legalnews/the-biden-administration-s-expected-8632285/ [Accessed 28 June 2021].

Ramsay, M., Baker, P., Goulden, C., Sharp, C. and Sondhi, A. (2001) *Drug misuse declared in 2000: Results from the British Crime Survey*. London: Home Office.

Ren, M., Tang, Z., Wu, X., Spengler, R., Jiang, H., Yang, Y. and Boivin, N. (2019) 'The origins of cannabis smoking: Chemical residue evidence from the first millennium BCE in the Pamirs', *Science Advances*, 5(6): 1–8.

Research and Documentation Centre (the Netherlands) (2013) *Het Besloten Club en het Ingezetenencriterium voor Coffeeshops: Evaluatie van de Implementatie en de Uitkomsten in de Periode Mei-November 2012, Tussenrapportage* [The Private Club and the Residence Criterion for Dutch Coffeeshops: Evaluation of the Implementation and Outcomes in the Period May-November 2012, An Interim Report], Den Haag: WODC.

Reynolds, J.R. (1890) 'On the therapeutical uses and toxic effects of cannabis indica', *The Lancet*, 135(3473): 637–8.

Ritter, A. and Bammer, G. (2010) 'Models of policy-making and their relevance for drug research', *Drug and Alcohol Review*, 29(4): 352–7.

Ritter, A. and Sotade, O. (2017) 'Explaining the declining rates of past year cannabis use in Australia: A first pass', *Drug and Alcohol Review*, 36(5): 602–8.

Ritter, A., Lancaster, K., Grech, K. and Reuter, P. (2011) *An Assessment of Illicit Drug Policy in Australia (1985–2010): Themes and Trends*, Drug Policy Modelling Program, Monograph 21, Sydney: National Drug and Alcohol Research Centre, UNSW Sydney.

Room, R., Fischer, B., Hall, W., Lenton, S. and Reuter, P. (2008) *Cannabis Policy: Moving Beyond Stalemate*, Oxford: The Beckley Foundation.

Rose, N. (2000) 'Community, citizenship, and the third way', *American Behavioural Scientist*, 43(9): 1395–411.

Ryan, M. (2003) *Penal Policy and Political Culture in England and Wales*, Winchester: Waterside Press.

Rychert, M. and Wilkins, C. (2020) 'How not to legalize cannabis: Lessons from New Zealand's experiment with regulating "legal highs"', in T. Decorte, S. Lenton and C. Wilkins (eds) *Legalizing Cannabis: Experiences, Lessons and Scenarios*, Abingdon: Routledge, pp 116–30.

Rychert, M. and Wilkins, C. (2021) 'Why did New Zealand's referendum to legalise recreational cannabis fail?', *Drug and Alcohol Review*, [Online], Available at: https://onlinelibrary.wiley.com/doi/10.1111/dar.13254 [Accessed 20 June 2021].

Rychert, M., Wilkins, C. and Witten, K. (2018) '"Lost in translation": Issues with the establishment of a legal market for "low risk" psychoactive products ("legal highs") in New Zealand', *Drugs: Education, Prevention and Policy*, 25(3): 254–61.

Rychert, M., Emanuel, M. and Wilkins, C. (2020) 'Issues in the establishment of a therapeutic cannabis market under Jamaica's Dangerous Drugs Amendment Act 2015', *International Journal of Drug Policy*, 86: 102945. doi: 10.1016/j.drugpo.2020.102945

Sabatier, P. (1988) 'An advocacy coalition framework of policy change and the role of policy-orientated learning therein', *Policy Sciences*, 21(2/3): 129–68.

Sandel, M. (2010) *Justice: What's the Right Thing to Do?* London: Penguin.

Sare, J. (2009) 'Labour is in denial over cannabis row', *The Guardian* [Online], 2 November, Available at: http://bit.ly/1qT0UtS [Accessed 15 January 2014].

Sayer, A. (2000) *Realism and Social Science*, London: Sage.

Sayer, A. (2011) *Why Things Matter to People: Social Science, Values and Ethical Life*, Cambridge: Cambridge University Press.

Scarman, L. (1982) *The Scarman Report: The Brixton Disorders 10–12 April 1981*, Middlesex: Penguin.

Schlag, A., Baldwin, D., Barnes, M., Bazire, S., Coathup, R., Curran, H.V., McShane, R., Phillips, L., Singh, L. and Nutt, D. (2020) 'Medical cannabis in the UK: From principle to practice', *Journal of Psychopharmacology*, 34(9): 931–7.

Schwartz, D. (2013) 'High federalism: Marijuana legalization and the limits of federal power to regulate states', *Cardozo Law Review*, 35(2): 567–641.

Seddon, T. (2006) 'Drugs, crime and social exclusion: Social context and social theory in British drugs-crime research', *The British Journal of Criminology*, 46(4): 680–703.

Seddon, T. (2008) 'Risk, security, and the "criminalization" of British drug policy', *The British Journal of Criminology*, 48(6): 818–34.

Seddon, T. (2020) 'Immoral in principle, unworkable in practice: Cannabis law reform, the Beatles and the Wootton Report', *The British Journal of Criminology*, 60(6): 1567–84.

Sentencing Council (UK) (2011) *Drugs Offences*, London: Sentencing Council.

Sentencing Council (UK) (2012) *Drug Offences: Definitive Guideline*, London: Sentencing Council.

Shanahan, M. and Cyrenne, P. (2021) 'Cannabis policies in Canada: How will we know which is best?', *International Journal of Drug Policy*, 91: [Online], Available at: https://doi.org/10.1016/j.drugpo.2019.09.004 [Accessed 7 July 2021].

Shanahan, M., Hughes, C. and McSweeney, T. (2017) *Australian Police Diversion for Cannabis Offences: Assessing Program Outcomes and Cost-Effectiveness*, Canberra: National Drug Law Enforcement Research Fund.

Sherman, L. (2009) 'Evidence and liberty: The promise of experimental criminology', *Criminology & Criminal Justice*, 9(1): 5–28.

Shiner, M. (2003) 'Out of harm's way? Illicit drug use, medicalization and the law', *The British Journal of Criminology*, 43(4): 772–96.

Shiner, M. (2009) *Drug Use and Social Change: The Distortion of History*, London: Palgrave Macmillan.

Shiner, M. (2015) 'Drug policy reform and the reclassification of cannabis in England and Wales: A cautionary tale', *International Journal of Drug Policy*, 26(7): 696–704.

Shiner, M. and Newburn, T. (1997) 'Definitely, maybe not: The normalisation of recreational drug use amongst young people', *Sociology*, 31(3): 511–29.

Shiner, M. and Newburn, T. (1999) 'Taking tea with Noel: The place and meaning of drug use in everyday life', in N. South (ed) *Drugs: Cultures, Controls and Everyday Life*, London: Sage, pp 140–59.

Shiner, M., Carre, Z., Delsol, R. and Eastwood, N. (2018) *The Colour of Injustice: 'Race', Drugs and Law Enforcement in England and Wales*, London: StopWatch; Release.

Single, E., Christie, P. and Ali, R. (2000) 'The impact of cannabis decriminalization in Australia and the United States', *Journal of Public Health Policy*, 21(2): 157–86.

Sischy, J. and Blaustein, J. (2018) 'Global drug policy at an impasse: Examining the politics of the 2016 United Nations General Assembly Special Session', *International Journal of Drug Policy*, 60: 74–81.

Smyth, B. and Christie, G. (2021) 'Opposition to cannabis legalization on public health grounds', *The Lancet Regional Health – Western Pacific*, 9: 100142 [Online], Available at: https://doi.org/10.1016/j.lanwpc.2021.100142 [Accessed 20 June 2021].

Snippe, J., Bieleman, B., Kruize, A. and Naayer, H. (2005) *Hektor in Venlo: Eindevaluatie: Inspanningen, Proces en Resultaten 2001–2004* [Hektor in Venlo: Efforts, Process and Results 2001–2004], Groningen: Intraval.

Sosa, K. (2012) *Proceed with Caution: Use of Out-of-Court Disposals in England and Wales*, London: Policy Exchange.

South Wales Police (2011) *Policing Plan 2011–2015*, Bridgend: South Wales Police.

Spicer, J. (2021) *Policing County Lines: Responses to Evolving Provincial Drug Markets*, Cham: Palgrave Macmillan.

Squires, P. (ed) (2008) *ASBO Nation: The Criminalization of Nuisance*, Bristol: Policy Press.

Standing Committee on Health, Ageing and Community Services (Australian Capital Territory) (2019) *Inquiry into Drugs of Dependence (Personal Cannabis Use) Amendment Bill 2018*, Canberra: Standing Committee on Health, Ageing and Community Services.

Stenson, K. (2002) 'Community safety in middle England: The local politics of crime control', in G. Hughes and A. Edwards (eds) *Crime Control and Community: The New Politics of Public Safety*, Cullompton: Willan, pp 109–39.

Stenson, K. and Edwards, A. (2004) 'Policy transfer in local crime control: Beyond naïve emulation', in T. Newburn and R. Sparks (eds) *Criminal Justice and Political Cultures: National and International Dimensions of Crime Control*, Cullompton: Willan, pp 209–33.

Stevens, A. (2007) 'Survival of the ideas that fit: An evolutionary analogy for the use of evidence in policy', *Social Policy and Society*, 6(1): 25–35.

Stevens, A. (2011) *Drugs, Crime and Public Health: The Political Economy of Drug Policy*, Abingdon: Routledge.

Stevens, A., Hughes, C., Hulme, S. and Cassidy, R. (2019) 'Depenalization, diversion and decriminalization: A realist review and programme theory of alternatives to criminalization for simple drug possession', *European Journal of Criminology*, [Online], Available at: https://doi.org/10.1177/1477370819887514 [Accessed 15 October 2020].

Stoned Again (2012) Radio Programme, BBC Radio 5 Live, 28 November.

Tak, P. and van Kalmthout, A. (1998) 'Prison population growing faster in the Netherlands than in US', *Overcrowded Times*, 9(1): 12–16.

Taskforce on Cannabis Legalization and Regulation (2016) *A Framework for the Legalization and Regulation of Cannabis in Canada*, Ottawa: Health Canada.

Taylor, S. (2008) 'Medicalizing cannabis: Science, medicine and policy, 1950–2004: An overview of a work in progress', *Drugs: Education, Prevention and Policy*, 15(5): 462–74.

The Mainichi (2021) 'Japan to criminalize cannabis use, but allow medical marijuana: Expert panel report' [Online], 12 June, Available at: https://mainichi.jp/english/articles/20210612/p2a/00m/0li/018000c [Accessed 17 August 2021].

The Times (1969) 'Cannabis penalties not to be reduced', 24 January, p 8.

Thomson, D. (1965) *England in the Twentieth Century, 1914–63*, Harmondsworth: Penguin.

Tilley, N. (2009) 'Sherman vs Sherman: Realism vs rhetoric', *Criminology & Criminal Justice*, 9(2): 135–44.

Tomaney, J. (2000) 'End of the empire state? New Labour and devolution in the United Kingdom', *International Journal of Urban and Regional Research*, 24(3): 675–88.

Tonry, M. (2009) 'Explanations of American punishment policies: A national history', *Punishment & Society*, 11(3): 377–94.

Townley, B. (2008) *Reason's Neglect: Rationality and Organizing*, Oxford: Oxford University Press.

Transform Drug Policy Foundation (2022) 'Drug diversion in the UK' [Online], Available at: https://transformdrugs.org/drug-policy/uk-drug-policy/diversion-schemes [Accessed 2 March 2022].

Transnational Institute (2014) *The Rise and Decline of Cannabis Prohibition: The History of Cannabis in the UN Drug Control System and Options for Reform*, Amsterdam: Transnational Institute.

Trench, A. (2008) *Devolution and Power in the United Kingdom*, Manchester: Manchester University Press.

Tsurutani, T. (1998) 'The national bureaucracy of Japan', *International Review of Administrative Sciences*, 64(2): 181–94.

Uitermark, J. (2004) 'The origins and future of the Dutch approach towards drugs', *Journal of Drug Issues*, 4(3): 511–32.

UK Cannabis Social Clubs (2022) 'Official UK cannabis social clubs list' [Online], Available at: https://ukcsc.co.uk/official-ukcsc-list/ [Accessed 2 March 2022].

UK Drug Policy Commission (2012) *Politicians' Views on Drug Policy* [Online], Available at: https://www.ukdpc.org.uk/wp-content/uploads/politicians-views-on-drug-policy1.pdf [Accessed 2 September 2021].

UN High Commissioner for Human Rights (2020) *Situation of Human Rights in the Philippines: Report of the United Nations High Commissioner for Human Rights*, Geneva: OHCHR.

United Nations (UN) (1961) *Single Convention on Narcotic Drugs 1961*, New York: United Nations.

United Nations (UN) (1971) *Convention on Psychotropic Substances 1971*, New York: United Nations.

United Nations (1973) *Commentary on the Single Convention on Narcotic Drugs, 1961*, New York: United Nations Secretariat.

United Nations (1988) *Convention against the Illicit Traffic in Narcotic Drugs and Psychotropic Substances 1988*, New York: United Nations.

United Nations Development Programme (UNDP) (2015) *Perspectives on the Development Dimensions of Drug Control Policy* [Online], Available at: https://www.unodc.org/documents/ungass2016//Contributions/UN/UNDP/UNDP_paper_for_CND_March_2015.pdf [Accessed 3 June 2021].

United Nations Office on Drugs and Crime (UNODC) (2009) *Political Declaration and Plan of Action on International Cooperation towards an Integrated and Balanced Strategy to Counter the World Drug Problem*, New York: United Nations.

United Nations Office on Drugs and Crime (UNODC) (2016) *Outcome Document of the United Nations General Assembly Special Session on The World Drug Problem*, New York: United Nations.

van Amsterdam, J., Opperhuizen, A., Koeter, M., van Aerts, L. and van den Brink, W. (2009) *Ranking van Drugs: Een Vergelijking van de Schadelijkheid van Drugs* [Ranking of Drugs: A Comparison of the Harmfulness of Drugs], Bilthoven: RIVM.

van der Giessen, M., Moolenaar, D. and van Ooyen-Houben, M. (2014) *De Export van in Nederland Geteelde Cannabis* [The Export of Cannabis Cultivated in the Netherlands], Den Haag: WODC.

van der Gouwe, D., Ehrlich, E. and van Laar, M. (2009) *Drug Policies in the Netherlands*, Utrecht: Trimbos-Instituut.

van der Stel, J., Everhardt, V. and van Laar, M. (2009) 'Ontwikkeling van het Nederlandse drugsbeleid' [Development of Dutch drug policy], in M. van Laar and M. van Ooyen-Houben (eds) *Evaluatie van het Nederlandse Drugsbeleid* [Evaluation of Dutch Drugs Policy], Utrecht/Den Haag: Trimbos Instituut/WODC, pp 45–68.

van Dijk, J., Mayhew, P. and Killias, M. (1990) *Experiences of Crime across the World: Key Findings of the 1989 International Crime Survey*, Deventer: Kluwer.

van Hout, M.C. and Bingham, T. (2014) 'Responsible vendors, intelligent consumers: Silk Road, the online revolution in drug trading', *International Journal of Drug Policy*, 25(2): 183–9.

van Kessel, S. (2011) 'Explaining the electoral performance of populist parties: The Netherlands as a case study', *Perspectives on European Politics and Society*, 12(1): 68–88.

van Laar, M. and van Ooyen-Houben, M. (eds) (2009) *Evaluatie van het Nederlandse Drugsbeleid* [Evaluation of Dutch Drug Policy], Utrecht/Den Haag: Trimbos-Instituut/WODC.

van Mierlo, H. (1986) 'Depillarisation and the decline of consociationalism in the Netherlands: 1970–85', *West European Politics*, 9(1): 97–119.

van Oorschot, W. (2006) 'The Dutch welfare state: Recent trends and challenges in historical perspective', *European Journal of Social Security*, 8(1): 57–76.

van Ooyen-Houben, M. (2006) 'Hoe werkt het Nederlandse drugsbeleid? Een evaluatieve verkenning van een decennium drugsbeleid' [How does the Dutch drug policy work? An evaluation exploring a decade of drugs policy], *Justitiele Verkenningen*, 32(1): 24–45.

van Ooyen-Houben, M., Bieleman, B., Biesma, S., Snippe, J., van der Wagen, W. and Beelen, A. (2009) 'Drugsgerelateerde overlast' [Drug-related nuisance], in M. van Laar and M. van Ooyen-Houben (eds) *Evaluatie van het Nederlandse Drugsbeleid* [Evaluation of Dutch Drug Policy], Utrecht/Den Haag: Trimbos-Instituut/WODC, pp 293–314.

van Os, J., Bak, M., Hanssen, M., Bijl, R., de Graaf, R. and Verdoux, H. (2002) 'Cannabis use and psychosis: A longitudinal population-based study', *American Journal of Epidemiology*, 156(4): 319–27.

van Schendelen, M. (1978) 'Verzuiling en restauratie in de Nederlandse politiek' [Pillarisation and restoration in Dutch politics], *Beleid en Maatschappij*, 5(2): 42–54.

van Swaaningen, R. (2005) 'Public safety and the management of fear', *Theoretical Criminology*, 9(3): 289–305.

van Swaaningen, R. (2006) 'Criminology in the Netherlands', *European Journal of Criminology*, 3(4): 463–501.

van Swaaningen, R. (2013) 'Reversing the punitive turn: The case of the Netherlands', in T. Daems, D. van Zyl Smit and S. Snacken (eds) *European Penology?* Oxford: Hart, pp 339–60.

Vaughn, M., Huang, F. and Ramirez, C. (1995) 'Drug abuse and anti-drug policy in Japan: Past history and future directions', *The British Journal of Criminology*, 35(4): 491–524.

Verweij, K., Huizink, A., Agrawal, A., Martin, N. and Lynskey, M. (2013) 'Is the relationship between early-onset cannabis use and educational attainment causal or due to common liability?', *Drug and Alcohol Dependence*, 133(2): 580–6.

Volkskrant (2008) 'Drugsoverlast te groot om door de vingers te zien' [Drug nuisance too big to condone] [Online], Available at: http://bit.ly/1dT85uU [Accessed 3 March 2014].

Wacquant, L. (2004) 'Decivilizing and demonizing: The remaking of the Black American ghetto', in S. Loyal and S. Quilley (eds) *The Sociology of Norbert Elias*, Cambridge: Cambridge University Press, pp 95–121.

Walsh, J. and Ramsey, G. (2016) *Uruguay's Drug Policy: Major Innovations, Major Challenges*, Washington DC: Brookings Institution.

Warburton, H., May, T. and Hough, M. (2005) 'Looking the other way: The impact of reclassifying cannabis on police warnings, arrests and informal action in England and Wales', *The British Journal of Criminology*, 45(2): 113–28.

Webster, P. (2018) 'Debate over recreational cannabis use legalisation in Canada', *The Lancet*, 391(10122): 725–6.

Weiss, C. (1977) *Using Social Research in Public Policy Making*, Lexington, MA: Heath.

Welsh Government (2008) *Working Together to Reduce Harm: The Substance Misuse Strategy for Wales 2008–2018*, Cardiff: Welsh Government.

Welsh Office (1996) *Forward Together: A Strategy to Combat Drug and Alcohol Misuse in Wales*, London: Stationary Office.

Wibberley, C. and Price, J. (2000) 'Young people's drug use: Facts and feelings – implications for the normalization debate', *Drugs: Education, Prevention and Policy*, 7(2): 147–62.

Wilkins, C. and Sweetsur, P. (2012) 'Criminal justice outcomes for cannabis use offences in New Zealand, 1991–2008', *International Journal of Drug Policy*, 23(6): 505–11.

Wilkins, C. and Rychert, M. (2021) 'The rejection of cannabis legalization in New Zealand: Issues with the Cannabis Legalization and Control Bill or wider concerns?', *Addiction*, 116(2): 236–8.

Wilson, D. (2015) 'Dangerous Drugs (Amendment) Act 2015 to come into effect April 2015', *Jamaica Information Service* [Online], Available at: https://jis.gov.jm/dangerous-drugs-amendment-act-2015-come-effect-april-15/ [Accessed 28 June 2021].

Wilson, D. and Game, C. (2011) *Local Government in the United Kingdom* (5th edn), Basingstoke: Palgrave Macmillan.

Windle, J. (2013) 'How the East influenced prohibition', *The International History Review*, 35(5): 1185–99.

Wisselink, D., Kuijpers, W. and Moi, A. (2012) *Kerncijfers Verslavingszorg 2011: Ladis Landelijk Alcohol en Drugs Informatie Systeem* [Addiction Key Figures 2011: Ladis National Alcohol and Drugs Information System]. Houten: IVZ.

Withuis, J. and Mooij, A. (2010) 'From totalitarianism to trauma', in J. Withuis and A. Mooij (eds) *The Politics of War Trauma: The Aftermath of World War II in Eleven European Countries*, Amsterdam: Aksant, pp 193–216.

Working Group on Narcotic Drugs (the Netherlands) (1972) *Rapport van de Werkgroep Verdovende Middelen* [Report of the Working Group on Narcotic Drugs], Den Haag: Staatsuitgeverij.

World Health Organization (WHO) (1952) *Third Session of the World Health Organization Expert Committee on Drugs Liable to Produce Addiction*. Geneva: World Health Organization.

World Health Organization (WHO) (2003) *WHO Expert Committee on Drug Dependence, Thirty-Third Report*, Geneva: World Health Organization.

World Health Organization (WHO) (2006) *WHO Expert Committee on Drug Dependence, Thirty-Fourth Report*, Geneva: World Health Organization.

World Health Organization (WHO) (2014) *Consolidated Guidelines on HIV Prevention, Diagnosis, Treatment and Care for Key Populations*. Geneva: World Health Organization.

World Health Organization (WHO) (2017) 'Joint United Nations statement on ending discrimination in health care settings' [Online], 27 June, Available at: https://www.who.int/news/item/27-06-2017-joint-united-nations-statement-on-ending-discrimination-in-health-care-settings [Accessed 20 May 2021].

Wouters, M. and Korf, D. (2011) *De Wietpas en het Social Clubmodel: Meningen en Verwachtingen van Coffeeshopbezoekers in Utrecht* [The Weedpass and the Social Club Model: Opinions and Expectations of Coffeeshop Visitors in Utrecht], Amsterdam: Rozenberg Publishers.

Wouters, M., Benschop, A. and Korf, D. (2010) 'Local politics and retail cannabis markets: The case of Dutch coffeeshops', *International Journal of Drug Policy*, 21(4): 315–20.

Yin, R. (2014) *Case Study Research: Design and Methods* (5th edn), Thousand Oaks, CA: Sage.

Youdell, D. and McGimpsey, I. (2015) 'Assembling, disassembling and reassembling "youth services" in austerity Britain', *Critical Studies in Education*, 56(1): 116–30.

Young, J. (1971) *The Drugtakers: The Social Meaning of Drug Use*, London: Paladin.

Young, J. (1999) *The Exclusive Society*, London: Sage.

Young, J. (2002) 'Searching for a new criminology of everyday life: A review of "The Culture of Control"', *The British Journal of Criminology*, 43(1): 228–43.

Zammit, S., Allebeck, P., Andreasson, S., Lundberg, I. and Lewis, G. (2002) 'Self-reported cannabis use as a risk factor for schizophrenia in Swedish conscripts of 1969: Historical cohort study', *British Medical Journal*, 325(7374): 1199–201.

Zedner, L. (2002) 'Dangers of dystopias in penal theory', *Oxford Journal of Legal Studies*, 22(2): 341–66.

Zedner, L. (2007) 'Pre-crime and post-criminology?', *Theoretical Criminology*, 11(2): 261–81.

Index

References to tables appear in **bold**.
References to endnotes show both the page number and the note number (179n3).